ENGLISH CHURCH MUSIC
1650–1750
IN ROYAL CHAPEL, CATHEDRAL AND PARISH CHURCH

STUDIES IN CHURCH MUSIC

General Editor: ERIK ROUTLEY, B.D., D.Phil.

Other volumes in this series

TWENTIETH CENTURY CHURCH MUSIC
by Erik Routley, B.D., D.Phil.

CHURCH MUSIC IN THE NINETEENTH CENTURY
by Arthur Hutchings, Mus.D.

MUSIC AND THE REFORMATION IN ENGLAND 1549–1660
by Peter Le Huray

THE MUSICAL WESLEYS by Erik Routley, B.D., D.Phil.

THE CHORAL REVIVAL IN THE ANGLICAN CHURCH
by Bernarr Rainbow

CHRISTOPHER DEARNLEY

ENGLISH CHURCH MUSIC
1650–1750

IN ROYAL CHAPEL, CATHEDRAL AND
PARISH CHURCH

1970
OXFORD UNIVERSITY PRESS
New York and London

Contents

Acknowledgements		ix
Introduction		xi
1	The Background of English Church Music 1650–1750	1
	"Better sailors than fiddlers, more farmers than contrapuntists"	1
	"An innocent luxury"	5
	"Pulsation, Voice and Blast"	11
2	Royal Music—1	19
	The Restoration of the King	19
	Charles II and his Chapel	22
	The Chapel Royal Choir	27
	The "Children of the Chapell"	33
3	Royal Music—2	40
	The "four and twenty violins"	40
	"Wind-musique"	48
	The decline of the Chapel Royal	52
4	The Cathedrals—Renovation	61
	"Psalm-roaring Saints"	61
	Restoration	65
	Varying standards	69
	Striving for excellence	77
5	The Cathedrals—Decay	82
	Much thrushed	82
	Supporters of the old style	84
	New influences	88
	Subsidence	92

v

6   "Cathedral Musick"—The Order of Service   96
       The daily round   96
       Psalms   102
       Canticles   107
       Anthems   109

7   "Cathedral Musick"—The Musicians   116
       The Organist   116
       Organ music   125
       The Singer   129

8   "Parochial Musick"   135
       "One grand scream of treble voices"   135
       The "Musickers"   146

9   The Organ in Church   156
       "A dangerous and antichristian Machine"   156
       "Neat, rich, and melodious Organs"   160
       "The Lawfulness and Use of Organs"   169

10   List of Composers   176

Appendixes   278
     A   Royal Chapels   278
     B   The music repertoire of cathedral choirs   281
     C   Psalm chants, 1661–1771   285
     D   The working life of a cathedral organist   288

References   290

Index   301

Plates

Appearing between pages 148 and 149

1 A chorister of the Chapel Royal
2 Frontispiece to Weldon's *Divine Harmony*
3 The choir of Oxford Cathedral
4 The choir of Ely Cathedral
5 & 6 Procession of musicians of the Chapel Royal and Westminster Abbey
7 *Prospectus Londinensis:* the City at the beginning of the eighteenth century
8 The opening page of Locke's–*The King shall rejoice*
9 Monument to Robert Pierrepont
10 Monument to Sir John Evelyn
11 A solo movement from *Bow down thine ear, O Lord*
12 The Renatus Harris organ in St. John's, Wolverhampton

vii

Acknowledgements

Adequately to express gratitude to the many people who have helped me gather material for this book is impossible. All who have supplied information and encouragement I wish to thank. Particular mention, however, must be made of my wife, Bridget, for her patient understanding of my preoccupation, Helen Compton for secretarial assistance, and Dordie Daniels who so ably transcribed crabbed handwriting into orderly typescript. The Dean and Chapter of Salisbury Cathedral also, acting like good midwives, considerably eased my labour by allowing time which enabled much of the preliminary work to be completed.

One thing only I ask of this book, using the words of an eighteenth-century writer: "May God grant that it may be as helpful and pleasing to you as it was troublesome to me."

C.H.D.
Salisbury. 1968

Introduction

This book is a series of studies rather than a comprehensive history of English church music from 1650 to 1750. There is, of course, a need for definitive biographies of the more eminent composers and an exhaustive survey of their music. Even now Purcell is the only composer of the period honoured with a complete edition of his music, a project which has taken eighty-nine years to complete. All I can hope to do is to encourage an attitude that will consider further research and documentation worthwhile. I have done a little scraping around in "slags and cinders of the past", but at this stage, useful as it may be to learn on what day and in what year a composer was baptised, it is much more important to try to understand the environment within which he grew up and worked, and how it affected his music.

In pursuit of this objective the matter of each chapter has been allowed to range freely, darting across chronological divisions in an attempt to let the subjects speak for themselves. Rows of date-defined categories, tidy though they may be, do no good to a topic by cooping it up inside artificial pens which, in any case, demand the greatest ingenuity to construct. The year 1660, for instance, has for long been conveniently used in this way with the consequent assumption that English church music at that time finally set the seal on a defunct "Golden Age" and began a new era perverted with all sorts of unwholesome influences, whether of foreign or secular origin.

These pages adopt the structure of a suite in preference to that of a symphony, containing a number of discussions on selected aspects rather than a development of related and contrasting themes. Their content, with liberal quotation from the writings and ideas of contemporary authors, bears the nature of a pasticcio. Whatever the form and material, there is a singular purpose: to dispel unfair criticism of church music of this period by promoting a basis for a better appreciation its of aims and limitations.

The century following the Restoration is a fascinating one whose problems are not unfamiliar to us today. Church musicians were fighting antagonism without or apathy within and, in addition, were striving to keep pace with many significant musical trends. The process of change from the hopes raised by the music of the late seventeenth century to the polite and well-ordered writing of eighteenth-century composers presents at times a depressing drama. Yet the tedium of some of the later music is offset by the actors' colourful lives, and the whole scene can interest the musician, churchman, and student of English history.

For anyone who is concerned with music's place in worship these years hold a particular relevance. Divinity reduced to deism, or God to the role of a benevolent fairy, accompanied an underestimation of the place of music in a discipline of life that bears on a two-way intercourse of God and man, and with the never-ending problem of finding adequate means of expression to formulate this conversation. The chances that were missed in the eighteenth century of using music to supplement the limitations of words provide an object lesson to us. We do not have the excuse of inexperience of the problem and we are no longer hindered by an art deemed inferior to others and inessential.

"Some books are to be tasted, others to be swallowed, and some few to be chewed and digested." This one tries to spread the fare, keeping, wherever possible, the less digestible portions to one side. References are numbered and then tabulated discreetly at the end. The notes at the foot of a page contain only supporting comments. They are placed there as optional matter, because incorporating them within the text would have been a disservice to the reader who expects a book to be reasonably entertaining and free of persistent interruptions, like unasked-for telephone calls, and who, having little time to spare, needs to steer through his subject without being sidetracked by horrid little facts.

The Background
of
English Church Music
1650—1750

The speed of change in England of the seventeenth and eighteenth centuries may seem slow in comparison with the present century, but the changes are nonetheless obvious. Society was expanding from rural into urban. Wealth was accumulating and, accompanied by an increasingly empirical approach to life, was building up the wherewithal for Britain's later explosion into greatness as an industrial power and one of international pre-eminence. The wars of the seventeenth century, civil and otherwise, gave place to many years of peace after the Treaty of Utrecht had been signed in 1713. Relative stability and security sheltered the nation's growth.

Parallel with this transition went an inner movement, if not from God-centred to materialistic thinking at least towards a new emphasis on the practical. The scientific orderliness of Newton, the rational philosophy of Locke became acceptable to those who were finding it possible to place life in manageable compartments rather than experience it with all its depth and variety, illogical suffering and extraordinary happiness.

In the centre of this progression from mediaeval to modern, on a less nebulous plane, stood London. "One was wont to say often of London, that it was a marvelous fine sweet place if it stood but in the country";[1] yet even if disliked by its inhabitants it was for them the political and social, as well as intellectual and cultural capital. In any case some of them could escape the city's confines, and they were not entirely out of touch with the country. In the summer months not only did the royal court go to Windsor but the gentry went to their estates and the bishops to their dioceses. This two-way interchange between country and city, although fruitful in many ways, had its disadvantages. For all its powerful rulers, high life, extravagant fashions, the capital did not altogether lose a rustic stamp. The village green was not all that far distant from London's pleasure gardens, the local inn from its fashionable coffee houses. In the world of music a coal-merchant's room and taverns were not the most suitable concert halls for promoting high standards of taste or performance.

The court's sphere was so diminished by the infiltration of democracy following the 1688 "Glorious Revolution" that it never had the chance to dominate as did that of Louis XIV in France. Few that had wealth, extravagant though they were, cared to spend it on musical luxuries. One only, the Duke of Chandos, for a brief moment at his residence at Cannons, supported a musical establishment that provided a temporary home for Handel. But Cannons was short lived; there were no successors, and no more Chandos anthems. In any case had there been strong centres to further the fine arts their influence would have been limited by the temper of an age which discouraged anything that was not rational or served no obvious purpose.

Rough edges were smoothed over with a surface veneer of elegance, but little attempt was made to grind them out of existence. Poverty, for instance, was no less a feature in eighteenth- than in seventeenth-century England; what was different was the increasing awareness of it. The eighteenth century witnessed the promotion of many charitable works but, apart from the satisfaction these gave to uneasy consciences, their aim was not so much to eradicate poverty as to bring it under control, if only for the practical reason that a sound economy relied on healthy, reasonably contented artisans.

Death was treated with a similar callousness. A corpse could be viewed as an object of curiosity, "like boyld Brawne". What once had been accepted as a gateway to a higher state was left with the "cool indifference you quit a dirty inn". Being one thing that reason could not explain away, it was treated lightly, even facetiously.

The veneer was most thinly spread over behaviour and morals. The uninhibited seventeenth-century doctor who "kept a pretty young wench to wayte on him, which I guesse he made use of for warmeth-sake as King David did"[2] could not have acted so openly once puritan ideologies had firmly insinuated themselves into English life. The wenches were kept, but hidden in a cupboard. The reaction after the strictness of the Commonwealth days was at first towards an open laxity; but this in turn was superseded by a self-conscious awareness of shortcomings. A late seventeenth-century list of such reads like a catalogue of faults in modern society: "Baudy houses and light huswifes . . . corrupters of youth . . . multitudes of ailhouses . . . extravicancies in apparell . . . lying and swearing . . . atheism . . . disrespect to seniors . . . sawciness . . .".[3] But talking and preaching did not remove the offences which led, on the one hand, to a lack of serious purpose, a loss of true dignity and earnestness in life, "all, forsooth, must be gentile and neat"; and, on the other, to hypocrisy. If immorality could not be mended, it could at least be glossed over.

A great artist does not have to live in a holy land, though the air he breathes must circulate freely and be fresh, if not pure. Mists of hypocrisy interfere with his vision. A composer explores territory not usually reached in any mundane approach to living, and in his search he is neither ashamed nor afraid to view every corner of total experience.

English church musicians thrived more in the vigorous life of the Restoration period than in that of the ordered, mannered eighteenth century. Lacking then the vitality of genius to burst through codes of politeness they were further handicapped by the preoccupations of their compatriots who, sailing the seas in search of wealth and renown or farming the fields to feed the baser appetites, were too busy to encourage musicians, whether fiddlers or contrapuntists. Music, it was felt, "wastes so much of a young man's time . . . and engages him often in such odd company".

There was no shortage of energy for a variety of activities but it was most likely to be spent in making a fine country estate out of rank ground, "a pleasant fertile island . . . in the middle of a naked sea of land", or on the less beneficial delights of eating and drinking.

> The large halls of corporations, and trading companies, are, in general, as void of decorations by the arts, as the members which assemble in them are often void of taste, eating and drinking excepted. . . . They would look upon the sum paid to an artist, for ornamenting their hall with an excellent picture, as a most idle and unpardonable expence; they would enquire how many fine haunches of venison, how many well-fed turkies, how many delicious turtles, how many dozens of excellent old wine might have been bought for such a sum?[4]

Such parsimony has for long continued to dog the arts. The notorious and extended penury of English music was not only due to the shortage of homebred Beethovens and Wagners. However much the applied arts flourished, music was disparaged. Earlier generations had been able to live on the reputation described by Erasmus: the English "particularly challenge to themselves Beauty, Music and Feasting", and this could still at the end of the seventeenth century sustain one composer of supreme genius, Purcell. But he was beyond compare for very many years. Although church music had the support of a firm tradition, even this was inadequate in the face of eighteenth-century attitudes. With so much against them, from the sphere of aesthetics down to humdrum problems of performance, the achievements of composers like Croft, Boyce and Greene are all the more remarkable.

"AN INNOCENT LUXURY"

Music was discussed in the eighteenth century, but the approach was very different from that voiced by Henry Peacham in 1622 (*The Compleat Gentleman*): those who do not love music "are by nature ill disposed and of such a *brutish stupidity* that scarce anything else that is good and savoureth of virtue is to be found in them". Two generations later another writer looked back wistfully, "in my younger time, we had Musick most excellently choice, and most eminently rare",[5] and contrasted the decadent trends of his day. One such was the anti-social change from music in parts, consort music amongst friends, to "some-single-soul'd Ayre", a concerto for soloist with figured-bass accompaniment. With a premium placed on extravagant display music ceased to be appreciated as a stimulating discussion amongst equal intelligences and became merely an entertaining monologue.*

The impact of virtuosi players, and especially that of operatic singers, was more of a body blow than beneficial massage. So, at first, was the complementary change from domestic to concert music, amateur (in the best meaning of the word) to professional. Standards are essential; but the experience of active participation in music should always be the bedrock of passive listening. Unless these two are commingled, a wholesome musical life is unattainable. In the eighteenth century the musician, no longer respected for his sociable and enlightening

---

* "This last grand Revolution in the Musicall State hath made great alterations . . . it is deterierated, and in great danger to be utterly lost, or so deformed as to become ridiculous. Anciently musick was in some sort pastorall, that is plain, practicable, and good. Now it is set up drest in superlatives brought from I know not whence, at imense charges in profuse salarys, pensions, subscriptions, and promiscuous courtship and flatterys into the bargain."[6]

accomplishments, became an entertainer charged with upholding the surface elegance, disguising unwanted emotions or anything that undermined a reasonably ordered existence.

It was said in 1711: "We are transported with any thing that is not *English* . . . *English* Musick is quite rooted out, and nothing yet planted in its stead".[7] Handel later filled the void, but there were no native composers of sufficient stature and maturity to combat the loss of a sense of purpose. Neither were there any writers who could overcome a fundamental deficiency in musical aesthetics. Roger North, at the beginning of the eighteenth century, was perhaps the first to tackle this subject and question the wide acceptance of limiting theories. That he felt obliged to do so indicates not so much a new approach to music, that it should be appreciated seriously *per se*, as a defensive reaction against inroads on this very thing. Music being in danger of passing "for whimsye, that every trifler may pretend to", North struggled to raise its esteem as "an art requiring a sound judgement and discretion in its professors, as well as other arts and sciences have required". A skilful protagonist, his arguments nonetheless show how circumscribed was musical thinking in his day.

The main contention was based on music's efficacy in "moving affections and exciting passions in men".* Joined to this was the common experience of music's capacity to please, to entertain. This needed no proof, but its automatic acceptance tended increasingly to exclude a more serious purpose.

The "affections" were limited to respectable ones. They had to "pour in upon the Mind a silent and serene Joy", to "fix the Heart in a rational, benevolent, and happy Tranquillity". Invoking an emotional response came to mean stilling "every unquiet Passion", and encouraging only those that were deemed civilised. Any that were not in this category had to be

---

* Widely used terms. In general, "affections" implies mental, and "passions" emotional states. Music which moves the "affections" stirs the mind, and that which touches the "passions" stimulates feelings of joy, sorrow, etc.

repressed. "It is the peculiar Quality of Music to raise the *sociable and happy Passions*, and to *subdue* the *contrary ones*."[8]

Such well-meaning pragmatism excluded realms of experience to the great loss of much eighteenth-century music. It achieved prettiness at the expense of profundity; banished the devil and, at the same time, lost sight of God.

Handel's last oratorio, *Jephtha*, shows a great artist brazenly breaking through the limitations of his age. The libretto he was given twists the harsh realities of a primitive Bible story with all its tragic implications into a harmless fairytale, and provides a fictitious happy ending. Handel used it, drawing on the depths of his own experience, to create a masterpiece of wide-ranging significance, boldly facing up to the tragedy and sparing none of its bitterness. Lesser composers than he did not have such courage and safely skimmed the surface of emotion or hid behind the skirts of a major key.

The approach to this position was a gradual one. North was still enough in touch with the seventeenth century to say that music is a true "resemblance of Humanity in all its states, actions, passions and affections". Though he says "all", he later adds a qualification: "the utterances of extream pain, torture, or fright in any creature can never be represented in musick, for they are always the worst of discord". He does, however, illustrate his point: "the common passions of joy and sorrow" can be most appositely expressed in the major and minor keys. This was an acceptable device that composers did not fail to use sensitively.* But they too often abused another means of description—word painting. Literal representation of individual

* Seventeenth-century composers, particularly Purcell and his contemporaries, used the minor key because it provided greater scope than the major (the melodic minor scale having nine different notes as against the major's seven). Though writing in the minor key for subjects expressing grief and sorrow, they did not use it exclusively so. Eighteenth-century composers, in addition to limiting the minor key for a single expressive purpose, showed a distinct preference for the simplicities of the major key. Boyce even went one stage further by eschewing modulation: "the skill of the artist is best shewn, not in departing from the original key, but in keeping within it".[9]

words often made nonsense of the underlying mood. Effective enough when handled with care and discretion, "humouring the words" too frequently led to excesses, "as when any thing is sayd to *rise*, the musick must needs advance in the scale, which comonly proves too short to reach the skyes, tho' a voice is made almost to crack, and the air is wounded almost to death, yet it will come short".

The power of music both to resemble and to stimulate emotion was strongest in the setting of words for voices. Vocal music long remained pre-eminent for this reason, but its position became undermined when it was argued that instrumental music too had this capacity, although to a less obvious extent. The maxim, "make the Sound eccho to the Sense", was applied to both. Without the help of words to make explicit the representation of human feelings, instrumental music relied more on the total effect of a movement, its pervading mood: the "Harmony, which runs thro' the whole work and like the soul animates the man".

Lest this seemed too vague a concept, North instanced the theory in practice. In the movements of an instrumental sonata (Italian style) the opening *Grave* "most aptly represents seriousness and thought", the following *fuge* "hath a cast of business or debate", and the *Adagio* "is a laying all affaires aside, and lolling in a sweet repose". After this there is a return to activity in the concluding dance movements, representing "the various humours of men diverting themselves", generally ending with "a *Gigue* which is like men (half foxed) dancing for joy, and so good night".*

A too literal approach to music was a symptom of a dangerous disease. If a composer wanted to talk about serious thought

---

* A programme note such as this can partly elucidate the late seventeenth-century instrumental anthem. Many of them bear out North's statement that the best music "is found at the beginning, for then the master's spirit and invention are fresh, and in full vigor, which in the process will in some measure abate". And no better description can be found for those lightweight concluding choruses, triple time settings of repeated "hallelujahs", than "half foxed"!

debates, sweet repose and light diversions, he would have said so in so many words and not in musical notes. But it seems that the eighteenth-century rationale could not allow for disclosing something in music which could be expressed in no other way. The most it could do was to admit that, in its ability to voice thoughts and excite response, music resembled the arts of poetry and painting.

North gave as an example Raphael's picture, "The Pest House", as invoking the type of response that music had the power to stimulate.[10] A later writer, Avison, took the analogy further when he said that both music and painting are "founded in Geometry, and have Proportion for their Subject"; melody and harmony in the one have their equivalents in design and colouring in the other.* It is hardly surprising that in English church music of the period subjects requiring an obvious, literal interpretation fare better than those demanding depth of insight. The imagery of the sun striding around the heavens like a giant stimulated Boyce to write one of his best solos in the anthem, *The heavens declare*, and even a minor composer like Travers could rise out of a rut at the prospect of the earth being glad, the sea making a noise and all the trees of the wood rejoicing.[14]

* Avison gave six instances of painting and music parallels:
1. Chiaroscuro, the "mixture of light and shade"—the "judicious mixture of concords and discords".
2. Fore, mid and background—Bass, tenor and treble.
3. Principal subject—main theme.
4. Secondary subjects—supporting material.
5. Viewed from a distance—listen from a distance.
6. Various styles—various instruments.[11]
This is not as far-fetched as Hayes's comparison of music with the hunt. "A good Fugue may very justly be compared to a good Chace", represented in the fugue subject and the false scents in the episodes:
1. "A well matched Pack of Harriers"—the performers.
2. "The artful windings and doublings of the hare"—the composition.
3. "The Huntsman"—the conductor.[12]
More profoundly Hawkins wrote in his *History* (1776) of the "immediate reference" of harmony (i.e. music) "to those principles on which all our ideas of beauty, symmetry, order and magnificence are founded".[13]

The weaknesses inherent in music as mere pictorialism were sensed by Hawkins who wrote his *History* to remove this, amongst "numberless prejudices", by asserting the dignity of music as a *science*, "worthy the exercise of our rational as well as audible faculties".[15] That this needed to be emphasised at all is evident when set against the theories of a thoughtful writer such as Harris[16] for whom music, together with the arts of painting and poetry, was an inessential appendix to living, distinct from those "arts" such as medicine and agriculture which contributed to life's necessities. Even in this redundant category it was only an "ally to poetry", in vocal music disposing the mind of an audience to receive the ideas of the verbal text.

Contemporary with Harris, a doctor argued that music had indeed an indispensable function, and was not to be "cultivated merely for amusement", on the basis that music controls mind, and mind controls matter. Anxious to demonstrate music's practical value, he went so far as to affirm that it regulates "dissipation of the animal spirits" and promotes longevity.[17]

Such views were not unique to the eighteenth century. The seventeenth-century philosopher, Thomas Hobbes, at night when he was sure nobody heard him, "sang aloud (not that he had a very good voice) but for his health's sake: he did beleeve it did his lunges good, and conduced much to prolong his life".[18] Even today an excellent music shop can advertise its wares on similar lines: "Tired? Nervy? Unable to unwind after a hard day at work? Consult a specialist. Get a prescription from Suttons for a Hammond Organ".

The general approach to music in the eighteenth century was to treat it as "a mere recreation, and an amusement for vacant hours". At times it seems that even the theorists pleaded in vain that music must instruct as well as please. North's feline irony was apparently ineffective when he reminded listeners to extend not only "their long ears to an enterteinement of musick, but a regulated understanding also". Then they would gain both a richer awareness and a sounder basis for criticism than those whose enjoyment was entirely superficial. Whosoever indiscriminately praised what they heard, whether it was good, bad or indifferent merely because they liked it, did not stop to ask "why or wherefore; all which a catt may pretend to as well as a man".[19]

Even Boyce could confess that he knew music to be of an "excellent Kind" whenever "I feel my back begin to open and shut".[20] Others could say that "no musick is pleasant, but when you can chuse your distance, or time of attention".[21] Shallow attitudes too easily passed unquestioned and it was left to Samuel Johnson to redress the balance.

> The science of musical sounds, though it may have been depreciated, as appealing only to the ear, and affording nothing more than a momentary and fugitive delight, may be with justice considered as the art that unites corporal with intellectual pleasure, by a species of enjoyment which gratifies sense, without weakening reason; and which, therefore, the Great may cultivate without debasement, and the Good enjoy without depravation.[22]

"PULSATION, VOICE AND BLAST"

In other words, rhythm, melody and harmony. One Hanoverian cleric made these the musical equivalents of the Three Persons of the Trinity and, as such, the subject of a sermon. Yet not all thinking on the relationship of music and worship was as naïve as this. Many preachers applied themselves to the matter with great thoroughness and their opinions still make interesting reading for us today. Our own experiences are not so remote from theirs as to make it difficult to imagine features of English church life two hundred or so years ago.

First, the setting: this can be pictured by looking at a typical eighteenth-century parish church. Inside it is cosy, neat and homely. Though lacking the comforts of modern heating, it is quite possible to settle snugly within the box pews. There are no effigies of saints to direct our minds to the next world but enough elegant monuments to remind us of the transitoriness of this. The walls are whitewashed clean, and light streams in through plain windows. There is little coloured glass, no fragrant incense to create an atmosphere of mystery, and even the altar is too barely adorned to attract our gaze being in any case overawed by the tablets of Moses' law. The only other object that vies with them is the pulpit.

As we leave the church a prominent royal coat of arms impresses on us a due respect for the powers that be, and the clock face on the outside wall reminds us of the dignity of our faith with some such motto as "Time consecrates, and what is grey with age becomes religion". In the churchyard the parson continues to preach to us posthumously from the epitaph on his grave: "Mr. William Lowth, late Rector of this Church, who died May ye 17th 1732. And being dead desires to speak to his beloved parishioners, And sweetly to exhort them constantly to attend public worship of God, frequently to receive the Holy Sacrament and diligently to observe the good instruction given in this place".[23] Alternatively, for more direct advice, his successor may be found if not in the church at least close by in the vicarage garden. A visitor to Banstead discovered him there: "the parson of the Parish has diverted himself in his garden these fifty yeares, is now old and doates".[24] He might even be pleased to enjoy friendly conversation with us about horse racing, Roman history and ecclesiastical tittle-tattle: "After prayers waited upon Sir Henry Bunbury, very civilly entertained. . . . Talked about Horse Races. . . . Sir Henry Bunbury very desirous to shew his skill in Roman History etc. . . . The Chancellor entertained us with the Dispute he had with the Bishop about Rural Deans etc, till near 12".[25]

The church did not reach this comfortable state easily. In the seventeenth century men were prepared to kill, or be killed, for their faith and, indeed, for their particular version of the faith. The reaction from such bitterness was towards some degree of tolerance for those outside the established church and to peace and quiet for those within. There was nothing abhorred in the eighteenth century so much as the "enthusiasm" of the dissenters, and the Church of England tried to steer a careful course between this and the dangers of popery, "free from the Extream of Irreverance or Superstition".

Preserving much that was essential against outlandish claims and striving to be "most primitive, apostolical, and excellent",* the Anglican church lost more than the 1,760 worthy clergy who refused to take the oath at the passing of the Act of Uniformity in 1662, and the 400 non-jurors in 1689. It forfeited its vitality. Its authority became emphasised as stemming not only from a natural excellence but also from an established position. This left no safety valve to channel the later fierce eruption of Methodism, and did everything to encourage the bland acceptance that "every alteration in so well an ordered constitution [as that of the Church of England] will be for the worse". The church became shackled to its seat, dulled by its respectability. There was more than a little truth in an unkind quip of Charles II about Presbyterianism being no religion for a gentleman, and Anglicanism no religion for a Christian.

Energy was spent primarily in providing safeguards against extremism and then, later, in efforts to accommodate the new scientific and intellectual discoveries. The passage from a mysterious to a natural, reasonable religion was inevitable, but it was unfortunate that in the voyage more than ballast was thrown overboard. What, in faith, could not be illuminated by reason, "the candle of the Lord", was left in darkness and pushed out of sight like disquieting fantasies of the night. In the seventeenth century even one of puritan sympathies could write of "holy angels bright" and "blessed souls at rest". Some years later it was no longer the angels that declared God's glory but the "spacious firmament on high", the "spangled heavens" and "all the planets in their turn".

* This was claimed by that inveterate sermon-crawler, Evelyn, in 1685, though he was less bold then than he had been in 1661, when he had recorded: the Church of England is "for purity of doctrine, substance, decency and beauty, the most perfect under Heaven".[26] However disparaging to the church's reputation were later criticisms, it must be remembered that there were always some good men who furthered the "solemn service of God in *his Church*, by Prayers, Praises, and *Sacramental* celebrations".[27]

> . . . In reason's ear they all rejoice,
> And utter forth a glorious voice;
> For ever singing as they shine,
> "The hand that made us is Divine".[28]

The Age of Enlightenment did not encourage abstract forms of expression. Explicit and reasonable statements do not come within the province of the fine arts. When the philosophers welded language into a vehicle for rational thought, and the scientists legislated nature into an orderly constitution, music, of all the arts the most ephemeral, evaporated into thin air with a "most melodious twang".*

A change of approach was most evident in vocal music. When the tidy logic of words came to dominate other means of expression, a text could no longer be used by the composer as a tailor's dummy to be clothed with the richest material of his mind. The personal mysticism that is revealed in Byrd's motets was fragmented in the struggle for order in the music of Blow and Purcell and disappeared entirely in the neat, symmetrical writing of the Georgian composers. By their time English church music was no longer in a position to enrich the symbolic expression of great mysteries but was limited to a literal and descriptive function, intensifying speech rather than by-passing words in the articulation of otherwise inexpressible thought and feeling. Furthermore the fire of faith seared less fiercely the imagination of later composers. There are examples to show that the spark was not entirely extinguished, but it flickered fit-fully in the changing conditions that caused Purcell, for instance, to devote himself to music for the theatre in the latter part of his life. Even Blow, for whom church music was of prime import-ance, felt obliged to maintain a variety of professional interests. By Boyce's time church music had become merely a respectable activity that clothed other musical pursuits like a well-cut frock-coat.

* No self-respecting writer in the eighteenth century would have recorded the experience of one who, in 1670, met an "Apparition" that "disappeared with a curious Perfume and most melodious Twang. Mr. W. Lilley believes it was a Farie".[29]

The hitherto profound and wide influence of the Bible was diminished; it ceased to be the source book of Divinity and became accepted as a partner, so described by Thomas Browne, with "Nature, that universal and publick Manuscript".* For the dissenters the Old Testament still retained a particular relevance; their beliefs were "bottomed on the Scriptures". Equating their semi-outlawed condition with that of the Israelites, tolerated but not accepted, they struggled hard against the philistine forces of their world to gain the promised land. Excluded from the highest positions of office and influence, they tried to improve their lot with hard-working industry. Left with neither leisure nor inclination to pursue the finer points of living, the non-conformist middle classes settled into a prim stolidity which infiltrated, in course of time, the established church. Even spontaneous holiness became commuted into piety for practical purposes. By 1746 an Anglican minister could maintain that a neglect of church going is a "melancholy proof of a *national* decay of piety; of which, a national decay of trade . . . is both a natural and judicial consequence".[30]

Defenders of church music had first to join the battle to prevent the faithful from degenerating into the "Gross Sub-Beastical Sin of Atheism", and only then could they strive to protect choral services against the "Zealots" who would destroy them, and the "Sleighters" who would suffer them to die of neglect as not worthy of sustenance. Were music such a *"Low Inferiour Despicable Thing"* as both zealots and sleighters esteemed it, then certainly King David "was some *Silly-Conceited-Idle-Headed-Intoxicated-Brainsick-Inthusiast"*.[31]

Church music could not escape the effects of trends in aesthetics and religious belief, and it is not surprising that its defence weakened from forwarding serious purposes, through furthering music as a beneficial refreshment against

---

* In any case God was no longer considered a proper object for study.
    "Know then thyself, presume not God to scan;
    The proper Study of Mankind is Man."
                (Pope's *An Essay on Man, Epistle II*)

temptation, to finally selling it as an inducement to charity. The sermons preached at the Three-Choir Festivals in the eighteenth century show how the clinking of coins became a more pleasing sound than the praises of God.*

At the time of the Restoration it was accepted unquestionably, by musician and divine, that "the first and chief Use of *Musick* is for the Service and praise of God, whose gift it is; the second Use is for the Solace of Men". God stands first.

"So sweet, so *Angelicall*, so *heavenly*, and *divine*" a gift is God's absolute due. To exclude music from His services and limit it to secular use, is to place "a Jewel in a swine's snout".

"The Holy Ghost, . . . in his Wisdom, mingled Heavenly Mysteries with pleasing Melody." Sacred music "accommodates" the soul, heightens "our dull minds to speak, hear, pray". And those who object that they cannot understand music, that they have no stomach for it, must recollect that it is the appetite, not the food, which is at fault.

As the years passed, such opinions were voiced less frequently. Church music became a means of mitigating "moroseness and austerity", of emphasising religion as "the most entertaining thing in Nature", and of relieving "the Weariness of a long Attention, to make the Mind more Compos'd and Chearful, to endear the Offices of Religion".

By 1712 the influence of new aesthetic theories can be seen behind the statement that religious music "raises noble Hints in the Mind of the Hearer, and fills it with great Conceptions. It strengthens Devotion and advances Praise into Rapture". A little later another writer on church music emphasised the

---

* Such emphasis had been placed on music as a shallow entertainment that increasingly it had to be linked to an altruistic purpose. Aided by the rising influence of non-conformist attitudes, consciousness of enjoying oneself for apparently no worthwhile reason was eased by the opportunity to do good. Still, today, many concerts are promoted under the wings of a charitable aim.

It is not too far-fetched to think that the success of Handel's Foundling Hospital performances was in part due to their charitable object. This may be putting the cart before the horse, but the proceeds of nearly £7,000 from the composer's eleven performances of *Messiah* at the Foundling Hospital are considerable by any standards.[32]

"irresistible power of harmony when united with poetry". Words alone cannot "affect" nor awaken "our natural passions" so much as when allied to music. Those who have hearts "too tough and dry" to appreciate music, or who are "too bound up in the low purposes of getting, to be moved with anything beside", must hide this as a defect of a depraved and distorted nature.

More typical still of the eighteenth century was the view of music as "the chief among the delights ordained for the sons of men", legitimately so used in church; in fact, a means of attracting people to the practice of religion.

One Three Choirs Festival sermon (for Gloucester in 1727) showed unusual awareness of the purposes of church music which, the preacher said, not only provides "necessary Refreshment, or innocent Diversion" but is also "an Occasion of magnifying the Goodness of God". Viewing worship in its sacramental aspect as a "Privilege and Means of drawing near" to God, as well as an "act of Duty, and Honour", he added: "musick, if it be not wholly spiritual, neither is it wholly carnal; but of a middle Nature between both; and is therefore best qualified to receive the Impressions of the divine Goodness, and convey them to our Perception . . ." "There is something so peculiarly heavenly in the Pleasures of Musick, as makes the divine Original of them to be more readily confess'd, than of any other Pleasures."

Such insight, in its time, was uncommon; and it became rarer still. That there was a shift in accent is indicated clearly enough by the very title of the sermon at the 1753 Hereford Festival (preached by William Parker): "The Pleasures of Gratitude and Benevolence improved by Church-musick". Less is heard of the latter, in this and other sermons, than of alms-giving.* Music's task, with its power to stir

---

* Worcester Festival, 1755, "The Harmony of Benevolence" (Robert Eden); Hereford Festival, 1756, "Music a rational Assistant in the Duty of Praise when united with charity" (Digby Coates). Benevolence and charity take up so much of the preachers' time that neither have anything to say worth recording on church music.

the emotions, was to stimulate praise to God *and* "gratitude", i.e. charity.

The apologists in the Church of England could at least take comfort that music, of some sort, was accepted in their services. This was more than their brethren in the non-conformist churches could even begin to do. A Baptist who tried to promote the simplest form of singing in his congregation was rapped for lusting "after the Onions and Garlick of Egypt"; something so inessential to the practice of religion as singing had to be rejected outright, or confined to a "silent" or "inward" sort.[33]

Facing antagonism without and shallowness within, it is understandable that musicians writing for the Church of England appeared to achieve so little. Their work, therefore, must be measured not so much against that of another age as with a knowledge of the limitations of their own. Only then can the settings and anthems of the late-seventeenth and eighteenth centuries be heard afresh, freed from the must and mildew of many years' ill-founded criticism.

In the course of our period English music was diverted from a mainstream into lesser channels, and church music was forced into the smallest, having to negotiate all manner of obstacles before being diluted in a watery morass. But at the outset it had been part of a strong current cascading in fountains in the gardens of kings' palaces. So splendid was this display that our attention must first be drawn to it at its source: the Chapel Royal of Charles II.

Royal Music—1

THE RESTORATION OF THE KING

The restoration of the monarchy in 1660 has for long been considered a vital moment in the development of English cathedral music. The event has been adopted as a convenient dividing line marking the beginning of a new era, an era that has been said to have inaugurated a type of church music smacking of levity and secularity, almost indecent when set against the impeccable pattern of the "Golden Age". The truly great achievements of the Elizabethan and early-Stuart period are allowed not only to overshadow the works of later composers but also to shed an aura of respect over its own lesser satellites, so that writers like Farrant, Batten and Tomkins are treated with a seriousness not accorded to their successors.

The striking feature of church music by Purcell and his contemporaries is not its assumed secular overtone but its whole-hearted acceptance of styles that were by then common currency in European music, in particular the use of a *basso-continuo* idiom. Earlier anthems had been scored for solo voices, but always in a polyphonic context; single melodic lines over a figured bass were a new departure. No political upheaval, however drastic, could have prevented such an innovation.

Assimilation of revolutionary principles, however, was not achieved easily. But there is no excuse for withholding our considered attention of post-Restoration church music because much of it is obviously experimental. Its neglect has been due not only to an unwillingness to view it in its own light but also to the way it has been rough-handled by incompetent performances which unthinkingly repeat stylistic anachronisms.

Inhibiting ideas about its suitability in church and preconceptions that it can be measured by the yardstick of this or that period have been followed by a search for a scapegoat to be held responsible for deterioration in taste.

Charles II very conveniently fitted the part. He liked lilting French dances; the voluptuous sound of twenty-four fiddlers caught his fancy much more than the austere tones of a consort of viols; therefore the music written for his entertainment in court and chapel was in some way also depraved—or so the theory goes. A prejudiced view of Restoration church music still persists, though not now expressed as blatantly as it used to be: "In place of simple vocal counterpoint . . . there was gradually introduced the verse and solo anthems, with their independent symphonies and ritornellos, often graced (as the King fancied) or more possibly disgraced, with twiddles and turns enough to upset the reverence of the music and mar the serious character of the words".[1] "Many otherwise admirable works were marred by faults of taste and judgement which to minds nurtured on the artistic products of later generations appear almost ludicrous."[2] Such opinions need not detain us. But it is necessary to take a closer look at the notorious monarch, his influence on the music written during his reign, and his Chapel Royal.

There is no doubt that Charles II, directly and indirectly, did influence church music. His personal delight in music and his concern to maintain standards and magnificence in his chapels, even though this was often way beyond his means, ensured the first step—the reconstitution of an interrupted tradition. And he was not the only one who longed for the recovery of former splendours.

However many people had welcomed the setting up of a commonwealth at its outset, few could have been left to mourn its departure in 1660. The change of government that followed

the Civil War did not prove to be popular, and there was a
growing desire, by the end of the Interregnum, to return to the
stability of a traditionally ordered society. Thomas Fuller voiced
this in his prayer that "God in due time set us right, and keep us
right, that the head may be in its proper place. Next the neck
of the nobility, then the breast of the gentry, the loins of the
merchants and citizens, the thighs of the yeomanry, the legs and
feet of artificers and day-labourers".[3] In addition, the asperities
of government based on puritan principles had begun to wear
thin and, after too many years of drab propriety, there was a
growing demand for pomp, pleasure and gaiety. The "intervall
way—which was long, tedious and too practicall", had lost
appeal.

The restoration of the monarchy, when it came, was greeted
as though it were a return to peace after a long drawn-out war,
and it was celebrated with widespread rejoicing. Hopes were
set high for a new life of light and gaiety after years of gloom.
That the gaiety went to extremes of licence, and that dis-
illusionment soon followed as the light became sullied, is neither
here nor there. By then the Church of England was restored,
with its form of service and musical establishments making
church-going once more a pleasurable activity and not solely a
ponderous duty. The King's Music had been speedily re-
established, and the Chapel Royal led the way for other
choirs.

The court soon became the vortex of fashionable life, whose
tastes and manners, both good and bad, were aped elsewhere.
The personal character of the King may have left much to be
desired—he certainly earned his epithet, "the merry monarch",
and the things that made him merry were not always of the
purest; but it was also admitted that Charles II was "the
pattern of courtesie, and first brought good manners into
England", and that city life centred on his court provided a
focal point of cultural and intellectual activity which could not
flourish outside London, where, for lack of such stimulus,
"one's witt growes mouldy".[4]

B

CHARLES II AND HIS CHAPEL

At the Restoration the Chapel Royal once again assumed that pre-eminence in English cathedral music which it had held until the Commonwealth. Leading musicians were drawn to it, and the combination of their talent with the King's interest led it to a brief moment of glory comparable with any period during the previous century. That this moment was only brief can be directly related to the duration of Charles II's reign—little over half that of Elizabeth I. During those forty-four years the conditions that had emboldened the growth of a central church music tradition had enabled it to flourish also under the early Stuarts. So strongly that, even though it was cut down to the roots at the time of the Commonwealth, it sprang up again at the Restoration with full vigour and fresh growth. Charles's court provided again the continuous encouragement that had done so much for earlier musicians, but, just as the results were beginning to become apparent with the formation of a new school of composers developing fresh styles and forms, this lively growth was nipped in the bud. The sharp reaction at the time of the Restoration, combined with the hot-house stimulus of Charles II's interest produced a plant that could have matured into a product much more able to stand comparison with the solid achievements of the previous century, had it not been put out in the cold by Charles's immediate successors.

This does not controvert the fact that the Restoration composers secured brilliant results. They built up a position where once more the music of the Chapel Royal held the centre of informed musical interest. The services in the royal chapels were a resort of fashion and taste; entries in Pepys's diary show what they meant to an enthusiastic amateur such as he. Furthermore, they maintained this central position not merely by providing good entertainment value but by refusing to let their anthems become a backwater of the main stream of music, a specialist sphere unrelated to secular music and developing styles. Obviously they recognised the distinction in purpose of music for chamber, church and theatre, but they also allowed little dichotomy between sacred and secular, naturally and without false embarrassment in their anthems feeding the appetite for instrumental music, exciting vocal solos, rhythm and tunefulness, discarding in the process the old-style polyphony. But at the moment when they were beginning to establish their own identity, forging a church music which embraced liturgical purpose and also new and expanding secular tastes, Charles II very inconveniently died. The quarter-century of his reign did not prove long enough to make the new building weatherproof and the whole edifice began to crumble, first under James II who, as a Roman Catholic, had no interest in an Anglican Chapel Royal, and later under William and Mary, when royalty's power or inclination to lead national tastes was diminished. Queen Anne had the inclination, but by then it was too late to do more than patch up the half-finished building and limit its use to the barest practical essentials, devoid of the ostentatious extras that had been planned originally.

There was no further place for a significant development that had taken place in Charles's Chapel: the verse anthem with strings. Like an expensive new aircraft that has already made its maiden flight only to be axed on grounds of economy, the instrumental anthem never passed the prototype stage. Without a flourishing Chapel Royal providing a weekly platform there was little pressure for further extension of this type of anthem as a central feature in choral services. The opportunities for performance being few, the tender tradition wilted. The instrumental anthem survived only as a side line, produced for special thanksgivings and celebrations, being eventually resuscitated in a much altered and revolutionary way as an ingredient in Handel's oratorios. Composers for the church service fell back on the verse anthem with organ accompaniment and tried hard to explore further the possibilities of the full anthem, though this vein had been deeply dug by the Elizabethans and early Stuarts.

The far-ranging outlooks of Cooke and Locke had prepared

the way for a high-powered group of composers whose potential in church music was never fully realised. Humfrey and Wise died too young, Purcell, who was similarly short-lived, had already switched his attention from church to theatre music in the latter years of his life, and Blow became the "establish-ment" composer, holding a variety of metropolitan posts, who provided the congratulatory ode or thanksgiving anthem as occasion demanded. Their successors in the eighteenth century knew that in composing liturgical pieces they were writing for a tradition that was becoming more and more confined and which was in the process of segregating itself from secular music. Nothing could help them combat this trend, least of all the Chapel Royal whose influence had long since abated.

No native school of opera can survive for long without the nucleus of a well-endowed, central repertory opera company; in its day the Chapel Royal was just as essential to church music. Although it is common practice to speak of the English *cathedral* music tradition, the achievements of the sixteenth and seventeenth centuries properly belong to the Chapel Royal rather than to the cathedrals, which could not match the court's more ample resources and relatively informed patronage.

The bestowal of this patronage was enjoyed by Charles II and he employed it for a variety of reasons, not the least being that he himself liked music. Roger North disparagingly admitted that "King Charles II could not bear any other music than what he could daunce or keep time to".[5] That was preferable to com-plete barbarism. A more reliable testimony from one of the King's favourite singers, John Gostling, was handed down to an eighteenth-century writer: Charles II "had some knowledge of music . . . and sang, to use the expression of one who had often sung with him, a plump bass".[6]

Tudway, having been a chorister of the reconstituted Chapel Royal, can be illuminating. But, writing fifty years after the Restoration, his experiences were tempered by his subsequent opinions. He was concerned primarily with the state of cathedral music at the beginning of the eighteenth century and, being conscious of the rising feeling that sacred music must be kept clearly distinct from secular, he was one of the first to voice the myth that Charles II, through the music of his Chapel, was behind a noxious contamination of church music. "This secular way was first introduced into the service of the chappell, And has been too much imitated ever since." But he did admit that "the King took great delight in the service of his Chappell, and was very intent upon establishing his Choir", making places for both those "who had bin sufferers, and had survived the wars, and also for the best voices that were then to be found". Tudway proceeded to reveal his view that

> His Majesty who was a brisk, and Airy Prince, coming to the Crown in the Flow'r, and vigour of his Age, was soon, if I may say so tyr'd with the Grave and Solemn way, And order'd the Composers of his Chappell to add Symphonies etc. with Instruments to their Anthems; and thereupon established a select number of his private music to play the Symphonies, and Ritornellos, which he had appointed.
> The King did not intend by this innovation to alter anything of the established way; he only appointed this to be done, when he came himself to the Chappell, which was only upon Sundays in the Mornings, on the great Festivals, and days of Offerings. . . .

If the King really did attend church as frequently as this the composers must have had to work hard to keep up a flow of new music for his delight, but they would not have needed royal commands to make them write instrumental symphonies. They would have been familiar enough with the precedent of the early Stuart composers' verse anthems for viols and voices, and the chance of using a modern orchestra of violins would have been too good to be missed. Tudway in fact recognised this when he later added:

> Some of the forwardest, and brightest Children of the Chappell, as Mr. Humfreys, Mr. Blow, etc. began to be masters of a faculty in composing: This his Majesty greatly encouraged, by indulging their youthful fancys, so that every month at least, and afterwards

oftener, they produced something New, of this Kind; In a few years more, severall others, Educated in the Chappell, produced their Compositions in this style, for otherwise it was in vain to hope to please his Majesty.

Tudway stated that the anthem with instruments was discontinued after the death of Charles II; but, for him, the damage had been done, as the instrumental flourishes and interludes continued to be perpetrated on the organ.[7]

Whether or not the "restoration style" would have become so popular without such a sympathetic audience is open to question. It was natural enough that these young composers should strive to be up-to-date and conversant with contemporary continental developments. If this led, as it did for Humfrey, to a visit to France at government expense this probably served only to reinforce existing inclinations. Nonetheless, Charles II's tastes would have been well known and his musicians happily pandered to them—he paid the piper, or tried to. And he was not the only one tired of the "grave and solemn way"; other members of the royal family held similar views. Pepys followed suit. He rarely missed a chance of going to one of the royal chapels when there was something worth hearing. Occasionally, however, he was disappointed. He has recorded how on St. Peter's Day, 1668, he "did hear an anthem of Silas Taylor's making; a dull old-fashioned thing, of six and seven parts, that nobody could understand: and the Duke of York, when he came out, told me that he was a better store-keeper than an anthem maker, and that was bad enough, too". This reaction is not surprising considering how Pepys had already stated that "singing with many voices is not singing", and displayed his fashionable delight in the rapidly evolving verse-anthem style and consequent distaste for polyphonic music: "the manner of setting of words and repeating them out of order, and that with a number of voices, makes me sick".

Another writer said of Silas Taylor* that "he was very

* Silas Taylor, 1624-1678. Antiquarian, civil servant, and minor composer. A captain in Cromwell's army.

musicall, and hath composed many things, and I have heard
Anthems of his sang before his Majestie, in his Chappell, and
the King told him he liked them".[8] This, probably, was an
example of Charles II's tact and courtesy; for a more discerning
observation of the King's natural reactions we must again rely
on Pepys: "after sermon a brave anthem of Captain Cooke's
which he himself sung, and the King was well pleased with it".
Two months later—"an anthem, ill sung, which made the King
laugh". In 1663, "the anthem was good after the Sermon, being
the 51st psalme, made for five voices by one of Captain Cooke's
boys, a pretty boy. And they say there are four or five of them
that can do as much. And here I first perceived that the King is
a little musicall, and kept good time with his hand all along the
anthem."[9]

THE CHAPEL ROYAL CHOIR

A former chaplain to Charles I and Archbishop Laud, indicated
at the Restoration the task before the royal court. By pointedly
referring back to the good old days of Queen Elizabeth he
showed who should lead the way in the proper observance of
the Church of England liturgy.

> Nor is it much to be admired that such a general conformity to those
> ancient usages was constantly observed in all Cathedrals and the
> most part of the parish-churches, considering how well they were
> precedented by the Court itself, in which the Liturgy was officiated
> every day both morning and evening, not only in the public
> Chapel, but the private closet; celebrated in the Chapel with
> organs and other musical instruments, and the most excellent
> voices, both of men and children, that could be got in all the
> Kingdom.[10]

Such a hint was hardly necessary. The complete ceremonial
and splendour of the Church of England services accompanied

the re-establishment of the church as automatically as did the full panoply of the court in the train of the King.

Appointments were quickly made to the King's Music, and the Chapel Royal choir did not lack singers glad of employment after the Commonwealth years. It was quickly grasped that the court would once again be the centre of musical activity. Indeed, it was many years before a musical career in other spheres could offer serious counter-attractions. An increase in salary in 1662 for a Gentleman of the Chapel Royal from £40 to £70 per annum obviously helped, and the records show singers being drawn from a variety of provincial establishments.*

Fortunately the right man was appointed to find and train the choristers. It may have been necessary to supply and reinforce the treble parts with cornetts immediately after the Restoration but, within his first year as Master of the Children, Captain Cooke had already obtained five boys from Newark and Lincoln, and had filled all the twelve places. In 1662, as a precaution against the departure of many of the first batch all at the same time, he also admitted an extra, thirteenth chorister.†

* 1662. George Yardley, "a base from Worcester".
  1663. Charles Husbands, "a counter tenor from Windsor".
  1664. Mr. William Hopwood, "a basse from Exeter".
  1664. Mr. Andrew Carter, "a Priest of Salesbury".
  1669. Mr. William Turner, "a counter tenor from Lincolne".
  1669. Mr. Edmund Slauter, "a base from Windsor".
  1670. Mr. James Hart, "a base from Yorke".
  1671. Mr. Andrew Trebeck, "a basse from Worster".
                                                    etc.[11]

† Two left in the summer of 1663, and four more in 1664 (Thomas Price and Michael Wise, Michaelmas, 1663; Thomas Edwards, 25th March, 1664; Pelham Humfrey, John Blow and John Blundivile, Christmas Day, 1664).

A little too much has been made of the seeming callousness of "press-ganging" boys from provincial cathedrals into the royal choirs. This prerogative was widely exercised and, though not always popular, it must generally have been considered an honour to provide boys for the King's own choir. No better start in a musical career could have been found anywhere else, considering not only the training the choristers acquired at the Chapel Royal but also the after-care they received when their voices broke.

Apart from fetching boys from Newark and Lincoln, Cooke is promised payment in April 1665 for "going into the country looking after boyes for

That Cooke had both an eye for musical talent and the ability to make the most of it when he found it is evident from the fact that amongst his earliest boys were Wise, Humfrey, Blow and Turner. With choristers of this calibre one cannot explain the predominance of alto, tenor and bass verses in the Restoration anthem as being due to shortage of skilled trebles. Solos for trebles are a regular feature in music that would take a permanent place in the repertoire, such as settings of the canticles and many full anthems. Yet a large number of the verse anthems would have been written for a different purpose: a vehicle to display the vocal prowess of a favourite singer, or a novelty item to delight the King. It would be an uneconomic use of time to teach boys extensive verses which might be sung only once or twice before being discarded for something else, whereas for the men, being able and experienced sight-singers, such solos would provide a refreshing musical stimulus.

There was, however, no time to wait for the first batch of boys to be trained. Within weeks of the King's restoration the Church of England services were in use once again. Evelyn stated that on Sunday, 8th July, 1660, "from henceforth, was the Liturgy publicly used in our churches, whence it had been for so many years banished". The organ had already been played a month earlier at Whitehall, but on 8th July Pepys, too, recorded: "here I heard very good music, the first time that

the Chappell", in April 1668 for "going to Windsor, for two boyes", in May 1669 for "fetching and bringing up boyes from severall places", in June 1670 for "fetching of boyes from Rochester, Lyncolne, Peterborough, Worcester, and other places", in May 1671 for "going to Westchester, Litchfield, Canterbury and Rochester to look for boyes". The sole reference to this practice during Humfrey's brief rule as Master of the Children is significant in marking an exception: 2nd May, 1673, "In this warrant was nothing for fetching children from several cathedrals, as is sometymes". Blow made use of the custom; but on three separate occasions he went all the way to Cambridge, Salisbury and Lincoln to fetch only one boy each time (unless he was using this as a pretext to visit friends in the country), and only once is he recorded as making a larger catch. This would imply that he was accepting no boys other than those who had been recommended as being specially deserving of a Chapel Royal education, and not greedily skimming the cream of the cathedral choirs.

B*

ever I remember to have heard the organs and singing-men in surplices in my life". Although Evelyn was to be very critical of later developments he also noticed with gratification, in November of the same year, that at the royal chapel "now the service was performed with music, voices, etc., as formerly".[12]

Following the reinstatement of the liturgy, attention was soon directed to placing the royal choir on a well ordered basis. Barnard's *First Book of Selected Church Music*, published in 1641 just before the Civil War, provided much of the music to be sung. Surviving manuscript copies of services and anthems were re-employed until augmented or replaced by later additions to the repertoire.*

On 3rd December, 1660, a warrant was made out "to provide three score and four surplices of fine holland cloth for the Gentlemen of the Chappell and twelve surplices for the musicians and thirty-four surplices of the like fine holland cloth for the children of the Chappell". Subsequently every effort was made to keep the men, boys and instrumentalists smart in the chapel, judging by frequent entries in the records referring to the provision of surplices. From these it would seem that

---

* £5 18s. od. was paid on 24th March, 1662, "for a book of the services and anthems for his Majesty's use". Subsequent payments were made of £73, in 1669, to the subdean "for paper books, pricking services and anthems for his Majesty's service, and for other things, from May 1662 to 10 December, 1668"; of £15 to William Tucker's widow "for her husband's writing in fifteen books the Anthems with Symphonies for King Charles the 2nd's use in his Chappell Royal"; and of £12, in 1681, to the subdean "for some parts of anthems and services written in the books, belonging to his Majesty's Chappell Royall, from 12 February, 1676 to 25 December, 1680, and for books and ruled paper for the children of the Chappell".

This latter sentence indicates that, on occasions, the boys copied music into part-books. An ex-Chapel Royal bass part-book (1682–1685) which formerly belonged to Richard Border of Pulborough, Hants, contains eighteen instrumental anthems by Humfrey (8), Blow (4), Purcell (2), Locke (2), Turner (1), Tudway (1), and seven complete services by Blow (3), Aldrich, Purcell, Child, Humfrey, and part of Tallis's short service. Pencilled on one page is: "This is the book which my Lord Keeper bespoke of a Child of the King's Chappel, and was pay'd £1 10s. for since his death".

surplices were ordered on four separate occasions in twenty-five years: in 1660, 1667, 1672 and 1685.

The allowance for the annual expenses of each chorister, "for the diett, lodging, washing, and teaching of each of the Children", was raised in 1661 from £15 4s. 2d. to £30; and, in the following year, the salary of a Gentleman of the Chapel Royal became £70 per annum. The men had previously petitioned for an increase on the grounds that, with the rise in the cost of living, the £40 per annum of King James I's reign had lost half its value. Perhaps it was intended that this increase should be linked with improved efficiency as, a year later, detailed rules were laid down concerning attendance, order and discipline in the Chapel. The enforcement of these (restating an earlier set of regulations made at the beginning of King James I's reign) was placed in the hands of the sub-dean for the express purpose "that the great neglects in God's service may be redrest in his Majesties Chappell Royall".[13]

It was now felt reasonable to expect the gentlemen to treat the Chapel Royal as a full-time occupation and not combine it with singing duties in other choirs. Reasonable it may have been in theory. Nonetheless it soon became apparent that an award of a salary increase did not guarantee its receipt. As arrears began to accumulate, it became essential to hold other posts as an insurance against dilatory payments from the king's coffers. The authorities at Worcester Cathedral would not have been alone in officially recognising the mutual advantages to their choir and its members when, in 1673, they condoned membership of two choirs: "such of the choir as are related to his Majesties Chappel shall be freed from the sayd mulct [for absence] during the time of their service there, and for two weeks more in respect of their journeys".[14]

The gentlemen of the Chapel Royal were ordered to attend services punctually (at 10 a.m. and 4 p.m. on weekdays, 9 a.m. and 4 p.m. on Sundays and sermon days), come "decently habited in their gownes and surplices (not in cloakes and bootes and spurrs)", enter the chapel "orderly together", and not leave before the end of the service. If they did not arrive until the end of the first psalm they were fined sixpence; if they came after the first lesson they were fined one shilling, as though they had missed the whole service. The fine for absence on Sundays and feastdays was double this. In King James's reign the proceeds from these fines had been given to those who had the best attendance record; in 1663 they were left to the dean to dispose of as he thought fit. The whole choir was expected to attend on Sundays, feastdays and their eves; but on "working days" they went by a monthly rota, drawn up at the beginning of each year in collaboration with the sub-dean. They were only permitted to provide deputies, in the event of sickness or for an officially approved reason, from amongst their own number. Holidays, however, were generous and included, in addition to three months in the summer, at least five separate weekly periods before Christmas, in the New Year, at the beginning of February, after Easter, the end of April, and "all removing weekes".

A new member of the choir would generally be admitted into an "extraordinary" place, where he would undertake a probationary period until a full place became vacant. This he would gain on being approved "for manners, skill, and voyce". It was considered necessary to order all the men to join in the spoken parts of the service and the hymns as well as sing the settings and anthems: they were to "use their bookes and voyces in the Psalmodies and Responsalls according to the order of the Rubricke, and in the hymnes of the Church in the time of Divine service, and answer the Amen in a loud voice".

All three organists were bidden to attend at the major feasts, the senior one always playing on the actual feastday and its eve. On other days two were considered sufficient: one to play the organ, the other, "in his surplice in the quire, to beare a parte in the Psalmodie and service". The choice of music was placed not in the hands of the musical director but in those of the dean or sub-dean. The master of the children was only entitled to give his advice when anthems were considered that involved the trebles.

There were thirty-two gentlemen of the Chapel Royal, and this number included both clerical and lay singers as well as the three organists. The complete establishment probably was present only on special occasions, and it is likely that a working strength was a reduced choir of the proportions of that accompanying the King on his summer visits to Windsor. Choir practices were not considered a matter requiring the attention of official regulations although, at the beginning of Charles II's reign, the master of the King's Music was given authority to arrange whatever rehearsals he considered necessary for "all his Majesty's musicians", and was empowered to punish all who refused "to wayte at such convenient tymes of practize and service as he shall appoint". Further commands than this were unnecessary, and the only other reference in thirty years to extra rehearsals is to those in preparation for the coronation of Charles II called by Cooke, who was promised payment of " £2 16s. for torches and lights for practising the musick against his Majesty's coronation".

THE "CHILDREN OF THE CHAPPELL"

One of Cooke's first noted appointments was "master of the boyes in the private musick", an office distinct from that of master of the "children of the Chapel". In the former capacity he was allowed £10 a quarter "for keeping and teaching 2 singing boys", and Cooke and his successors combined this responsibility with their other duties apart from one occasion, in 1668, when it was taken over by Louis Grabu (for some time director of the whole of the King's Music).*

* In a list of payments for 9th January, 1669, Cooke is owed £48 as "master of the boys" and, in addition, £40 "for 2 boys in the private musick". A royal order dated 21st February of the same year places the twenty-four violinists, the Master of Music, with "two boyes, two composers, and Monsieur Le Grange for a basse" in a separate category from "our musick in our chappell".

These two "singing boys" may have been trained to sing as soloists in some of the Chapel Royal services, and may at times have sung for the Queen's separate establishment, but their main task was more likely to have been the provision of informal music for the King. Certainly, two skilled trebles and a bass with instrumental continuo would have provided an ideal ensemble for performing some of the *Psalms* of Child and Lawes as well as the sacred songs and motets of Locke, Blow and Purcell. A modern edition of an anthem by Porter, *Praise the Lord*, provides a striking instance of the elaborate music these boys might have been expected to sing.[15] Pepys was particularly impressed by a performance of music of this nature at Lord Sandwich's residence on 21st December, 1663: "Captain Cooke and his two boys did sing some Italian songs, which I must in a word say I think was fully the best musique that I ever yet heard in all my life".

Cooke's gift for training two boys in the King's Private Music equally benefitted the twelve children of the royal chapel. The singing of the choristers as much as that of the men would have drawn Pepys there to enjoy "a good anthem" (he certainly did not find a comparable attraction at Westminster Abbey or St. Paul's Cathedral). It is unfortunate that one of his more familiar accounts of the boys' singing refers to efforts made by three whose voices had broken. Yet however excruciating the sound on that occasion, Pepys did not fail to admire the evidence of exceptional musical ability.

This morning come two of Captain Cooke's boys, whose voices are broke, and are gone from the Chapel, but have an extra-ordinary skill; and they and my boy, with his broken voice, did sing three parts; their names were Blaew and Loggings; but nottwithstanding their skill, yet to hear them sing with their broken voices, which they could not command to keep in tune, would make a man mad—so bad it was.[16]

If "Blaew" is a mis-spelling for Blow, as has been generally assumed, it must indeed have been a rough noise. Blow had already left the choir nearly three years before and was by then eighteen and a half years old.

As a singer and teacher of high repute, Cooke could be expected to know all about voice production; as a lieutenant in the army in the Civil War, later promoted to captain, he would have no problem with discipline. In addition he also had to be music master, school teacher, matron and general factotum to the boys. Even if some tasks were deputed to others, the office of master of the children was no sinecure.

The instruments the boys were taught after the Restoration were generally the lute, violin and theorbo (a tenor lute, used as a continuo instrument to provide accompaniments). No doubt emphasis was placed on the violin right from the start, and Humfrey, Blow and Purcell must have gained useful first-hand experience of string idiom from this early instruction. Cooke may well have taught all the instruments to the boys himself, although his immediate successor, Humfrey, delegated the teaching of four pupils "on the violl and theorbo" to a colleague for £30 per annum. The master of the children had to keep his pupils' instruments in playing order, and replace any that were broken beyond repair. £20 spent by Cooke on a theorbo in 1662 would have bought a very good instrument for use in the chapel services; student instruments would have cost less. For no more than £22 Humfrey, in 1673, bought two theorbos and two bass viols "for teaching the children of the Chappell".

Alongside this practical instruction the boys were also taught to write music (or so one would gather from frequent references in the accounts to the provision of "ruled paper, penns and ink"). The organ was taught, but only during two defined periods. As the first of these coincided with the time when Wise, Humfrey, Blow and Turner were choristers (up to March 1667) and the second, Purcell (from March 1668 to March 1671) it would seem that only the more promising boys had organ lessons.

The choristers' musical training was thorough and comprehensive. Equal care was taken over their general education, although it was only in the first years of Cooke's tenure of the office that the master of the children assumed direct responsibility for this. Cooke discovered there was not time to do everything and consequently drew the line at teaching Latin, preferring to pay out £30 a year "to masters for teaching the said children to write and to learne and speake Latine".

Practical matters needing attention included making arrangements for transport and accommodation when the choir accompanied the King to Windsor and elsewhere, the heating of the practice room, and the provision of "Common Prayer books in octavo, for the Children to doe their service in his Majesty's Chappell". General administration, routine ordering of the daily services, and much incidental business would have been enough without having to look after "diett, lodging, washing", yet the welfare of the boys was one more concern of the master of the children. He had to see that they were equipped with suitable clothes, varying from the special "scarlet cloth" uniform for a coronation, "perfumed cord gloves", to such ordinary items as "strong waxt leather shoes" (six pairs each!). In fact the uncertain state of the royal finances would have made it a problem to keep the boys' uniforms from falling to pieces, let alone smart and tidy. As late as 1693 Blow had to be paid for "cloth, buttons, silk and thread for mending the cloths and linen several times".

The boys' health was a serious responsibility. 1665 was the year of the Great Plague, so it is not surprising to read then of the "nursing of three boys that were sick of the small pox". Six years later Cooke had to be recouped for calling in "doctors, nurses, and for looking to severall of the Children when they were sick". "Nursing one of the children being sick of the small pox" (1673), "a nurse, chamber rent and firing for keeping of John Cherrington, one of the children of the Chappell, being sick of the spotted fever" (1676), and "the cure of a broaken legg" (1677) completes the health record for the remainder of the seventeenth century apart from one final entry in 1684:

to Dr. John Blow . . .
For a nurse for one of the children   —   £3 12. 0.
For burying Edward Frost —   —   —   £7 5. 8.*

For the choristers that survived their time in the Chapel Royal choir, well-meant attempts were made to further their education. When a boy's voice broke he was maintained for three or four more years by the master of the children, or by a colleague on his behalf. £30 a year was due for the "charge and expense of keeping" the boy during this period; and it was intended that this allowance should be supplemented with a complete trousseau.† The intention was admirable. In fact the money was not always forthcoming, and an ex-chorister was fortunate if he received his full set of clothing. Over seven years after William Turner had left the choir a warrant had to be made out to pay £120 to him direct; even then it is unlikely that he received it. The master of the children would hardly be in a position to abuse the system under these circumstances. He would probably try to keep the more promising boys

* The complete account dated 1st November, 1684, will show both details of the annual out-of-pocket expenses incurred by the Master of the Children, and the nature of his responsibilities:

	£	s.	d.
For the children's learning on the lute	30	0	0
For the violin	30	0	0
For the theorbo	30	0	0
For fire and strings for the musicke roome in the chappell	20	0	0
For ruled paper and penns and inke, etc.	2	10	0
For strings for the lutes and theorboe	2	10	0
For 6 days travelling to Lyncolne and bringing a boy	6	0	0
For a nurse for one of the children	3	12	0
For burying Edward Frost	7	5	8

£131 17 8

† A warrant dated 17th January, 1673, gives particulars: ". . . for the use of Henry Hall, late child of the Chappell, whose voyce is changed and is gon from the Chappell, two suites of playne cloth, two hatts and hatt bands, four whole shirts, four half shirts, six bands, six pair of cuffs, six handkerchiefs, four pair of stockings, four pair of shoes, and four pair of gloves." No small leaving gift, and known to cost £18.

himself so as to continue their musical training, though there
was at least one occasion when he had to find a friend who
would undertake this expense for him. Pepys did this gladly for
Cooke when asked to take in Thomas Edwards who had left
the choir in March 1664.

> So doing some other small errands I home, and there find my boy,
> Tom Edwards, come, sent me by Captain Cooke, having been
> bred in the King's Chappell these four years. I propose to make a
> clerk of him, and if he deserves well, to do well by him.
>
> So home and find my boy a very school boy, that talks inno-
> cently and impertinently, but at present it is a sport to us, and in
> a little time he will leave it. So sent him to bed, he saying that he
> used to go to bed at eight o'clock, and then all of us to bed, myself
> pretty well pleased with my choice of a boy.

Edwards was well able to tackle Porter's elaborate treble
parts to Pepys's satisfaction:

> . . . the boy and I again to the singing of Mr Porter's mottets,
> and it is a great joy to me that I am come to this condition to
> maintain a person in the house able to give me such pleasure, as
> this boy do by his thorough knowledge of musique, as he sings
> anything at first sight.

Cooke still kept a watchful eye on his former chorister's
musical studies, as is shown by one further remark of the diarist:
"Captain Cooke met me, and did seem discontented about my
boy Tom's having no time to mind his singing nor lute . . .".
Pepys, however, set his mind at rest. At any rate, two years
later, Tom Edwards was able to hold his own with Blaew and
Loggings.[17]

There was one significant exception to the annual maintenance allowance of £30, and this was when £40 yearly was
promised on Humfrey's behalf. Either this was intended as
recognition of exceptional ability (Humfrey had already enlarged the Chapel Royal repertoire with his anthems), or it was

an instance of understandable favouritism. Humfrey later married one of Cooke's daughters, and the pupil–teacher relationship must have been unusually cordial to encourage such a match.

The allowance for an ex-chorister was reduced from 1687 onwards, when he received a single "suit of plain clothes" and a flat payment of £20. It was no longer worth while for the master of the children to continue the boys' education after their voices had broken (many years of erratic payments of expenses had probably already caused this system to lapse). Subsequently this diminished emolument was made out to the boy or his parents as a reward for good service.[18]

Even with the decline in the importance of the Chapel Royal that followed the end of Charles II's reign, the education of the choristers continued on lines similar to those already described and, in this way, offered the best available training and introduction to a musical career. The boys, in 1715, were being taught by Croft to play an instrument, to compose, and to handle figured-bass accompaniments.[19] Their work prospered under the tuition of gifted choirmasters such as Croft himself and his successors, Gates and Nares. Their singing excelled at the many state occasions that called for the Chapel Royal choir—public thanksgivings, coronations, royal weddings and funerals; in addition, they later frequently took part in London performances of Handel's oratorios.

Yet, in the long run, none of these activities gave the Chapel Royal that pre-eminence in English musical life it had enjoyed under Charles II. The distinctive feature of the services in his chapel was not just the excellence of the choir, the high-calibred musicianship of its members, but the regular use of instruments. This aspect now demands closer attention.

3

Royal Music—2

21st December, 1962.

After which, instead of the ancient, grave, and solemn wind-music accompanying the organ, was introduced a concert of twenty-four violins between every pause, after the French fantastical light way, better suiting a tavern, or play-house, than a church. This was the first time of change, and now we no more heard the cornet which gave life to the organ; that instrument quite left of in which the English were so skilful.

Although Evelyn the squire accepted traditional, aristocratic instruments in church, the puritan in him abhorred the devilish implications of twenty-four violins. An antipathy to instruments, other than the organ, accompanying a church service has remained with us ever since. Why else our scant experience of Viennese orchestral Masses, of the authentic sounds of bells and banging in mediaeval sacred music, and of the English instrumental anthem?

Regardless of Evelyn, these violins provided for a short time a creative stimulus within English church music. Of all the avenues that had been opened since the Reformation, most had been fully explored: the "short" service by Gibbons, the "great" service by Byrd, and the full anthem in many instances by these composers and their contemporaries. There remained little to add to their achievements. The verse anthem, however, despite its hundred years' history, was the one structure which left scope for further expansion. More than the other forms it allowed natural expression of the evolving musical styles of the seventeenth century: the departure from many-voiced music to an air supported by a single bass part, from a continuous interweaving to the clear-cut definition of sections with cadence and modulation, and from the inner intensity of polyphony to the dramatic contrasts obtainable from the juxtaposition of various combinations of solo and ensemble. Weelkes and Gibbons, amongst others, had begun to investigate the various possibilities, but it was left to the Restoration composers to explore them to their fullest extent.

Viols had already been much used in verse anthems, but their idiom and associations were too closely linked with old contrapuntal styles. Violins, on the other hand, being new in the context of the church anthem, did not have this drawback. Instead of continuing the vocal line, part and parcel of the same musical argument, the violins now assumed a dramatically independent role. The structure of a verse anthem could no longer be built solely on a succession of cadences, or sentences of a text, but required the pillars of instrumental sections to add cohesion, contrast and colour. It is not surprising if, in some instrumental anthems, the opening symphony should be but an impressive portico disguising a very ordinary building, since mastery of new materials and ideas was not gained without a struggle. Those works, however, which won through were in their way as remarkable as Wren's great churches.* The massive

---

* To pursue further this architectural analogy: the change in style from the elaborate baroque of Archer's churches (e.g. St. John's, Westminster) to the neat, well-proportioned but far less imaginative churches of the later eighteenth century (e.g. Gibb's St. Martin's-in-the-Fields) has obvious parallels in music. This comparison can be extended to include, for instance:

Inigo Jones — Palladian   — Lawes and Locke
Wren   — half Baroque   — Purcell
Van Brugh — whole Baroque — Blow
Burlington — polite Palladian
                        reaction   — Boyce.

architecture of Locke's *The King shall rejoice*, Blow's *God spake sometime in visions*, and Purcell's *My heart is inditing* is in no small way inspired by the diversity of the materials used. Given full rein, the Restoration composer could be stimulated by the possibilities of using large forces of voices and instruments to produce works of extraordinary stature. But these three works with their fulsome scoring were written for special occasions; on a smaller scale was the instrumental verse anthem, maintaining a less lavish function in the routine services of the Chapel Royal. That here also composers revelled in writing for the violins is readily apparent in the quality of the string symphonies and interludes by Turner, Humfrey and Blow. In many anthems these short symphonies still appear fresh to us, even where the vocal writing has faded with age.

This is digressing from Evelyn's attitude. He could not foresee the potential of combining a choir with an ensemble of violins, and he was too much of a conservative in matters touching the Church of England to welcome such a dramatic innovation in its regular services. The violin in secular use had, during the Commonwealth, already begun to gain in popularity and to make inroads on the position of the viol. Nonetheless, the latter was for many still the gentleman's instrument, far superior to the violin, the plaything of the "common fiddler". Not even the use of violins at the state funerals of Queen Elizabeth and James I in 1603 and 1625 had succeeded in raising that instrument's status.

Charles II was not over-much concerned with such rival reputations. The violin's qualities—"lowdness a great ingredient, together with a strong snatching way of playing, to make the musick brisk and good"[1]—may have accounted for the King's preference for it. But that this helped to make a vulgar instrument fashionable was incidental to his primary aim: to re-establish a court life which he could enjoy, and one that could impress by its exuberance and splendour both the unruly people he had returned to govern and his rivals amongst foreign powers. In exile Charles II would have admired Louis

XIV's *Vingt-quatre violons du Roi* as a striking status-symbol and for the value of their musical performances. He wasted no time ordering the equivalent for himself, and saw that he had an orchestra of twenty-four violins ready to play at his coronation on 23rd April, 1661.*

It is important to emphasise that the violins were established to play for state functions, or for the entertainment of the King on public or semi-public occasions. Roger North reminds us: "after the manner of France, he [Charles II] set up a band of twenty-four violins to play at his dinners"; and Anthony à Wood reinforces this: "the King, according to the French mode, would have twenty-four violins played before him while he was at meales, as being more airie and brisk than viols". This is not an attempt to whittle down the celebrated fiddlers to post-prandial players; they also provided music for court theatricals and other occasions as and when required by the King. But these, and not the chapel music, were their primary employments. Tudway, for all that he blamed the King for the innovation of instrumental interludes in anthems, stated that Charles II did not plan any alteration of services in the Chapel Royal, requiring the instruments to attend no more than once a week, and then only a "select number of his private music".

A look at indications of the actual number of players thus selected will help correct the impression created by Evelyn's reference to a "concert of twenty-four violins". This, in any

* (Here, and subsequently, "violins" comprehends the complete orchestral family.)

Only a month after the coronation a royal order expressed the King's concern for quality as well as quantity. Being aware of some inadequacies in the performing standards of "his band of violins", he deputed orders for the better regulation of "their practize and performance of musick to prevent their former neglects".

The coronation would have seen the first appearance of the twenty-four violins (23rd April, 1661).[2] This does not contradict Evelyn's statement at the beginning of this chapter which refers to their introduction to the Chapel Royal services (21st December, 1662), nor necessarily that of Pepys (see note page 45) referring to the addition of symphonies played by "violls and other instruments" (14th September, 1662).

case, may not have been the literal number that Evelyn heard but the general title by which the band was known. It is conceivable that Charles II originally called for all his violins to attend on him at the Chapel, and then later accepted the reduced numbers discussed below. But it is more likely that (on the majority of occasions) only a section of the complete band played at the chapel services, and that it was with the breakdown of working arrangements as to who should play when that it became necessary to produce specific regulations.[3]

In May 1670, and again at the end of 1671, the names of fifteen members of the King's violins, drawn up in three lists of five, are included in an order that they "doe wayte and attend in his Majesty's Chappell Royall as they are here sett down, five in one month and five in another. Soe that each person attend every third month, or they will answere the contrary". In March of the following year there is a similar order, only this time the numbers are increased to six in each list. Six would provide two players to a part in some anthems; otherwise the symphonies would have to be played by a solo ensemble. Obviously these lists give the minimum number for the routine performances of string anthems in the Chapel Royal. If the master of the music required more players, he could arrange for this; but there is one revealing clue that he generally managed with either six or twelve. Amongst frequent references in the court records between the years 1660 and 1685 to the provision of surplices for the "gentlemen" and the "children" of the chapel, twelve are allotted to the "musicians". Wear and tear on the boys' surplices was such that a set of three each (thirty-six for twelve children) was considered necessary. The men managed with two (sixty-four for thirty-two gentlemen). One would assume that the instrumentalists were no less careful than the men with their surplices.*

_____

* Also apparent from this source is an indication that the instrumentalists ceased to take a *regular* part in the Chapel Royal services after the reigns of Charles II and James II. From the Restoration onwards until 1685 the number of surplices mentioned always includes twelve for the "musicians",

The number twelve brings us to the "select band" mentioned by Tudway. Soon after the Restoration John Banister was directed "to make choyce of twelve of our four and twenty violins to be a select band to wayte on us whensoever there should be occasion for musick". Choice was duly made, and the names appeared in a list dated 14th March, 1667. A year later, the twenty-four violins are set out in two, monthly, rosters, twelve to "wayt and attend" each month alternately. Although there are different names in the lists for the two years, there are twelve players in each, and this number would have been available for the chapel.*

together with those for the choir. The only other reference to the provision of surplices between 1685 and the end of the century is an account (dated 1692) from the reign of William and Mary "for making sixty-four surplices for the gentlemen . . . and thirty-six surplices for the children of the Chappell Royall", which noticeably excludes the musicians.

* A warrant dated 20th March, 1665, indicates one reason for this division into two bands: "severall coloured silkes for four and twenty violins, twelve of them being for his Majesty's service in the theatre Royall, and the other twelve habitts for his Majesty's service in his Highness the Duke of York's theatre".

In another context, even in the middle of the eighteenth century one writer felt that an orchestra of twelve players was adequate for the performance of a concerto grosso (consisting of one solo instrument, four ripieno players, four ripieno basses, two double basses and one harpsichord).[4]

In any case it would have been an impossible squash to have all twenty-four instruments and their players in the organ loft, where Hawkins was told they played. Charles II "commanded such as composed for the chapel to make also Symphonies and Ritornellos to many of the anthems in use, which were performed by a band of instruments placed in the organ-loft".[5]

Pepys, unfortunately, does not enlighten us on this question. Although he had heard, three months before Evelyn did, anthems with instrumental interludes at the Chapel Royal, he neither specified how many violins were used, nor, indeed whether they were used at all.

7th September, 1662.

". . . most excellent anthem, with symphonies between . . ."

14th September, 1662.

". . . Thence to White Hall chapel, where sermon almost done, and I heard Captain Cooke's new musique. This was the first day of having violls and other instruments to play a Symphony between every verse of the anthem; but the musique more full than it was the last Sunday, and very fine it is."

When the Chapel Royal dispensed with instruments in its regular services, the symphonies of the string verse anthems were truncated and replaced by cursory organ introductions. Blow preferred them performed this way rather than not at all, and made his own adaptations accordingly; eighteenth-century taste followed his precedent, and succeeding generations did not stop to question it. Now that these anthems are no longer acceptable in this mutilated form, any more than the organ is agreed to be an adequate substitute for strings, it becomes essential to reach a clear idea (even if precise numbers cannot be ascertained) of the relative strengths of singers and instrumentalists.

Too large a body of strings can easily give the false impression that an anthem's opening symphony is a miniature orchestral overture, weightily setting the stage for ensuing dramas of vast import. A group of only twelve or six players comes within the province of chamber music, a match for the vocal ensembles with which they alternate. Symphonies played by such numbers would lead naturally, without any sudden change in scale or dynamic level, into verses for solo voices with continuo accompaniment. Ritornelli binding the vocal sections together, often by repeating their phrases, would be within the same proportions. Then the final choruses place their emphasis not by length or musical interest (they are never long and rarely of exceptional interest) but by sheer force of numbers. The size of the full choir would be at least double that of the band; and the change from a few solo voices to a full chorus would have an obvious and immediate impact. Not very subtle, admittedly. But for the Restoration composers the subtleties were expressed by the chamber-music groups of instrumentalists and solo singers, and the chorus was intended to provide no more than an emphatic full-stop to an argument already fully discussed.

Official records give the numbers of musicians who accompanied Charles II to Windsor on three separate occasions. Generally incorporating the celebration of St. George's Feast on 29th May, these excursions of the court, lasting a month

or two, would present the King and his household with a
welcome change of air at a time of year when London became
none too healthy. The musicians, too, benefited from these
summer holidays. As the King insisted on having music where-
ever he went, it is not likely that for any extended period he
would tolerate a choir and orchestra seriously reduced in size
from that which he was accustomed to in London. In the
summer of 1671 the following attended at Windsor: twenty-
four gentlemen for the week ending with St. George's Feast,
24th to 30th May, and half that number for the remainder of
the time, 30th May to 15th July. In attendance for the whole
period of seven and a half weeks were the organist, in this
instance, Blow, "two base violls and four violins", and six
children with their Master. Cooke, with all twelve boys, was at
Windsor for a further, unspecified fortnight.*

That Charles II was determined that his music out of town
should not be below par is evident from an order dated 16th
May, 1674. By excusing at that particular time some of his
choir from weekday duties at Windsor, he clearly implied that
such absence would not be granted under other circumstances.†
In 1674 the court was at Windsor for a total of three and a half
months. From 18th May to 3rd September fourteen violins
were in attendance together with eighteen men, increased by

* Possibly services carried on as usual in Whitehall Chapel during the
King's absence from London, and the musical establishment was split to
maintain this double routine. For instance, after a preliminary period at
Windsor (two weeks for the boys, one for the men) when the whole choir
assembled for rehearsal, culminating in the actual celebration of St. George's
Feast, half the choir would return to London to sing at Whitehall, possibly
alternating with the Windsor half by weeks or months, leaving twelve men,
six boys and six strings at either place.

† "It is his Majesty's pleasure that Mr. Turner and Mr. Hart or any other
men or boys belonging to his Majesty's Chappell Royall that sing in the
Tempest at His Royal Highnesse Theatre doe remaine in towne all the weeke
(dureing his Majesty's absence from Whitehall) to performe that service,
only Saturdayes to repair to Windsor and to returne to London on Mun-
dayes if there be occasion for them. And that [they] also performe the like
service in the opera in the said theatre or any other thing in the like nature
where their helpe may be desired upon notice given them thereof."

six for the week of St. George's Feast, and eight boys with their master. Fourteen violins had been used in 1662 at Hampton Court. Certainly a band of fourteen players is more conveniently divided than one of twelve, but it seems that in 1674 these players had some particular music to perform at Windsor. A special entertainment before the King was presented on 4th July which may have been one that had been previously rehearsed in London under the French composer Cambert's direction.

It was during this period that Humfrey died suddenly, at the age of twenty-seven, and that Blow was quickly appointed to be his successor. The relevant "list of the gentlemen of the Chappell that are to wayte and constantly attend his Majesty's service at Windsor during his residence there" is particularly informative, and gives the choirmen's names set out both in sides (i.e., Decani and Cantoris) and in voices (six altos, six tenors and six basses).

When the King was accompanied by his music at Windsor four years later, for all six weeks from 14th August to 26th September he had twelve violins, eight boys and sixteen gentlemen. In addition Blow was present as both organist and master of the children.[6]

Summary of the numbers of singers and string players in attendance on the King at Windsor

	1671	1674	1678
Boys	6	8	8
Men	12	18	16
Strings	6	14	12

"WIND-MUSIQUE"

The complete musical establishment of thirty-two men, twelve boys, twenty-four strings and the wind music met together only on rare occasions; so it is fortunate that we have the Windsor lists to indicate what was considered an acceptable allocation of strings and voices for the services of the Chapel Royal. But consideration of this matter and preoccupation with violins must not entirely divert our attention from the use of other, less novel, instruments.

Evelyn, for all his agitation about "the French fantastical light way", had no objection to "the ancient, grave, and solemn wind-music accompanying the organ". Indeed, at Charles II's coronation, he had been quick to appreciate "rare music, with lutes, viols, trumpets, organs and voices". A consort of wind instruments delighted Pepys. It is doubtful whether the recherché violins could ever have excited him as much as "the wind-musique" he heard at an entertainment in 1668: "so sweet that it ravished me, and indeed, in a word, did wrap up my soul so that it made me really sick; just as I have formerly been when in love with my wife; . . . and make me resolve to practice wind-musique, and to make my wife do the like". A short time afterwards Pepys went to the Chapel Royal in search of more: "to White Hall, and there to the Chapel expecting wind musick".[7] Whether or not he was satisfied is irrelevant; the fact remains that there was nothing unusual in his going to the Chapel Royal for wind-music, even in 1668.

The king's musicians had played in the chapel for many years before the Civil War. At the Restoration the older instruments once more came back into use. In 1661 three double sackbuts were bought "for service in his Majesty's Chappell"; a year later an order was made "that Robert Strong and Edward Strong are to attend with their double curtolls in his Majesty's Chappell Royall at Whitehall, and Thomas Bates and William Gregory with their [bass] violls, every Sunday and Holy day, and all the rest to wayte in their turnes". A theorbo was bought especially for the chapel in 1673. These, as continuo instruments, would "accompany" the organ. Treble instruments, such as the cornett, would play with the voices, except in the rare instances when music was written specially for them, as William Lawes's *Before the mountains*, "an anthem with verses for cornetts and sackbutts".*

A novel use for sackbuts and curtalls was discovered by Cooke at the St. George's festival held at Windsor in 1661. Two choirs took part: those of the Chapel Royal and St. George's, Windsor. An anthem was specially composed by Cooke, to be sung during "the grand procession". By his direction "some instrumental loud musick was at that time introduced, namely, two double sackbuts and two double curtalls, and placed at convenient distance among the classes of the Gentlemen of both choirs, to the end that all might distinctly hear, and consequently keep together in both time and tune: for one sackbut and courtal was placed before the four petty canons who began the hymn, and the other two immediately before the prebends of the College".[9] Cooke thus not only maintained reasonable precision during processional singing but also, by a skilful manoeuvre in the artful placing of the wind instruments, successfully separated his own able choir from the Windsor singers.

The Chapel Royal was not alone in having a tradition of using instruments at its services. Viols, recorders and other wind instruments were used in some cathedrals earlier in the seven-

---

* There are sufficient indications that the theorbo supplied the harmonic framework in continuo passages well into the eighteenth century. It was recognised as an alternative to the organ or harpsichord for this purpose in printed collections of vocal music. Musically it is much better suited for continuo in solo sections of instrumental verse anthems than the organ, which may have been reserved for the choruses.

Cornett: A wooden instrument, with finger holes, played with a cup-shaped mouthpiece. "It is a delicate pleasant wind musick if well played and Humored" (Randle Holmes, 1688). "Nothing comes so near, or rather imitates so much an excellent voice, as a cornet pipe; but the labour of the lips is too great, and it is seldom well sounded" (Roger North, 1742).

Sackbut: The cornett's bass companion. A trombone, in fact, though possessing a softer tone than the modern instrument.

Curtall: A now obsolete equivalent of the bassoon, with double tube, keys and reed. Bass to the hautboy.

Child and Wise were still, in 1684, being paid a daily wage as "musicians in ordinary for the cornet".[8]

teenth century. Cornetts and sackbuts were known to have
been played at Worcester in 1619, Salisbury in 1625, and
Durham in 1633.[10] Their use was revived for a time at the
Restoration: Westminster Abbey employed a cornett player
from 1661 to 1667; Exeter Cathedral, in 1664, spent £19 on
"shagbutts and cornetts procured at London by Mr. Travers for
the use of the church".[11] At provincial cathedrals cornetts came
in very useful for remedying deficiencies in the treble line, and it
was perhaps because they were forced into such a subsidiary
function, and were no longer appreciated for the tone colouring
they could add to a vocal ensemble, that they gradually fell into
complete disuse. The sackbut and cornetts at Durham referred
to in the Smart-Cosin controversy of 1628 were used to give
the musical services maximum splendour, and were thoroughly
in keeping with the high-church tendencies of that cathedral.*
Later in the century, however, these instruments were demoted
to filling in missing voice parts, it having become difficult in
some areas to find adequate singers. Writing in 1676 of York
and Durham, Roger North stated:

> They have the ordinary wind instruments in the Quires, as the
> cornet, sackbut, double curtaile and others, which supply the
> want of voices, very notorious there; and nothing can so well
> reconcile the upper parts in a Quire, since wee can have none
> but boys and those none of the best, as the cornet (being well
> sounded) doth; one might mistake it for a choice eunuch.

Some years later these eunuch substitutes had disappeared.
Before the publication in 1742 of *The Life of the Right Honourable
Francis North* the above passage had been significantly altered to
read: "In these churches, wind musick was [sic] used in the choir;
which I apprehend might be introduced at first for want of
voices, if not of organs; but, as I hear, they are now disused."[13]

*John Cosin "has divided the morning service into two parts; the 6
o'clock service which used to be read only and not sung, he chants with
organs, sackbuts and cornetts, which yield a hideous noise. . . . The Second
Service at 10 o'clock he calls Mass. . . ."[12]

Thus was marked the cutting of the final link with the mediaeval practice of combining instrumental and vocal timbres in liturgical music. In the larger churches the organ arrogantly assumed its kingly rule. The wind instruments that once had added a touch of elegant colour to cathedral services were now dispensed with until their humbler relations were permitted to appear in the hands of the west-gallery "musickers" in parish churches.

The precedent set by Charles II's chapel in using a band of violins at its services was too short-lived to have any effect on the cathedrals. Those organists who had direct knowledge of this example may have wanted to use strings with their own cathedral choirs, but would have been thwarted by their authorities' lack of finance and unco-operative attitude. The absence of string parts in existing cathedral libraries bears this out. Only Durham, not surprisingly, appears to have ventured in this direction: one organ book of anthems (mainly by Humfrey and Blow) that survives there is a full score including string parts.[14]

THE DECLINE OF THE CHAPEL ROYAL

It is remarkable that the Chapel Royal flourished at all after the Restoration. Charles II had to have it equipped with music, whatever the expense, but he was rarely in a position to pay. His musicians found themselves at the wrong end of a defective hire-purchase agreement, and the cost to them, in terms of salary arrears, was considerable. One of their number, John Hingston, may have overstated the case in 1666 by telling Pepys, "many of the musique are ready to starve, they being five years behindhand for their wages"; but by the end of Charles's reign five years' arrears were as nothing. In September 1686 it was estimated that £2,484 16s. 3d. "remains due to musicians of his late Majesty". It was then ordered that debts be redeemed from a tax on tobacco and sugar.

The less well-paid members of the King's Music, and those lacking the flair to adapt to this situation, must have found money matters very trying. Cooke managed to organise his affairs well enough to die owning property. He had little else to bequeath. Salaries and expenses, payments owing to him from the King's exchequer (totalling £1,709 13s.!) he generously divided between his two daughters. In the year before his death Locke, perhaps realising he would never have the cash himself, astutely assigned three and three-quarter years' salary arrears to a creditor. Methods must have been found of living with the payments problems, in much the same way as today artful evasions are conjured to succeed each fresh tax law, but they would hardly have induced the best financial discipline in the private lives of the King's musicians. Even the Master of His Majesty's music, in the more solvent reign of William and Mary, ran up an account of £120 with his brewer for "bear and ale", the equivalent for many of three or four years' wages.

Economies had to be made by Charles II, but not, if he could help it, in the chapel music. In March 1668 he made a drastic cut in the number of his own trumpeters. Yet, after this and other retrenchments, an order of the following year expressed the royal pleasure that "our musick in our chappell be continued and paid for theire services there as formerly, any order of retrenchment to the contrary notwithstanding".[15]

However vast the financial problems, the Chapel Royal music survived, and thrived, under Charles II. At his death it possessed sufficient momentum to carry it through three years under a Roman Catholic monarch with no interest at all in Anglican worship. Soldier King William, too busy to listen to lengthy instrumental anthems, and a parliament much too democratically inclined to cultivate a minority interest like the Chapel Royal music, together eroded an institution from unrivalled status to the level of a cathedral establishment. The Chapel Royal, that formerly had provided musical stimulus and resources for the instrumental anthems of Humfrey,

C

Turner, Blow and Purcell,* by the eighteenth century had become little more than a London club for leading church musicians, offering its members professional respect but no vital incentives to experiment. A somewhat dimmed glamour remained; the substance had gone.

The coronation of James II in 1685 was the setting for one of the most splendid musical feasts that ever graced such an occasion.[16] All the progress of the previous twenty-five years culminated in the music for this service, written and performed by musicians who had developed their art during the dead King's reign. But the new King being an avowed Roman Catholic, the Anglican Chapel Royal went into eclipse. James II turned to his foreign musicians and Roman rites, and produced a completely new establishment for his service. When he went to Windsor in 1687 he was accompanied by "gentlemen and musicians and other officers of his Majesty's Chappell" (ranging from "Gregorians" to "one cushion man") hardly any of whom sang with the Chapel Royal choir at the 1685 and 1689 coronations.[17] The only exception was the counter-tenor, John Abell, who apparently became a Roman Catholic at this time and consequently did not regain his place in the Chapel Royal in the next reign.†

Anglican services continued, but only for the benefit of the princess Anne. It was not surprising that, lacking the King's interest, there was a deterioration in standards at "the Princess's Chappell". In 1687 the violins had to be reminded by official order of their continuing duties.

* Humfrey, having spent his short working life entirely in the service of Charles II's Chapel Royal, included strings in all but one of his seventeen known anthems.

Of Purcell's output of seventy-one anthems (of which only six remain undated) sixty-one were written before 1688.

† John Abell. 1660-1716. Gentleman of the Chapel Royal in 1679. Sent by Charles II to Italy in 1681 to cultivate his voice. Evelyn noted in his diary (27th January, 1682): "the famous treble, Mr. Abell, newly returned from Italy; I never heard a more excellent voice; one would have sworn it had been a woman's, it was so high, and so well and skilfully managed". Abell was selected to sing for James II at Windsor in 1685 and 1686.[18]

To Dr. Staggins, master of his Majesty's musick. Whereas you have
neglected to give order to the violins to attend at the Chappell at
Whitehall where Her Royal Highnesse the Princesse Ann of
Denmarke is present, these are therefore to give notice to them
that they give theire attendance there upon Sunday next and soe
to continue to doe soe as formerly they did.[19]

James II's brief reign was abruptly ended by the "Glorious
Revolution". The coronation of the new King and Queen was
celebrated in fine style. Yards of "scarlet cloth for coronation
liveries" were ordered for the singers; later their traditional
annual feast was restored (no doubt a popular move).* But fine
liveries and a forty-six pound sirloin of beef did not guarantee
musical well-being, and memorable hangovers for the gentlemen were quickly forgotten with the distasteful acceptance of a
reduced and unexciting role for the Chapel Royal choir. Far
from resuming its previous eminence in an extravagant court,
it became no more than an official adjunct to a constitutional
monarch.

Drums for the Grenadiers and trumpets for the Guards was
the King's music in the new reign. Accompanying these martial
strains the Chapel, now like any cathedral, prayed loyally for
the royal family, for victory in the nation's wars, and, when
this was granted, made appropriate noises with all the old
splendour of instruments and voices. Otherwise the strings
were mute. No longer needed every Sunday, the routine now
demanded "solemn" (i.e. vocal) music. An order of 1691

* "In the year 1690 . . . there Majesties were graciously pleased to restore
unto the Gentlemen of there Chapell Royall there antient annuall feast
which for some years beffore they had lost, and instead of three bucks which
they allways had at the said feast did then grant unto them twenty pounds in
money to be yearly paid unto them out of there Majesties Treasury Chamber,
with these perquisitts following, viz:—
    At the Salsary, fine flower 1bs 1d.
    At the Poultry, butter 36 pd.
    At the Pantry, Cheat [wheaten bread] fine 2 doz. Coarse 2 doz.
    At the Buttry, beer 1 hhd [hogshead]
    At the Cellar, clarett 2 gs. 2 ps.
    At the Larder, a sir loyne of beef 46 pd."[20]

declared that "the King's Chappell shall be all the year through
kept both morning and evening with solemn musick like a
collegiate church".[21] That is, services at 11 a.m. and 5 p.m.,
with full anthems at Matins on weekdays and verse anthems at
other times.

The number of singers was also reduced. Whereas there had
been thirty-three present at the 1685 coronation, in 1689 there
were only twenty-four men. This same number is listed in 1708
as consisting of one sub-dean, eight clerks of the chapel, twelve
gentlemen, two organists, and Dr. Blow as master of the
children. No adjustment was made to the salary for a gentleman,
which remained at £73 per annum, a figure little different
from that awarded in 1662 and still unchanged in 1776. There
was an addition of four men to the establishment in 1715, but
no attempt was made to reinstate the original number of boys
(twelve) once ten had been accepted.[22]

Not surprisingly attendance at choir practices became lax, and
on 5th April, 1693, "it was ordered that whatever Gentlemen
of the Chapel in waiting should absent himself from the practice
of the Anthem on Saturdays or other holiday eves, when the
King or Queen were to bee present on the morrow, or upon
any other occasions before the Wednesdays and Fridays in Lent,
being thereto ordered by the sub-dean to appear, should,
besides the usual mulct, forfeit half a crown for every such
absence". In fact "a notorious neglect of the duty of the
Chapell" had so offended the Queen that suspensions were
threatened.[23]

It does not seem that such measures were successful in
ensuring the maintenance of high standards. In 1728 six rules
had to be firmly specified, regulating everyday details in the
chapel services.[24] From these it can be gathered that:

The clergy gabbled the service too quickly.

A restrictive-practices attitude prevailed, preventing certain
parts of the music being sung by everybody. It was ordered that
priest and lay-singers were not to squabble about who sang
what, but to join together in singing the psalms, canticles and

choruses of anthems "with a due application and with a proper and decent strength and extension of voice".

The choirmen did not take the trouble to learn their notes; even solos in verse anthems were not receiving adequate preparation. Perhaps this was a consequence of their repertoire becoming too repetitive. (Chapel Royal manuscript part-books which had been assembled at the beginning of the eighteenth century were still being used over a hundred years later as is indicated by the presence in them of two pencilled dates, 1792 and 1826.)

The choir's appearance was so shabby that it had to be stipulated that the boys' surplices be washed every week, the men's fortnightly.

The selection of music for the canticles and anthems was haphazard. The choir were not notified until just before they should begin to sing, when the choice was passed round by word of mouth with obvious lack of dignity. To remedy this due warning was to be given before the service or, at the latest, during the voluntary between the psalms and the first lesson.

The choir stalls were untidy. Stools and hassocks were so placed that they prevented a clear passage through to the altar.

The existence of these official criticisms reveals not only the state the country's foremost choir had reached, but also a continuing, if intermittent, interest of the monarch in the Chapel Royal. Queen Mary had been aware of the shortcomings of church music in her reign, and one outcome had been the creation of a new office of composer for the Chapel Royal, first occupied by Blow in 1699. The Queen had originally intended that he should share the honour with Purcell and that between them they should regularly produce new anthems for her chapel, a design which was thwarted by Purcell's early death.*

* Hawkins relates that when the Chapel Royal was attending the Queen at Hampton Court during King William's absence in Flanders, Dr. Tillotson (Dean of St. Paul's) would give the sub-dean, Gostling, a lift "in his chariot".

"In one of those journeys, the dean, talking of church music, mentioned it as a common observation, that ours fell short of what it had been in the

Queen Anne, a sincere practising member of the Church of England, and supported by a tory administration, exercised a positive and beneficial influence on church music. As princess she had insisted on having the complete music in the Chapel Royal; and though she may have regretted the absence of weekly performances of string anthems by the time she came to the throne, she delighted in the various orchestral odes and thanksgiving pieces that were written to celebrate the major events of her reign. A burst of activity under Queen Anne was recorded by Tudway in the last of his six-volume collection of English church music. Omitting "very many which may be judged frivolous and common pieces" in his selection of "so great and so many voluminous" ones available, this final volume was largely devoted to those works "made upon the great Events and occurrences of her Majesty's reign wherein most of the composers of church musick, in all Cathedralls etc. as well as those of her own Chappell, were desirous to signalize themselves on those Publick occasions". Seven compositions alone were for the Peace of Utrecht, amongst them being Handel's celebrated *Te Deum and Jubilate*. So comprehensive a cross-section of services and anthems by Blow, his pupils Clarke and Croft, and many composers of lesser ability testifies clearly to the quantity, if not always the quality, of church music written during Queen Anne's reign.[26]

Under the Hanoverians composers were still indebted to the Chapel Royal for the presentation of their church music, and for some degree of encouragement. Blow previously had intended to widen his audience by printing some of his services and anthems, a "divine music" companion to *Amphion*

preceding reign, and that the queen herself had spoken of it to him. Mr. Gostling's answer was, that Dr. Blow and Mr. Purcell were capable of composing at least as good anthems as most of those which had been so much admired, and a little encouragement would make that appear. The dean mentioned this to her Majesty, who approved of the thought, and said they should be appointed accordingly, with a salary of £40 per annum, adding that it would be expected that each should produce a new anthem on the first Sunday of his month of waiting."[25]

Anglicus, but lack of assurance for the venture prevented him.[27] But it was Croft, aware of the lessening value of a court performance, who was the first to extend a shrinking platform by publishing his Chapel Royal anthems, though his dedications did not fail politely to express his obligation to both George I and the future George II. To the King: "I have composed the following Anthems, which having been Honoured with Your Royal Presence, in the Performance, and being now made Publick, are most Humbly offered to your Majesty."

To the Prince of Wales: "The Approbation Your Royal Highness has been pleas'd to shew of our Church-Service by Your constant Attendance therein, and serious Attention thereto, has encouraged me most Humbly to beg Your Protection on the Behalf of the following Performances".[28]

"Constant attendance" and "serious attention" by members of the royal family at services in their chapel may have provided encouragement, but could not alone create a situation in which the composers would be inspired to explore, break new ground, and stretch the experience of the worshippers. Charles II had managed somehow to effect just this for his chapel, but the willingness to maintain a similar establishment, even in his precarious manner, no longer existed in the eighteenth century. But by then it is doubtful whether the Chapel Royal's music, however extravagantly endowed, could possibly have rivalled the increasing appeal of secular musical entertainment. Church music, withdrawing to a cosily sacred corner, could not contend with changing tastes; and the Chapel Royal singers, despite their ability, were no match for the popularity of the castrato and prima-donna. The influx of foreign musicians that in the seventeenth century had grafted new strains on to English music now began to swamp it. Virtuoso opera singers fetched at vast expense from Italy ousted the fame of a Gostling or of prodigy organists and composers. The hub of musical life shifted from the court to aristocratic entertainments of opera and concerts.

Such a change did not pass without comment. Later in the

eighteenth century one writer voiced a reactionary, though revealing, attitude in no uncertain terms:

> The gay and the fashionable flock in crouds to places of public entertainment, to the opera, to the theatres, and to concerts, and pretend to be charmed with what they hear. It was once as fashionable to be alike attracted by the charms of choral music, where the hearers were sure of enjoying all the delight that could result from the united powers of sublime poetry, and harmony the most exquisite.[29]

As for the Chapel Royal, in 1762 a schoolmaster and self-styled teacher of psalmody could find it remarkable for nothing more than the example it gave of a bad practice in the performance of hymns.[30] His observation parodied the situation, but for the organist to be noted for his "long shakes" and "tedious Interludes" between the lines of a hymn was indeed a far cry from the reputation of Cooke's "brave musique", the "pretty anthems" of Humfrey, and the fame of "our Purcell, the delight of the Nation, and the Wonder of the World".

4

The Cathedrals

RENOVATION

"PSALM-ROARING SAINTS"

There was truth in this epithet: the Puritans liked a good sing
and wholesome psalmody was their best ditty. They were also
single-minded enough to admit no other. The practice of their
faith was not to be tainted with the dross of a common ballad,
and its expression was too unsubtle to have anything to do with
the skilled singing of anthems. Such artifice had no place in a
naïve, unaffected response to the word of God. The lusty singing of psalmody by the whole congregation may have provided its members with an acceptable outlet for religious
emotion, but it certainly deafened their ears to music in its
profounder forms. To be constrained to sit and listen to the
expert performance of extensive anthems was for them
unendurable; there was no realm of experience which could not
be read in Holy Writ, construed from the pulpit or answered in
the simple syllables of Sternhold and Hopkins.

For the Puritans who beheaded a king nothing could be
achieved by half-measures. Their successors in less violent days
might with a surfeit of congregational hymns reduce the efforts
of a few trained singers to impotency and, by lengthening
the sermon, render the anthem utterly ineffective. No such
compromise would have been acceptable to Cromwell's
fanatics, for whom cathedral choirs and their "curious singing"
were anathema. Whether visible or audible, adornments of any
sort were of no earthly use. Church music in its more developed

C*

forms, and with its too cunning insight into things unseen had to be crushed along with effigies of saints in stone or glass. Anything that stimulated the imagination other than the plain facts of Scripture and their honest exposition by the preacher was considered superfluous.

Only unison psalmody could fit such a narrow groove.* Outside church, however, music of a "proper" sort had its place in relaxation and sober entertainment. It has been convincingly demonstrated that during the Commonwealth certain aspects of music-making prospered,[1] and the songs and instrumental music written and performed during this time should be proof enough. Yet, a century later, Burney both blamed the Puritans for "much of the barbarism into which Music was thrown during the reign of James I and Charles I", and also levelled the accusation that during the Interregnum "the art of Music, and indeed all the arts but those of killing, canting, and hypocrisy, were discouraged". He could see through his blinkers far enough to admire music of ages other than his own, but that of the mid-seventeenth century he considered undeserving of prolonged scrutiny, notable only for the fact that it was written in times (as Burney thought) of ignorance and inexperience. He quoted Swift as being apposite: "we admire a little wit in a woman, as we do a few words spoke plain by a parrot".[2] Unfortunately, although Burney may have been ingenuously concerned to highlight by comparison the wonderful works of his day, his opinions have been adopted with little questioning even in the present century:

* A sentence from the Puritans' "directory for public worship" shows that at least this form of church music was actively encouraged: "It is the duty of Christians to praise God publicly by singing of psalms, together in the congregation, and also privately in the family. In singing of psalms the voice is to be tuneably and gravely ordered; but the chief care must be to sing with understanding and with grace in the heart."

It is necessary to mention here that throughout our period "psalms" or "psalmody" refers to metrical and not prose versions. Metrical psalms (the psalter in verse paraphrase) are similar to hymns (non-biblical words). The latter did not become common until the eighteenth century, eventually ousting the metrical psalms.

"the popularity of the Elizabethan school was killed by the ridiculous bigotry of the 'saints' of the Great Rebellion". Or: "When the Restoration came, English music, which had been the admiration of Europe, was dead. . . . From this date all music in England was imported."[3]

If some eighteenth-century writers overstressed the enforced hibernation of church music, it was for reasons other than those of historical criticism. The dangers to the established church of the Puritan attitude did not automatically dissolve at the Restoration; they were present for many years, even after Methodism had provided some sort of safety-valve. By the eighteenth century, church music had to face the oblique influences of submerged puritanism, not a frontal attack aiming for complete abolition but a subtle form of guerilla warfare directed at subversion from within. Music itself was considered the least of the arts, having no practical or rational purpose other than mere entertainment; the Christian accepted it for little more in his worship. Subtle arts which might open feelings to an uncomfortable depth, and paint truths in colours too vivid for a well-ordered palette of natural dogma, were entirely out of place in Sunday church, a weekly social occasion, fed on a round of Bible-reading and dispensed in subscriptions to charity. Burney's contemporary, Hawkins, was particularly apprehensive of this camouflaged assault and, thinking that it had its origin in Puritan opinions of the previous century, he directed his counter-attack against the Roundheads. In his attempt to preserve cathedral music in the eighteenth century, he praised the compositions of an earlier "Golden Age", and for deficiencies in his own day made the Commonwealth the culprit.

Perhaps at that time there was no other defence. General standards of performance gave little support; most choirs were stifled by miserliness and lack of sympathy. They were hardly in a position to demonstrate the richness that music can bring to church life, its capacity to complement simpler forms of worship, and the defenders of English cathedral music fell back on praising its great tradition in a vain attempt to save it from the impoverishment of one-tracked worship.

The "costly hired, curious and nice musitiens" that had so "chanted and minsed and mangled" Divine Service were inevitably dispossessed at the Commonwealth. Their "whorish harmony" and disreputable habits* had no place outside their former employment. Burney, with some licence, declared that out-of-work church musicians "were forced to sculk about the country, and solicit an asylum in the houses of private patrons". Hawkins more mildly put it that cathedral singers had to "betake themselves to some employment less offensive to God than that of singing his praises".† Obliged to find other ways of earning a living, they must have done much to spread the practice and enjoyment of music in the home. "Some went into the armyes, others dispersed about in the countrys and made musick for the consolation of the cavalier gentlemen. And that gave occasion to divers familyes to entertain the skill and practise of musick, and to encourage the masters to the great increase of composition."[6]

The closure of the monasteries a century earlier caused a comparable influx into the secular musical world, only on that occasion there had been no return. In the seventeenth century the changes from one sphere to the other and back again, sudden though they may have been, were not without benefits to secular and, later, church music.

The Civil War and changes of government did indeed bring

* Even a bishop of the established church could write: "the common singingman in Cathedrall churches are a bad society, and yet a company of good fellowes, that roare deep in the quire, deeper in the taverne".[4]

† Henry Lawes "lived in London and taught Ladies to sing"; William Webbe "instructed men and women, Boyes and girles to sing, merely for maintenance sake"; Simon Ives "stuck to his instruction in musick which kept him in a comfortable condition". The organist, Benjamin Rogers, not only "taught his profession at Windsor and in the neighbourhood" but also managed to secure "some annual allowance in consideration of his lost place". William Ellis kept himself and his wife "in a comfortable condition" by running a weekly music meeting at Oxford, which was popular with choirmen "being out of all employ". Etc.[5]

considerable distress to some musicians, particularly those least able, by age or temperament, to make the necessary adjustments. Walter Porter, a former Master of the Choristers at Westminster Abbey, had before his death in 1659 petitioned the Governors of Westminster School for relief; he and his children having since the Rebellion "lived in great want and necessitie And are at p'sent in debt and in a wanting condition...."

> In this sad case your Petitioner being 70 and odd yeeres of age his strength and faculties decayed, his wants dayly increased and his charitable freindes neere all deceased
>
> Humbly beseecheth your Honours in tender pittie and comiseration of his deplorable condition to bee pleased to give him a Share in the Monuments with the rest of the Singingmen or some other way of reliefe By which your noble Charitie hee and his Children will be relieved and the small remaynder of his dayes closed upp with comfort.*

Porter was optimisic enough (in view of his advanced age) to add that he could help by establishing "a meeting for Musick once a fortnight" and train "two or three boyes in the Art of Musick".[8]

RESTORATION

A number of church musicians survived the upheavals of the Interregnum to resume their former profession at the Restoration. Organs and music had been wantonly destroyed, but the former were quickly replaced, and the loss of the latter was not as widespread as has been supposed. Many manuscripts

* The cathedral revenues were not all embezzled by the Commonwealth government. Aubrey tells how they provided a student's grant for one Robert Hook in 1658 at Christ Church, Oxford, "where he had a Chorister's place ... which was a pretty good maintenance". A standard history of the Puritans states: "The parliament having ordered the sale of bishops' lands, and the lands of deans and chapters, and vested the money in the hands of trustees, appointed part of the money to be appropriated for the support and maintenance of such late bishops, deans, prebendaries, singing men, choristers ... whose respective offices, places and livelihoods, were taken away."[7]

met a natural end (a seventeenth-century antiquarian was not unduly surprised to find a valuable document missing—"I beleeve it haz wrapt Herrings by this time"—or to rescue another from "being used by the Cooke . . . destinated with other good papers and letters to be put under pies"[9]). Two choirs are known to have preserved their music books during the Commonwealth,[10] and for them and others less far-seeing Barnard's printed collection of *Selected Church Music* (1641) at last came into its own, replacing lost manuscript part-books or complementing those that were inadequate.

For singers who had forgotten the form of service, the organist of Christ Church Cathedral, Oxford, obligingly provided *A Short Direction for the performance of Cathedrall Service. Published for the information of such persons, as are ignorant of it. . . .* Not that the author, Edward Lowe, could have thought that fifteen years' disuse had erased all memory of previous practice, but he was astute enough to detect the advantage in publishing his precepts at that time.*

With or without advice, most cathedrals were soon back to

---

* "*A Short Direction* for the performance of Cathedrall Service. Published for the information of such persons, as are ignorant of it, and shall be call'd to officiate in Cathedrall or Collegiate Churches, where it hath formerly been in use." (By Edward Lowe, Oxford, 1661).

"To all Gentlemen that are true Lovers of Cathedrall Musicke.

It is too well known what hath bin practised in Cathedrall Churches (in order to the publique worship of God, for many years past) instead of Harmony and Order. And therefore it may be rationally supposed, that the Persons and things relating to both, are not easily rallyed, after so fatall a Route. But Since the mercy of God hath restored a Power, and by it put life into the Law, to promote and settle it as it was. It hath been judged convenient to revive the generall practise of the ordinary performance of Cathedrall service for the use of them, who shall be called to it, and are desirous to doe it with devotion and alacritie. To this end a Person is willingly employed, who hath seen, understood, and bore a part in the same from his Childhood: And therein thinks himselfe happy to be now a Meane Instrument to doe God, and the Church service, in such a time when there are so many Cathedralls to be furnisht, and so few Persons knowing enough (in this particular) to performe the solemnity requisite in them: He hath therefore put together and published, the Ordinary and Extra-ordinary parts, both for the Priest, and whole Quire. Hoping that his Brethren in the

normal. Within a year of the reinstatement of the Church of England liturgy on 8th July, 1660, the process of reconstruction had been completed at Worcester. By 31st August, 1660, the cathedral was ready for the first Morning Prayer, a said service. A new dean was installed on 13th September, with the responsibility of "settling the Church in order". By 7th November he had admitted ten choristers, and early in the following year (23rd February to 3rd April) added four lay-clerks to the six that remained from before the Commonwealth. The four minor-canons were joined by six more, admitted between January 1661 and May 1662.*

With the first essential achieved, a full-strength choir, the next matter was to equip them with music. £12 15s. 6d. was spent on Barnard's volumes of services and anthems, "for a sett of printed song-books for the quire, box and carriage". In 1662 £1 was paid to Loosemore of Cambridge for music, and £2 to one John Brown for copying.

By then the choir had been singing for some months. On 13th April, 1661, the "first quire service said and sung in the Cathedral Church of Worcester since the reducing of Worcester to the then parliamentary forces, 24th July, 1646". Perhaps the music did not go too well on that occasion, as a Chapter order was issued a fortnight later for the choir to meet for rehearsal twice weekly at least:

> That the members of the Quire doe attend the Quire service on
> Sundaies and holy daies Satterdaies in the evening the eves of

same Imployment will look on it as Candidly as he intends it, since what is done, is only as a help to those that are Ignorant of it."

Edward Lowe (c. 1610–1682) was a chorister at Salisbury Cathedral who later became organist of Christ Church Cathedral, Oxford, where he remained until his death. After the Restoration he was also one of the organists at the Chapel Royal, and professor of music at Oxford. Some of his anthems are included in Tudway's manuscript collection.

* This proportion of old and new choir members would have been fairly typical of other cathedrals. At Norwich, for instance, of the eight former lay-clerks five were reinstated at the Restoration, although here only one new member was admitted (thereby reducing the establishment to six).[11]

hollydaies and to meet twice a week att leste in some convenient place within the precincts of the said Cathedrall Church to exercise and to trie their voyces and fitt themselves for the more solemne and orderly performance of the service of God in the said Quire.

Also in April that year Charles II had written to the Dean and Chapter commanding that the annual stipends of the minor-canons and lay-clerks be raised to £16 or £20. On 23rd June the Chapter concurred. They awarded £16.

Finally, in July, the organ loft was finished and settlement was made with the builder, George Dallam, for setting up "a small organ". Now it was possible for an organist and master of the choristers to be installed and on 28th August, 1661, the young Giles Tomkins was confirmed in that office.[12]

There is, however, a postscript. Giles Tomkins was replaced in the following year. Even with weighty backing he could not, or would not, face up to his responsibilities at this tricky period. Maybe he found the preponderance of old lay-clerks in the choir too difficult to manage. A petition of theirs for more money soon after the 1661 award of a salary increase shows them to be hard-boiled sticklers for real or supposed rights. Tomkins stayed only half a year, and subsequently gave up his career as a cathedral organist. He then took orders, became rector of one parish for more than fifty years, and died at the ripe old age of ninety-two.*

* Giles Tomkins (1633-1725). A half nephew of Thomas Tomkins. (See Denis Stevens, *Thomas Tomkins*, 1957, pp. 19-20.)

Another bright young organist, Richard Henman, met difficulties at Exeter in 1695 similar to those experienced by Tomkins. Having only just left the Chapel Royal as a chorister (and probably full of high-flown ideas) he obviously did not go down well with the choirmen in a country cathedral. In his first year as organist he was "admonished to make himself capable and to qualify himself for his continuance [in] that place (complaint being made by the Quire of his unfittness)." A month later, in August, "upon complaint of Mr. Henman the organist's abilitys", he was further ordered to "endeavour to qualify himself for the performance of that office by Easter next".[13] Unlike Giles Tomkins, however, Henman learnt by his experience, improved his relations with his colleagues, and remained their organist for forty-seven years.

The restoration of choral services in other cathedrals doubt-less followed a similar sequence to the events at Worcester. But so speedy a return to old ways was not always effected without opposition; the "superexquisiteness" of cathedral music continued to be a subject for controversy. At Oxford the revival of music in college chapels stung the Presbyterians to compare "the organ to the whining of pigs", and the singing to "that of a joviall crew in a blind ale-house". In the same university, Edward Lowe, through his conscientious efforts to organise the proper performance of cathedral services, was the obvious victim for a peculiar practical joke which expressed, however crudely, still widely held feelings. Lowe had the reputation of being a "proud man", and his dignity must have suffered not a little from this attack.*

VARYING STANDARDS

The dust had settled, at Christ Church at least, by later in the century. Under a dean who was both conscientious and musical, the choir thrived and enjoyed an enviable and long-lived reputation.

Dean Aldrich was a rare cleric. Talented dilettantes were not so uncommon in days before specialised knowledge made it difficult to gain mastery in more than one field. Aldrich outdid even his contemporaries by being architect, musician, and antiquarian as well as dean of Christ Church, Oxford. It is in this latter capacity that he concerns us now.

* Some "varlets" of Christ Church went at midnight to the choristers' school-room, took all the surplices they could find and threw them into a "common privy house". The Dean and Chapter publicly complained. This in turn provoked a reply in the form of a lampoon entitled "Lowe's Lamentation":

> Have pitty on us all, good Lairds,
> For surely wee are all uncleane;
> Our surplices are daub'd with tirds,
> And eke we have a shitten Deane.[14]

A full account of the Dean's very practical interest in his choir was recorded by William Hayes in 1753. Earnestly concerned with a reform of defects in cathedral music in the middle of the eighteenth century, Hayes quoted Dean Aldrich's method of governing his choir (related by a member of the college contemporary with Aldrich) as the "noblest Model for his Successors and all others who preside over Colleges and Choirs".

This method comprised four points:

(1) Aldrich never admitted a chorister who had not had some preparation, and never without a trial.

(2) The adult singers had to be "properly qualified", and preference was given to those who had already proved their merit "in a lower Capacity". Aldrich thus ensured that "there was not an useless Member in his Choir; for Chaplains had then an equal share of choral Duty with the Singing-Men; nor was there the least Grumbling or Complaint on that Account; the Dean himself setting a noble Example to the former, by constantly singing a Part in all the Services and Anthems".

(3) Rehearsals were held weekly at the Deanery, the Dean both choosing the music and assisting in its performance.* He wisely combined hard practice, "to keep up the Spirit of the Music", with suitable refreshment, "to promote social Harmony". To such an extent in fact that a serious rehearsal became also a "musical entertainment" which the choir members were loathe to miss, and to which it was an honour for other members of the college to be invited.

(4) Discipline was an easy matter. Aldrich had no need for fines and reprimands; if a singer was absent without reason, he was banned from the next rehearsal; if late,

---

* That the organist's responsibility for directing and training the choir was at that time a limited one is also indicated by Tudway. It was the clergy who had to be "able to direct and govern Choirs etc. when they should arrive, or be promoted to be Deans, Prebendaries, Precentors of Cathedrals, etc. . . .".[15]

he was allowed to attend, but given "nothing to drink except Small-Beer".

Ordinary beer, however, was not the secret of the Dean's success as a choir director. This (for Hayes at any rate) lay in the care taken right at the source, i.e. the selection of "none but useful and properly qualified Boys to be Choristers". With a good education, a musical training, and the Dean's influence, the Christ Church boys grew up to be lay-clerks or minor-canons excelling in their professions and giving an example to all of "the decent and regular Performance of the Worship of the Deity".

Such a happy working relationship between dean and choir was rare in the eighteenth century. The unstated corollary of the four points of Aldrich's method—inadequate chorister material, perpetual friction between lay and ordained singers, unrehearsed music, general mismanagement—was borne out in Hayes's personal experience. He painted a very different picture of conditions in other choirs.

The organist, placed between an unmusical dean and illiterate singers, was ham-strung. He could expect little encouragement from his superior who had no "relish for Music", and who considered he was "placed in his Stall for no other Purpose, but *Bashaw* it over the inferior Members", more concerned with respect for his own person than God's. Such a one viewed "Brevity as the greatest Beauty in the musical Part of the Service", and made appointments to choir places less on merit than on the influence of the recommender, or even on the candidate's political colour.*

Thwarted in obtaining the singers he required, the organist

---

* "Some previous Questions must be answered to the Satisfaction of the Dean, before he will listen to the Voice of meritorious Pretensions: as, how did his Father vote at the last Election? Or how does he intend to vote at the next? I say, unless these, and such like Questions, are properly and satisfac-torily answered, no Arguments in favour of the Boy, or proving the necessity of doing something for the Good and Improvement of the Choir, will avail; nor shall we wonder at it, when we consider that the Dean probably was, and expects to be, preferred upon the same Principle."

was "obliged to endeavour to make singers of those, to whom Nature has denied the necessary Capacities". Furthermore, he was handicapped by "the mean and scandalous *Salaries* annexed to the office of Lay-Clerk" in most cathedrals. These, generally "the same as at the Reformation", bore no relation to a "competent Maintenance" or the considerable rise over the years in the cost of living. "The Deans with their Brethren of the Chapter, being careful to monopolize the Profits arising from the Improvements" of their estates to their own advantage, made totally inadequate provision for the musicians.* "The miserable Performances which we generally hear in Country Cathedralls" was a direct consequence of this, the singers, mere "Mechanics", being forced to eke out a living by undertaking some additional "Trade or Occupation". Not surpisingly, they had no time to "study the Art of singing properly". Though capable of improvement, if not great achievement, they would have had little inclination for practice when their wages barely covered their attendance.

"In this disgustful Situation" the organist had no desire to improve the service repertoire, seeing the "Impracticability of getting it performed with tolerable Decency. Upon the Whole, it appears, how little it is in the Power of the Organist to effect any thing, without the Concurrence not only of his Governor, but of his Brethren of the Choir also; and how little reason he has to expect the Concurrence of either."[16]

Cathedral choirs admittedly now earn greater respect, and have largely left behind the derision arising from centuries of neglect. But Hayes was not the first to bemoan the conditions in unskilled and underpaid choirs. Writing many years earlier,

* Hayes argued that Cathedral Statutes indicated exact proportions for the annual salaries of all the staff, as, for example, chorister, £5; lay-clerk, £10; minor-canon and organist, £20; residentiary-canon, £40; dean, £80. He then suggested, presumably with knowledge of available revenue, that these figures be multiplied by four. "The three former would be very well contented with it: Yet even this Increase will not satisfy the two latter: but without Scruple or Remorse they (by what Authority I know not) divide three Fourths of the Profits arising from the Portions alloted to their Inferiors, among themselves; a manifest Abuse of the Founder's Intention".

Thomas Mace complained feelingly of the poor health of cathedral music sixteen years after the Restoration and suggested a familiar medicine.

Mace traced the cathedral tradition of worship back to Solomon's temple, and argued how in his day it had the potential to equal, if not excel, such a glorious beginning. In theory, yes; in practice, no. Even with the unrivalled heritage of the music, the talent of many singers, "*stately* and *magnificent Structures*, ready *built*" for choral worship and generously endowed for that purpose, the hard fact was that in most choirs the music was "*Deficient, Low, Thin* and *Poor*", and that there was no hope of improvement.

And why? Firstly, "by the *General Thinness* of most *Quires*". When the general rule was but "one man to a part", the daily service could not be performed "but in a very ordinary manner" on account of frequent absenteeism (Mace listed such reasons as sickness, indisposition, business and—an authentic touch—colds and hoarseness). Secondly, by reason of the unskilled and unmusical singers, "Inferiour-low-capacitated Men".

Fundamental to these defects was the "*low Esteem*, and *great Disregard*" with which cathedral music was held by many people. Else the original endowments, no longer sufficient, would have been augmented by new benefactions. Not that the age lacked wealth and generosity, finding outlets in frequent bequests for maintaining lectures, schools, alms-houses, fellowships, and building of churches.

The statutory wages of £8, £10 or £12 a year for a cathedral singer, once a very ample maintenance, were utterly inadequate in those "*Miserable-hard-dear-Griping-Times*". The "*Poor-drudging-Clarks of Quires*" were forced to supplement their living in humble trades as barbers, cobblers, tailors and others more inferior; and, conversely, choice of choir members was limited to those already in some other employ.

Fortunately, there were some cathedral clergy who, when in residence, assisted with their knowledge and skill by singing with the choir (thus they "give *Example to others Profitably;*

Rectifie Errours Effectually; and *Reprove Ignorance or Insufficiency*").
But Mace knew from his own experience of an instance where
even this proved ineffective.

I have known a *Reverend Dean of a* Quire (a very *notable, smart-spirited Gentleman*) *Egregiously Baffled* by one of the present *Clarks*;
who to my knowledge was more *Ignorant* in the *Art of Song*, than
a *Boy* might be thought to be, who had *Learn'd* to *Sing* but only
One month; yet could make a shift to Sing most of the *Common
Services* and *Anthems*, by long use and habit, (with the *Rest*) pritty
well, (as *Birds* in *Cages* use to *whistle* their *Old Notes*.)

Yet I say, *This Dean* being known by *This Bold-Confident-
Dunce-Clark* (who you must know took himself to be a kind of
Pot-Wit) to have *No Skill* at all in the *Art of Musick; The Dean,* I
say, upon a *Time* (after *Prayers*) coming out and following *This
Great-Jolly-Boon-Fellow*, and as he was pulling off his *Surplice*,
began to *Rebuke him sharply*, (and indeed very *justly*) for a *Gross
Absurdity* committed by *Him* in *That very Service Time*, by reason
of his *Great-Dunstical-Insufficiency* in *Singing* of an *Anthem* alone;
in which he was so *Notoriously* and *Ridiculously Out*, as caused *All*,
or most of the *Young People* then present, to burst out into
Laughter, to the *Great Blemish* of the *Church-Service*, and the
Dishonour of *God* (at *That Time*, and in *That Place*.)

But *Thus* it fell out, (in short) viz. that after the *Angry Dean* had
Ruffled him soundly in very *smart Language*, so that he thought
he had given him *Shame* enough for his *Insufficiency* and *Duncery*;

How think ye *This Blade* came off?

Why, *most Notably*, and in such a manner as made all the
standers by *Wonder* and *Admire Him*; venting himself in *These
very Words*, (for I my self was both an Eye and Ear witness) with a
most *stern Angry Countenance*, and a *vehement Rattling Voice*, even
so as he made the *Church Ring* withall, saying, *Sir-r-r-r* (shaking
his head) I'd ha' you know I Sing after the *Rate of so much a Year*,
(naming his *Wages*) and except ye *Mend my Wages*, I am resolv'd
Never to sing Better whilst I live.

Hark ye *Here, Gentlemen!* was there *ever* a more *Nicking* piece of
shrewd Wit, so suddenly shew'd upon the *Occasion*, than *This
was?* Yae, or *more Notable* and *Effectual* to the *Purpose?* as you shall
hear, by the *Sequel*.

For the *Cholerick Dean* was so *fully* and *sufficiently Answer'd*, that turning immediately away from him, without *one word* more, He Hasted out of the *Church*, but *Never* after found the least *Fault* with *This Jolly Brave Clark;* who was *Hugg'd* more then sufficiently by *all the Rest* of the *Puny-Poor-Fellow-Clarks*, for *This* his *Heroick Vindication* and *Wit*.[17]

Neither the choleric dean nor the pot-wit lay-clerk deserve much sympathy, but the moral of the tale is perfectly clear. Wages had to be increased (even if this required the rearrangement of invested income) to such an extent that all choir singers could devote themselves entirely to their profession and the study of their art.

Honest Thomas Mace was no disinterested bystander. He had spent fifty years as a cathedral singer, and his experiences led him to exaggerate. Yet, in the main, other writers did not gainsay him.* It had to be admitted by Roger North that "except in St. Paul's and the Royall Chappell, there are few that care much to hear" cathedral music, redeemed by neither the dignity of its style nor the flattering acoustics of large churches (interestingly, he instanced an experiment in King's College Chapel, Cambridge, whereby "the organ with the Quire sounding, such a delicious musick shall be heard, as I may call the quintessence of Harmony"). North directed his attention to the imperfections of the singers and, in particular,

---

* In 1720 Tudway cited as one reason for the "decay of this Institution" (i.e. cathedral music)—"in all Cathedrals where Choirs were first founded, I dare say, then, their stipends were a maintenance; but Deans, and Chapters, since the Reformation, tyeing their clerks down to the same allowance, now, when money is not a 5th part in value, to what it was then, have brought a general neglect of the service, and a very mean and lame way of performing it, for want of encouragement."[18]

Hawkins, writing of the years following the Restoration, stated that in "cathedrals that were amply endowed, as St. Paul's for instance, in which a maintenance is assigned for minor canons and lay singers, the performance was little inferior to that of the royal chapel: in other cathedrals, where the revenues were so small as to reduce the members of the church to the necessity of taking mechanics and illiterate persons to assist in the choral service, it was proportionably inferior "[19]

their chanting of the psalms—"who expects better than the musick of Babell?" The old story again: "it is very hard to get voices to make a Quire" . . . "the failings of the men Quiristers, among whom is rarely found a tolerable voice" . . . "the Quires are poorly furnished, and one way or other the vocall performances are mean". But this time there is a different ending—"if female quiristers were taken into quires instead of boys, it would be a vast improvement of chorall musick".[20]

Praise of cathedral choirs was rare. The Hon. John Byng's comments made later in the eighteenth century may have accurately reflected poor standards, but they were harshly outspoken in their references to a service at Winchester as "more irregularly perform'd, than I ever remember to have heard it; and to a most shabby congregation"; to the psalms at Worcester as being "slurr'd over most irreverently, and the organ is a hoarse unpleasant instrument"; and to unfortunate experiences at Oxford—"we hurry'd away from our dinner in hopes of hearing an anthem sung by a famous singing boy of New College . . . we were baulk'd of our intention, as the anthem was very ill sung, and the service most idly perform'd, by such persons as I should suppose had never learnt to sing or read."[21]

Despite such criticism, cathedral music had its friends. One particularly devoted admirer was a certain lawyer, Humphrey Wyrley Birch, who never missed a chance to hear the funeral sentences by Purcell and Croft, even if it meant leaving his circuit and riding "many miles to Westminster Abbey". A somewhat morbid taste, but at the funeral of Queen Caroline he could not be close enough to the music. "For the greater convenience of hearing it, he, with another lawyer, who was afterwards a judge, though neither of them could sing a note, walked among the choirmen of the Abbey, each clad in a surplice, with a music paper in one hand and a taper in the other."[22] Not even the most ardent friend of cathedral music would dare claim such a privilege today!

The adverse comments on cathedral music came from without and within, and when those who were personally involved spoke of the sorry state of affairs they can not be doubted. They would not lightly speak of their colleagues as "Inferiour-low-capacitated Men", or as "Mechanics, and those of the lowest sort". And this harping on artisan status was only too well founded. The average annual wage for a choirman in the eighteenth century was in the region of £20, that of the organist and master of choristers ranging from this to about double the amount. In fact, equivalent to the hire of an agricultural labourer, or to the salary of the grossly underpaid country curate. An ambitious clergyman would sneer at this with his eyes on prebends worth anything from £200 to £800 per annum. Neither was there any comparison with salaries in the academic sphere. In 1698 the first master of the free school at Shrewsbury earned £150, the second £100, and the third £50. A fellow of an Oxford college earned £100 per annum, and even this was far short of "yeomanly Gentry" who, on £200 to £400 a year, could "eate and drink well and live comfortably and hospitably".[23] An organist at a fashionable London church could do very much better than the majority of his country colleagues, receiving as much as £50 a year for very little duty; and he could supplement this with a valuable teaching practice charging a guinea or more a lesson.[24]

STRIVING FOR EXCELLENCE

There were then, as now, the more adventurous choirs that both endeavoured to keep pace with new additions to their repertoire (as can be seen from a glance at those who subscribed to eighteenth-century publications of church music) and also tried hard to maintain the highest possible standards, however obstructed by lack of sympathy and finance.

If the services at Salisbury, for instance, had not been well sung it is unlikely that George Herbert would have left his parish duties to attend twice every week. Nor could he have said, apropos of these excursions, "that his time spent in Prayer, and Cathedral Musick, elevated his Soul, and was his Heaven upon Earth". After the Restoration, possibly under the fiery Wise's direction, the Salisbury choir regained its fame, and was noted then for having "produced as many able musicians, if not more than any quire in this nation".

In the eighteenth century the Salisbury authorities did their best to live up to this past, judging by various references to the music in the Chapter records. An order was made in 1711 "that the Perdition book shall be revived" for "observing and noting down in the said Book the Daily Absences of the Residentiaries, Vicars Choral, Lay Singers and other Officers". The other side of the bargain was struck with the organist and master of the choristers, whose salary was increased by £20 per annum. That business was meant is shown by the organist being admonished nine years later to instruct the choristers himself, and not by deputy.

Apparently the full number of the choir was maintained. Even during a vacancy in a lay-clerk's place, a temporary deputy was appointed to fill the gap. The choristers, too, received full attention. In 1713 it was ordered that their number "shall be eight, that the yearly salary of the two senior Choristers shall be £12 each, of the two not in seniority £10 each, and that they should all be new-cloathed once in every year", attending both the Grammar and the Singing Schools. (In 1681 there had been only six choristers, the top two being then paid £8 and the rest proportionately less.)

The boys were strictly disciplined (one was dismissed in 1717). Any irregularities in their admission, such as the abuse of contacts and influence to gain a place, were ruled out by an order of 1727:

> Resolved that no boy shall be for the future taught to sing in the Choristers' School longer than six months before he be brought to the Chapter to see if they approve of his being continued, and on their approbation he shall be entered on a List or Roll to be for that purpose kept by the Master of the Choristers, and for the

future the Chapter will in the Election of Choristers make Choice out of such only as shall be entered on such a Roll and have regard to none other.

Such precautions were effective, as it appears that no chorister was in serious trouble until one Wilkins had to be expelled in 1752 "for his bad behaviour and practices".

The St. Cecilia Festivals that were such a feature of Salisbury life in the middle of the eighteenth century would have provided an extra outlet for the choristers' talents additional to their daily cathedral routine. Master Norris was in such demand as a treble soloist as to sing in the 1761 Three Choirs Festival at Worcester. Unfortunately, his later career was marred by an unhappy love affair which drove him to drink and an early death. It was related that when he sang at Westminster Abbey in the year that he died "he could not hold the book from which he sang, and excited emotions of pity in place of the rapture that was wont to follow his performances".[25]

The Salisbury lay-clerks were either well behaved, or very discreet. There is no account of any misdemeanours. The vicars-choral fared not so well. In an attempt to halt the tendency of leaving the singing to their lay colleagues, in 1711 it was "resolved and ordered by the Dean and Chapter that on all Litany days for the future the Litany shall be chanted out by one of the Vicars Choral and not by two Lay Singers as it hath been usually done". Some years later it was "ordered unanimously that Mr. Lake, Vicar Choral, be oblig'd for the future to attend the Services of the Church constantly in his place as Vicar Choral and in his proper habit". This admonition was not entirely effective as, in 1753, another vicar-choral was rebuked for poor attendance, and told "to perform the Services in his turn with greater decency than he has sometimes done". Notwithstanding this, in 1755, three of the vicars-choral were reprimanded for frequent absences.[26]

In the long run it was the London choirs, particularly the Chapel Royal, that attracted the most talented church musicians. St. George's Chapel, Windsor, benefited from its royal connection. Not beset by too rapid a turnover of personnel (only three organists between 1632 and 1756 contrasts with the frequent changes in some cathedrals) the choir also prospered under experienced direction at the Restoration. Child remained in charge until his death at the age of 91 in 1697, and advancing years in no way affected the efficient discharge of his duties as he had before then prudently delegated some of these to an assistant.

It was as a result of Child's efforts that Pepys could admit in 1664 that Windsor had "a good Quire of voices", which is more than he said of the choir of St. Paul's Cathedral at that time—"the worst that ever I heard". The St. Paul's men had been singled out for criticism by Bishop Bancroft before the Restoration: "great undecencye in prayertyme, such as leaninge upon theyr elbowes, sleepinge, talkinge, and such-like", but this was all swept away by the Great Fire of London in 1666. A fresh start was made in 1697 when services were first sung in Wren's new building, and for many years afterwards the Cathedral was the resort of fashion and discerning worshippers.

Perhaps Steele parodied custom at St. Paul's when he wrote in the *Tatler* for 30th August, 1709: "five young Ladies, who are of no small Fame for their great severity of Manners, and exemplary Behaviour, would lately go no where with their Lovers but to an organ-loft in a Church; where they had a cold Treat and some few Opera Songs to their great Refreshment and Edification".

More accurately, the historian Hawkins observed that "it was very common for persons of rank to resort in the afternoon to St. Paul's to hear the service, and particularly the anthem; and to attend a lady thither was esteemed as much an act of politeness, as it would be now to lead her into the opera". Even Handel was attracted to Evensong at St. Paul's by the opportunity for playing the organ there, and particularly by the prospect of a convivial evening with the singers.

He has been known, after evening service, to play to an audience as great as ever filled the choir. After his performance was over it was his practice to adjourn with the principal persons of the choir to the Queen's Arms tavern in St. Paul's churchyard, where was a great room, with a harpsichord in it; and oftentimes an evening was there spent in music and musical conversation.[27]

Others had vouched for the excellence of the music at St. Paul's; apart from the Chapel Royal, North knew no rival to it other than Lichfield—"the service in that church was performed with more harmony, and less hudle, than I have knowne it in any church in England, except of late in St. Paul's".[28]

The one choir that still did more than most to advance the composition and satisfactory performance of cathedral music was that of the Chapel Royal. Well-meaning attempts were made by less favoured choirs to follow its example, though with little chance of success. The inescapable conclusion was that only "where there is encouragement or a maintenance, as at the Royal Chappell, St. Paul's, Westminster Abbey etc., they abound in good voices, and the Service is performed, with such decency and solemnity, that God is truly worshipped, as of old, in the beauty of Holiness".[29]

5

The Cathedrals

DECAY

MUCH THRUSHED

Mediaeval materials provided the substance for the liturgy of the national church at the Reformation. Its creators worked on these materials, moulded them anew, and with all the art and skill of great sculptors created a pattern of worship used and admired ever since. But the statue that was cast with such expert care was not invulnerable. Thrown down and cracked at the Commonwealth, it was, however, faithfully restored at the earliest opportunity and blemishes were disguised under a newly polished surface. Inevitably it became weathered by changing attitudes and tarnished by neglect.

It should already be clear from the previous chapters how the face of church music also crumbled under the corrosive actions of apathy and incompetence. In addition there were internal faults which, developing imperceptibly at first, later revealed themselves more clearly.

Elaborate music in church had its opponents at the Reformation, but it was still sufficiently familiar then to be accepted without too many qualms. The promotion of austerer musical forms did not succeed in stunting flourishing innovations such as the Elizabethan "great" service or the early Stuart verse anthem. Yet, by the end of the seventeenth century, there were no comparably significant developments, and church music became increasingly reactionary. As the contrast grew sharper between contemporary "airy" idioms and the old "Solemn and Grave

Musick", more reliance was placed on the past in an unimaginative attempt to counter modern trends.

Throughout the seventeenth century new melodic styles had been continuously evolving, but they failed to oust old contrapuntal methods. Composers such as Blow and Purcell, avoiding too free a mixture of new and old, nonetheless cultivated both in their verse and full anthems. In the eighteenth century the full style became almost nervously nurtured as an indispensable inoculation for the church composer, providing immunity against all sorts of secular diseases. He had no chance of gaining respectability in his solo anthems unless he offset these with a fair proportion of full anthems.

As new musical developments mostly took place within secular forms, and as it was in music for the church that contrapuntal part-writing was self-consciously encouraged, the composer of anthems and services was placed uncomfortably on a fence. Even Greene, who could write in an up-to-date aria style in the solo sections of his anthems, at times resorted to an unconvincing, antique language for his concluding choruses. More than he, his fellow composers in their struggle to find appropriate idioms were torn two ways. Eighteenth-century church music ran into a dangerous situation in much the same way as the driver of a car who, exceeding a speed limit, with one eye on the road ahead and the other on the lookout for a police patrol, risks crashing into a lamp-standard.

The popular approach in musical histories which assumes a continuous progression onwards and upwards with ever-increasing refinements of expression and artifice does not apply to our subject. If anything it was a journey in a downward direction, or at least a process of growing old, through the music of the Restoration to that of the Augustan composers, from lively adolescence to respectable middle age.

The very fierceness of the dislocation caused by the Civil War ensured an equally vigorous restoration. The composers at that time held no plans for cautiously rebuilding a tradition of English cathedral music, only a practical resolve to write freely for the needs of their day, uninhibited by limiting or antagonistic opinions. The terse contrapuntal technique evident in some of Blow's music may have owed a little to the Puritans' distaste for long-winded polyphony, but he could as naturally write an anthem like *My God, my God, look upon me*, far removed from the literal interpretation of a scriptural moral, and as abstract and poetic an expression in solely musical terms as the greater motets and anthems of his predecessors. It was not until later that restricting sectarian attitudes could insinuate themselves more subtly, and demand that the musical settings of the words of an anthem be didactic or superficially pictorial. This in itself was not fatal, but what eventually gnawed at the vitals of English cathedral music were events outside its control such as the gradual demise of the Chapel Royal and the dominance of Italian opera.

The defence of sheltering behind a glorious heritage led to the endless production of anthems and services that are negatively non-secular, avoiding anything that would cause offence or be unworthy of their past. What was first erected as a temporary blockade in the particular and inclement circumstances of the early eighteenth century became a permanent fortress more effectively imprisoning its defenders than keeping out its attackers. Looking inwards at themselves and backwards at their past, the defenders soon lost both vitality and vision. Even today the most lively church music is often that written by those outside the establishment. It is a sad reflection that the cathedral tradition might have generated sufficient energy to arouse native music in the eighteenth and nineteenth centuries but failed to do this by becoming so indrawn and preoccupied with its own self.

SUPPORTERS OF THE OLD STYLE

No time was wasted in constructing the fortifications. In 1696 a protégé of Dean Aldrich, the Rev. Sampson Estwick, preached a sermon defending "a due Esteem of *Church-Musick*, in an Age that seems hastening on apace to a neglect, if not a disuse of it".[1] Though Estwick may merely have had a painful memory of William III's 1689 commission that proposed the ending of chanting divine service in cathedrals, another supporter showed deeply felt concern. The Rev. Arthur Bedford, anxious that his contemporaries in 1711 should appreciate the more conservative examples of the previous century's church music, promoted the "excellent, solid, and grave, as well as harmonious Anthems" of Gibbons, Rogers and Child, and in his way contributed to a trend which led eventually to Boyce's publication of services and anthems. Boyce based his choice on grounds of historical and practical interest, and not the least of the aims he stated in his introduction was to preserve the music of the old masters "in its original purity". Modern scholarship may pick holes in his claim to have amended the grave errors of careless copyists, but cannot deny the sincerity of his intent, namely: to give "some reputable models" for composers to study of the "true style and standard" of church music.

Hawkins was quite clear in his mind where these models were to be found; for him the peak was reached in the generation after the Reformation (he instanced an anthem by Tye—*I will exalt thee*).[2] But it was Bedford who anticipated such an assessment and who was one of the first to analyse the ingredients of a church music style that could, or so he thought, withstand the advances of modern secular levity. Worried because "the Humour of the Age is turn'd from every thing that is solid to that which is vain, and our grave Musick vanishes into Air", he wished there were more anthems of sober quality.

A grave and serious Mind, which is the Temper of Devotion, is disturb'd by light and airy Compositions, which disperse the Thoughts, and give a gay and frisking Motion to the Spirits, and call the Mind off from the Praises of God, to attend merely on the agreeable variety of Sounds.

Full music, that is in three, four or more parts, was well suited
D

to keep the mind on God; but the excellence of cathedral music lay in its inherent possibilities for variety, not only in formal schemes which contrasted various combinations of solo voices with the full choir and organ, but also in stylistic features. Bedford was not so conservative as to exclude the use of elaboration and figuration in a vocal line in order "to strike upon the Passions, and increase our Rapture"; nor, on the other hand, did he fail to enjoy the skilful use of discords for variety's sake: "they are like some sharp sauces, which whet the Appetite, and make the Meat relish the better" (or, as Mace had earlier put it, as decorative as "Black-Patches, in Fair-Ladies Faces"). Further variety was ready to hand in such contrapuntal techniques as imitation and canonic writing. Bedford affirmed that "Dr. Blow's Excellency in Canon hath been inimitable", and bemoaned the fact that the use of this device in the Glorias of some canticle settings "is now wholly laid aside, nay, ridicul'd and expos'd".*

The eighteenth-century composer, although committed to a belief in the improvement of music and loath to accept that the compositions of his predecessors could equal or excel those of his own, had to admit, in Croft's words, that post-Reformation church music contained such commendable characteristics as "justness and exactness in the composure" and "sublimity and elegancy of style". Furthermore, Croft dared to recommend his own anthems on the grounds that he had "endeavoured to keep in my View the Solemnity and Gravity of what may properly be called the Church-Style (so visible in the Works of my Predecessors) as it stands distinguish'd from all those light Compositions which are used in Places more proper for such Performances".[4]

---

* Gibbons was the first to write a Gloria in canon (*Nunc dimittis* of his short service). The device was frequently used in similar contexts by later seventeenth-century composers.

About the use of discords, Bedford admitted that "this Art hath languish'd since the Death of Dr. Blow. . . . When Discords are rightly us'd, they have a pleasing seriousness or Gravity upon the Fancy. The Movements in both Parts must be solid, in order to carry on the same Humour."[3]

Byrd would surely have blushed at such emphasis on solemnity and gravity, and resisted too blatant an attempt to isolate a "Church-Style". He and his contemporaries freely set sacred texts for both liturgical and domestic performance, and we do not nowadays stop to discriminate between the two when singing them in church. But, over a century later, too many composers ("now everyone is become a Composer of Church Music") writing too many trivial pieces were debasing the church music coin. A tight rein had to be kept on style, and the best riposte to decadence was thought to be in the promotion of music of a less distracted era. Tudway's collection of services and anthems, although it grew to be predominantly of post-Restoration music, began life as a rescue operation designed to save from obscurity "our Ancient Compositions of Church Music; at this time so much mistaken, and despised". By the time he had finished his six volumes he had given their contents the status of "an Everlasting Memorial" to English church music, "the Glory of the Church of England's publick worship". Tudway obviously feared the worst, "particularly at this time, when Cathedral Service, lyes under so many and great discouragements and disregards; Nay ev'n when, (so little is Church Music understood), it is much to be feard, the use of it, may soon be going to be laid aside".*

---

* The contemptible result of departing from a respected style of church music is clearly delineated by Tudway.

"But above all, to the corruption of that solemn, and grave style, which was established as only proper to be used in Divine Service, there are composers, within the compass of this Age, that I defy the Stage to outdo in Levity, and wantonness of Style. . . ."

". . . such sorry, and injudicious composition, . . . instead of assisting, and improving the performance of the Service, as is pretended, by a greater variety, do but bring a disreputation, and contempt upon it, and is the occasion of that irreligious behaviour, which most people make appear at Cathedral Service, when they come, rather to be entertained, and diverted, than with a sence of Religion, or devotion; for finding such turns and strains of music, as they have been accustomed to hear at the PlayHouse, think it but reasonable, to make the same use of it in the Church; And this I conceive to be the very reason, why Church Music has lost so much of its former respect, and reputation, as well as the composers thereof, vis: by departing

NEW INFLUENCES

That disaster never came to fulfil Tudway's gloomy prophecy was due not so much to his (and others') condemnation of the anthem that was a diversion rather than devotion, as to the ability and drive of a composer like Greene who could successfully assimilate contemporary idioms, and the integrity of Croft or Boyce who could exclude the more extravagant fashions and at the same time write music of valid expressive content.

As for the growing distinction between sacred and secular, only a genius of Handel's stature could overcome such nicety. In his oratorios he could set a Biblical text and depict profound moral truths that went far beyond the literal subject matter, and at the same time make use of the devices and experience of the opera house. In church music lesser men never achieved this

from that peculiar gravity of Style Appropriated to it; If this had been strictly adher'd to, people had not come to church for diversion, but to say their prayers, which Cathedral Music was designed to assist them in."

Composers "never considered how improper such Theatrical performances are in religious worship; How such performances, work more upon the fancy, than the passions, and serve rather to create delight, than to Augment and actuate devotion; And indeed all such light, and Airy Compositions, do in their own nature, draw off our minds, from what we ought to be most intent on, and make us wholly attend, to the pleasing and Agreeable variety of the sounds and from hence sprang all that contempt which Cathedral service is fallen into; The fanaticks, and other enemies of our constitution, seeing the bungling work, that many, if not most of our Cathedrals made of the Service, by following a style which was neither suitable to devotion, nor capable of being performed by ordinary voices, have had the confidence to prefer their own heavy, and indeed shocking way, of Psalm Singing, to the best of our performances; whereas, such Compositions as are Grave, Solemn, and fitted to devotion, have always been valued and esteem'd even by our enemies. . . ."

Purcell's anthem *Thou knowest, Lord,* "composed after the old way", is the masterpiece that carries Tudway's point. All those present at Queen Mary's funeral heard this piece sung, "so rapturously fine, and solemn, and so heavenly in the Operation, which drew tears from all; and yet a plain Naturall Composition".

If people would go to church "with a pious and devout disposition, the old compositions of Tallis, Byrd, Gibbons, with such as have imitated them, would have the same effect as this as of Mr. Purcell's".[5]

synthesis. Either their style was too secular, and they were snubbed; or they rigidly eschewed this world and assumed such sobriety in the face of the next that they spawned out a profusion of pieces that were tedious, spineless and insipid. A little semolina pudding goes a long way, but cathedral choirs developed such a taste for it (admittedly often for the want of anything more substantial) that for many years stronger fare gave them indigestion.

Not that they had much choice. In Purcell's day sacred and secular idioms could intermingle to advantage and without embarrassment. Later composers had to accept the opinion that "there is a peculiar sort of Musick which ought to be consecrated for the Service of the Church . . . and very different from that of *Common* Use".[6] This resulted eventually in a limitation of the means of expression available to church music which inevitably gave the not altogether unfounded impression that it was suited to "melancholy tempers" and "smelt of the church".

Another emasculating tendency in the eighteenth century was a changing attitude to foreign stimulus. Musicians from the continent were, as always, hospitably welcomed, but whereas in the previous century this intercourse had provided fresh incentives to native music, it now began to swamp the little talent of those who slavishly followed modish but insignificant examples, or frighten into impotency those who were aware of their limitations in the face of real genius. The music of Croft and Greene had shown its indebtedness to that of Corelli and his compatriots, although this need not be over-accentuated; Italian was eighteenth-century music's lingua franca. More damaging effects came later, when such English composers as achieved any autonomy did so only in the shadow of European originals, as, for instance, Attwood of Mozart or S. S. Wesley of Mendelssohn (and Spohr). By that time English music had become so coddled by these comforting hot-water bottles that it had the utmost difficulty at the end of the nineteenth century in shaking itself out of its stupor.

There was nothing inherently at fault in Avison's recom-
mendation for church musicians to learn from the "best Chapel-
masters abroad" (although he quoted such little-known names
as Caldara, Lotti and Gasparini). Being aware that "many of our
best modern composers have generally deduced their Elements
of Harmony" from Corelli, he also urged the study of Corelli's
successors: Geminiani in instrumental and Marcello ("the
highest example") in church music. Yet this theme was over-
played. Avison's particular suggestion that a reformation of
English church music should follow Aldrich's precedent
of adapting works of Palestrina and Carissimi for anthems[7]
incurred the wrath of Dr. William Hayes, and provoked
such a reaction as to show how deeply isolationism had taken
root.

It is understandable that a leading church musician who was
also professor of music at Oxford should have felt piqued by
the forceful opinions of a parish church organist at Newcastle.
But it was not as simple as that. Hayes voiced firmly established
views and did not speak only for himself when he said: "the
present fashionable Froth, would only Corrupt and debase the
Sterling simplicity, which has been the Characteristic of our
Church Music". If it was already tainted that was because of
"too close an Imitation of the Italian style (or the Neglect of
Solidity for the sake of being genteel and fashionable)".

He admitted that "our Church Musick is capable of Improvement", but his remedy is the predictable one: "the further we
look back, the more excellent the Composition will be found,
and the most properly adapted to the sacred Purpose of
Devotion". Neither Marcello's Psalms, nor Aldrich's re-
gurgitated Palestrina, but Gibbons, Morley, Byrd and Tallis
are the proper models for English church music.[8]

From all this swaying to and fro between native and foreign,
sacred and secular, old and new, there arose a demand later in
the century for a church music style that was plain, simple and
free of distracting complexities. The ability to hear every part
in a piece of vocal music was considered beyond most listeners:

"Choral Singing is more of an alarming than an affecting Nature to the generality of an Audience".* It was not worth the trouble to appreciate Tallis and "his favourite Counter-Point"; rather let works in his style be "Exploded out of all Choirs". The favoured aim was to reduce cathedral music from its "complex and artificial style, to that of Simplicity and easy Execution". Neither old nor new idioms were relevant in this search for the plainest expression of the sense of the words:

> Too studious a Regard to *Fugues* and an artificial *Counterpoint* appears in the *old*, and too *airy* and *light* a Turn, to the Neglect of a grand Simplicity, in the *new*.[10]

An eminent precentor of York published an anthem book in 1782. In his preface he indicated that by then the church music of Elizabethan and early Stuart composers was out of favour, dismissed as "almost utterly unintelligible"; suited to an age of "metaphysical subtilties", its contrapuntal complexities confused the ear and obscured the words. He pleaded for music in no more than four parts, having little "fuguing" and possessing a "more simple kind of harmony", all with the exclusive aim of conveying the words with utmost clarity.[11] Admittedly, eschewing subtlety and ingenuity led to anthems that were plain and dull, but such was the consequence of this reaction from the two extremes of cunning polyphony and florid vocal extravagance.

* Said by the Rev. William Hughes of Worcester Cathedral, presumably in a Three Choirs Festival sermon (printed in 1763). Hardly very tactful for that occasion, though he did indicate that it was old-fashioned counterpoint he was criticising when he proceeded to name five anthems that were justly admired in his day.

Purcell: *O give thanks* ("it is clear, it is easy, it is natural").
Greene: *O Lord give ear unto my prayer.*
Boyce: *Blessed is he that considereth.*
Boyce: *If we believe that Jesus died* (which "deserves to be wrote in Notes of Gold")—tastes change! Two centuries later these Boyce anthems seem singularly trite and vapid.
Handel: *Zadok the Priest* (the highest praise of all is reserved for Handel).[9]

Surprisingly, Handel's example was not grasped immediately. Although he came to dominate English musical life later in the eighteenth century, at the time of his death his music was admired, but not necessarily copied. Even Greene, who has often been accused of being a mimic, was only speaking the same language. Handel's greatness was recognised; and, perhaps because of his very eminence, lesser composers realised their comparative limitations and at first did not try to compete on his terms.* His fame eventually rested on his oratorios, but the grandeur of their conception bore little relation to the humble aims of the English anthem which in any case, with increasing emphasis being placed on simplicity, had scant space for anything but the superficial trappings of that master's style.

SUBSIDENCE

As the years passed English cathedral music became more and more impoverished, weakened internally by arguments con-concerning style and purpose, by inadequate resources, and facing increasing indifference.†

Whereas Croft's publication of his anthems met with reason-

* Avison admitted that English composers had not in his time been altogether successful in their imitation of Handel, though he was a worthy enough model.

Hayes could foresee the invincibility of Handel's position, and that there was no point in anyone belittling this. "He might just as easily with the Palm of his Hand stop the Current of the most rapid River."[12]

† One cathedral organist commented in 1771, "how much *Cathedral-Service* is, at present disregarded . . . for few Singing-men care to be at the Trouble of practising any Thing new; and some had rather sing twenty Songs at a *Concert*, etc. than one Anthem at Church". He added, "'Tis, really, enough to give any Person, who understands Music, a Disgust to *Cathedral-Duty*, to hear the *Voluntaries* which are usually play'd, and those over, and over again; the chanting of the Responses, etc. Half a Note, all the Way, below the Reader; and other Things that might be mention'd, *Which are not taken the least Notice of*, tho' easily distinguishable, even to every common ear".

In short, "*Choir Music* never was at so low an Ebb".[13]

able success, and Greene's ran into six further editions within fifty-two years, Boyce could on no account be persuaded to publish his own church music, such a poor view had he of its likely reception. Even his historic collection, *Cathedral Music*, fared none too well. There was only one further edition in the eighteenth century, and that bore the conclusion, from the poor response the first edition had received and from the prevalent apathy towards cathedral music, that it "served to shew to what a low ebb the love of it had sunk".

When Samuel Wesley gave a lecture in 1827 the tide had gone right out, revealing a wide expanse of mud. He commented sadly on "the irreverent and indecorous musical weekday performances in our Cathedrals: The harmless Chords of Messrs. King and Kent in constant request all over England in the Cathedrals while Purcell's immortal service in B flat is very rarely performed". Even in London the weekday services were "galloped over" in debauched haste, the choirs often could not make up all four parts, and the music chosen was "for the most part the *shortest*, the *easiest*, and the least *valuable*".[14]

Barnard, in 1641, had felt no need to justify cathedral music other than on the grounds that it could "civilize the rough and boystrous fancies of a Nation, that is esteem'd of many, to be naturally somewhat of the sourest". By the following century all manner of excuses had to be invented in favour of cathedral worship. For instance: it contributed highly to the honour of God and was a splendid example to all reformed churches; it produced spiritual happiness for all members of a cathedral staff; it brought economic prosperity to cathedral cities; it was for the nation's good; it was offered on behalf of all the parishes in the diocese.[15]

Such diverse arguments made little impact on the average congregation which was content as long as an anthem provided a moment of light relief before a lengthy sermon. If the anthem was at all extensive it was made more palatable with a rousing finale, a boisterous Hallelujah or a humdrum fugue. (With such a conclusion the choir roused the congregation from its "pious

D*

Respite"* in much the same way as the preacher does who signals to a somnolent audience by winding up his address with a resounding "and now, finally . . .".)

Anthems were, after all, not alone in being so restricted at that time. Much music was designed merely as background entertainment or to grace a particular occasion. In such a capacity it can hardly sustain the serious analytical attention of our modern "Third Programme" approach to listening. This would have horrified rather than flattered the composer. An eighteenth-century audience did not subscribe to our conditions of excellence, nor was it accustomed to the wide range and variety that we enjoy, stretching from Indian Ragas to all kinds of electronic bleeps and blurps. Limited means of communication prevented musical development from being anything but gradual, and never without relation to accepted idioms. A by-product of this is the "sameness" and, to us, monotony of much eighteenth-century music. It is not surprising that when the basic idiom sounds so hollow and prosaic the third-rate composers should appear so much duller than their seventeenth-century counterparts. The short services of Patrick and Hunt are commended in a way that those by King and Kelway are not; to equate them is considered gross heresy. Admittedly the earlier settings possess a vitality common in their period (and an accepted antiquity) but apart from this neither in fact have much significance outside their workmanlike qualities.

In architecture a continuing, well-proved idiom had its advantages. Rule-of-thumb methods of the Georgian style enabled even a hack designer to conceive a building that was elegant and well-proportioned. Neither can literature be said to have been stifled by Augustan aims of "propriety, perspicuity, elegance, and cadence". But, for music, excessive reliance on Georgian proportions and Augustan elegance was disastrous. Once the "experimenting exuberance" of the

---

* "When the Spirits begin to languish . . . with a constant series of Petitions, she [the church] takes care to allow them a pious Respite, and relieve them with the Rapture of an Anthem."[16]

Restoration period had died down, music became almost suffocated in a smog of prim dullness. Being one of the most forthrightly expressive of the arts, it had the most to lose when the method became the substance.

6

"Cathedral Musick"

THE ORDER OF SERVICE

THE DAILY ROUND

Even without two guides that were published soon after the Restoration, the routine of the fully choral service at that time would not be difficult to reconstruct as it is not all that different today. The changes have been few and have consisted mostly in shifts of emphasis.

One important development has been the placing of a sung Communion service at the centre of Sunday worship. For years this service was little more than an appendage to Matins. In the seventeenth century the very name by which it was known indicated its subsidiary position: a nondescript "the Second Service".

English church music has undoubtedly been impoverished by this lack of a strong centre. It is no accident that the summit of the church music of Byrd and Palestrina is reached in their settings for the Mass, which even for Bach, a Lutheran composer, remained a sufficiently powerful influence to form the framework for one of the greatest works of art ever conceived. His *B minor Mass* contains the highest measure of inspiration within complete unity of expression, though what he expressed was so utterly comprehensive and overwhelming that it burst all liturgical bounds. By comparison the vehicle provided by the Church of England in the seventeenth century was puny. With the "Second Service" as a perfunctory adjunct to other heavy-gaited forms of worship, the music for it never had much chance to exceed the commonplace. A cropped little

Sanctus, threaded in between Litany and ante-Communion, and matched by a bobbed Creed cannot stand contrast with the wonderful tapestry of the great sixteenth-century settings of the Mass, adorning the liturgy and throwing into prominence its rich symbolism.

A composer for the church must be animated by the worship he sets out to illuminate if he is in his turn to add to its lustre. A service of Morning Prayer based on scripture readings, petitions and a sermon could hardly stir up any response in depth. To their credit and our good fortune English musicians have fallen back on the varied inspirations of the psalter, and found there a store of treasure.

The basic structure of the sung services was outlined by Lowe when he published his *Short Direction for the Performance of Cathedral Service* in the year following the Restoration, although in some details he proposed temporary remedies for the immediate situation:

Morning Prayer is begun with a monotoned introduction followed by unison preces and responses (the minister's part could be sung by either a counter-tenor or bass voice). Lowe also provided a four-part setting of the responses, with the plainsong in the tenor part, for festal use. Immediately after this the Venite and the psalms for the day are sung (antiphonally) to one of two simple unison tunes, one for weekdays and another for Sundays and festivals. It was not expected that the psalms would always be sung in this monotonous manner as "when Quiremen are well skild in song" then, on festival days, they may use for the psalms either of the three four-part "tunes" that are provided for the canticles that follow the lessons: Te Deum and Benedictus (or Jubilate) in the morning, Magnificat and Nunc dimittis in the evening. These prototype Anglican chants ("Canterbury Tune", "Christ Church Tune", and "For Boyes") could easily be arranged for accompaniment on the organ, and be played by any organist who had "but so much ability only as to play a Psalme" (i.e. a hymn tune). Following the second canticle, the Apostles' Creed and Lord's Prayer are monotoned, leading into unison responses and three collects with the choir singing "Amen" to each.

Lowe did not specify the order of service for Evening Prayer (it being similar to that for Morning Prayer) but went straight on to the Litany; "and then (upon Lettany dayes) the Lettany sung (in an ordinary way) by two of the Quire", answered in unison by the remainder. An alternative four-part setting of the Litany based on Tallis is provided, presumably for when choirs regained their former skill. A reminder is added that in harmonised responses the Amens are also to be in parts, except in the "Second Service" when they are to be in unison.

This service is dealt with next. After the priest has begun with the Lord's Prayer, reading it "in one grave tone, the deeper the better", the Ten Commandments are announced "in a higher tone", the choir responding after each "in the same tone" unless they are singing a setting with organ accompaniment. Then, before the Epistle, the Collects are read, the choir "answering Amen", and after the Epistle, the Gospel, the choir singing "Glory be to thee, O Lord". Next "the Priest (or whole Quire) say (or sing) the Nicene Creed". As Lowe gave no music for this, he presumably had in mind a harmonised setting or a simple unison version. He is uninformative about the way the service ended ("and after that the Priest reads the Prayer for Christ's Church Militant etc. and so goes on to the end of the Morning Service") so it would appear that it either concluded before the Communion, or else the choir was dispensed with altogether.

Neither psalmody nor anthems are mentioned. This deficiency is made good to some extent by James Clifford who published in 1663 a collection of the words of anthems sung at St. Paul's Cathedral (*Divine Services and Anthems*). Finding it so useful there, in the following year he made many additions for a second edition for the use of all choirs. Lowe's slender list of chanting tunes for the psalms and canticles is supplemented in Clifford's preface which gives thirteen unison melodies and four harmonised chants. The alternative canticles, Benedicite in the morning, Cantate Domino and Deus misereatur in the evening service, are now included. Clifford implied that specific settings were becoming more generally sung*, as the "chanting tunes" were only for "when more solemn composures are not used".

Of most interest, however, are his directions for the services "perform'd with the *Organ* in St. Paul's Cathedral on Sundayes etc.". Agreeing with Lowe on the order of service, he also indicated the place of anthems and organ voluntaries. One voluntary followed the psalms at Morning and Evening Prayer and another divided the composite morning service, being played after the Litany (which concluded the "First Service") and leading into the "Second, or Communion Service".

Two anthems are sung in the morning, the first after the third collect at Matins, the second after the sermon in the Communion service (following the Creed). This anthem concluded the choral service. At Evensong, in addition to an anthem in the usual place after the third collect, another was sung after the sermon.† It appears that St. Paul's was spared the strains of psalmody.

Neither Lowe nor Clifford mentioned the Sanctus and Gloria. The pre-Commonwealth practice of limiting the music at the "Second Service" to settings of the Creed and of the responses to the Commandments continued for a time at the Restoration. But room was soon found for the two eucharistic hymns, though not in their proper places: the Sanctus replaced the organ voluntary as a kind of introit to the Communion service, and the Gloria often served as the anthem concluding the choral part.

* In the course of discussing the evening service, Clifford named settings by Byrd, Tallis, W. Mundy, Bevin, Strogers, T. Tomkins, O. Gibbons, Batten, Giles, Portman, Child and C. Gibbons. It seems unlikely that St. Paul's and other cathedrals pursued the Bishop of Exeter's suggestion to say and not sing those parts of the service that are "*most plain, doctrinall, and fundamentall*", e.g. the Creeds and Commandments.[1]

† A full anthem before the sermon and a verse anthem afterwards was the prevailing custom at St. Paul's. The singing of two anthems in this way was not general.

In many churches a complete Mass was celebrated only on "sacrament Sundays" (which could, if wished, be limited to four a year: Christmas, Easter, Whitsun and harvest). Even in advanced churches that had a weekly celebration, the Communion hymns were only sung once a month, the choir presumably leaving when the communicants entered the chancel at the invitation "draw near with faith . . ." (a practice not unknown in the present century). More generally the service took the form of ante-Communion, finishing with a blessing after the prayer for the church militant.

Hardly surprisingly, a sung Creed gradually fell into desuetude and the Sanctus and Gloria were at worst "abandoned to a mode of recitation, adapted only to the most humble sanctuaries", and at best kept alive by Rogers's uninspired efforts.

Ex. 1

Existing settings of the Commandments and Creed were supplemented not long after the Restoration by new ones of the Sanctus and Gloria. Those in the key of G by Blow were included in leaves of Chapel Royal part-books transcribed between c. 1680 and 1687.[2] Other settings of the Sanctus were composed by Rogers, Child, Creighton, Golding and Aldrich, and the Sanctus and Gloria by Wise, Blow, Clarke, Croft and Weldon.

English cathedrals owe much to the Victorians, not the least for their beginning to place a due emphasis on the seriously neglected "Second Service". Without the stimulus of the Oxford Movement the worship in cathedrals would have continued in a debilitated way for many more years.

For instance, the matter of a choir's appearance. This had not always been overlooked, but a general improvement was certainly overdue. Open-fronted surplices covering ordinary clothes like a dust-sheet could soon become scruffy; not all choirs could or would replace them as often as the Chapel Royal did. Processions, or the lack of them, was another detail. It was hardly a reverent and decorous custom, however time-honoured, for clergy and choir to enter for a service in their own time, taking their places independently of each other and waiting for the clock to strike the hour like a starter's pistol. It was an obvious improvement to begin a service by all processing in together.

The choice of music, too, was haphazard and often completely disorganised. There were many occasions when choirs did not know what they were going to sing until the last possible moment. Anthems might be chosen by special request, and a good solo boy might collect for himself a little pocket-money by obliging somebody who could afford his favourite piece.* Perhaps it was in order to prevent such an irregularity that

---

* One organist, writing of the middle of the eighteenth century, said: "I generally had three, or four of them [boys] that sung *Solo* Anthems: Tho' I was not allowed to chuse them myself; (which was many Pounds out of my Pocket)."

Another money-spinner for the choristers was to provide a copy of the music for any distinguished, wealthy-looking visitor to a service. The Lord Chief Justice, Francis North, travelling the Northern Circuit in 1676 was caught this way. "His lordship was well enough knowne in all the Quires, where ever he came, and the boys failed not to bring him a fair musick book of the anthem and service, and sometimes the score, if they had it, expecting, as they always had, a compensation for their paines."[3]

Norwich Cathedral paid a lay-clerk five shillings a year "for nameing the Anthems".[4]

Where more care was taken over the choice of music it was left in the hands of the senior clergy in consultation, one hopes, with the master of the choristers. A weekly service list was rare; such a sensible system was not generally adopted until relatively recent times. Fortunately, a list of music sung at Durham Cathedral in the month of June 1680 has survived inside the cover of a part-book, but there are no further indications of this sort to show that other cathedrals organised their selection of music so efficiently. Incomplete as the Durham list is, it gives some information about a cathedral's working repertoire. On the whole it is conservative. The music of Charles II's Chapel Royal had not yet penetrated so far north, and there is a distinct bias towards that of the pre-Commonwealth period. Little-known writers are featured and there is, by modern standards, much repetition (eight of the services were sung twice within the month).

The congregation's contribution has not varied in essence. Doubtless a comment made by Robert Bridges would not have been inapposite. "It seems a pity that natur should hav arranged that where the people are musical they would rather listen, and where they are unmusical they would all rather sing."[5] But it is unlikely that in the eighteenth century the congregation took its task with the desired amount of seriousness, praying with the choir, meditating on the text and letting the mind be led by the music's insights. They unashamedly attended a choral service for entertainment. They even had to be reminded that to assume a "lazy sitting Posture" during the psalms and not to stand with the choir for the anthem was both indevout and bad manners.[6]

PSALMS

Psalms, canticles and anthems were the substance that filled the framework outlined by Lowe and Clifford. The "ordinary"

parts of the service were generally sung to specially composed
settings in harmony for the whole choir, which were frequently
repeated throughout the year, whether the responses to the
Litany, or the simple chants for the prose psalms that were
developing at this time, or the relatively elaborate music for
the canticles. But responses sung in unison for long rivalled
harmonised settings which were often reserved for Sundays and
festivals only. In the declining years of the eighteenth century
Merbecke's *Book of Common Prayer Noted* still provided a stop-
gap for choirs unwilling or unable to tackle more complicated
music.

> With scarce any variation, it continues to be the rule for choral
> service. . . . The musical notes . . . are very little different from
> those in use at this day, so that this book may truly be considered
> as the foundation of the solemn musical service of the Church of
> England.[7]

It is the chants for the psalms that are most curious to us, as
these have subsequently become such a prominent feature in
the choral service. Although Anglican chant has its roots in
plainsong, being originally a simple harmonised form of the
tones, it was in the years immediately following the Restoration that it became firmly established in its present form.

Prose psalms had been performed in various ways. Apart
from choir settings for festivals by such composers as Tallis,
Byrd and Gibbons, there were three basic methods: first,
sung to plainsong tones antiphonally by the choir (or, in the
parish churches, by the minister and the people); secondly, read,
or sung to plainsong, by the clerk and priest; thirdly, and more
simply, read by the priest, the congregation tacitly following
and assenting with an Amen at the end. The first of these three
was the progenitor of the Anglican chant, and a relic of the
third survives in cathedrals to this day, where the congregation
participate silently in the singing of the psalms.

It is ironic that the last method was one that non-conformists pressed for at the Restoration. Although their opinions were not accepted, experience of mumbled plainsong and mauled chant in parish churches has shown that the vocal participation of a congregation is more appropriate in hymns than psalms. Those who urged at the Savoy Conference in 1661 the abolition of "the repetition and responsals of the clerk and people, and the alternate reading of the Psalms and Hymns [i.e. canticles], which cause a confused murmur in the congregation", were rebuffed by the terse reply of the Anglican bishops: "If the people may take part in Hopkin's why not David's psalms?"[8] The bishops' simple contention prevailed.

Consequently, the revised Prayer Book of 1662 encouraged the antiphonal way of singing or reading the psalms with the whole congregation. This was the first edition that officially included, with the various orders of service, the psalter which previously had been printed separately as an appendix. Attention was drawn to this innovation on the title page announcing "The Book of Common Prayer and administration of the Sacraments, and other rites and ceremonies of the Church, according to the use of the Church of England", and adding, for the first time, "together with the Psalter or Psalms of David, Pointed as they are to be Sung or Said in Churches".

Cathedrals gradually replaced the unison plainsong tones for the psalms with harmonised settings. Dependent on the so-called "pointing" in the prayer book (a colon dividing each verse into two halves) choirs were restricted to the simpler tones that presented the least number of practical difficulties.* These formed the basis of the earliest four-part chants, and it was only as more chants were composed that the connection with plainsong was cast aside. In rhythm alone is the original pattern revealed. For instance, Tone i, fourth ending, has in its

---

* Lowe used the plainest Sarum tones (i and viii) for his two unison melodies, and added three simple harmonised chants. Clifford gave thirteen unison melodies of a similar nature and four harmonised chants: two found in Lowe, "Canterbury Tune" and "Christ Church Tune", another very similar to the latter ("Mr. Adrian Batten's Tune") and one new one, "Imperial Tune".

first half a reciting note followed by two other notes, in its
second half a reciting note followed by four. With slight
variations this formula persisted, and is immediately recognisable in the Anglican chant's final shape.

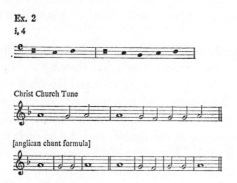

Ex. 2
i, 4

Christ Church Tune

[anglican chant formula]

Both Lowe and Clifford emphasised that the use of specific
note-values did not carry any particular rhythmical significance,* though such sound advice became difficult, if not
impossible, to follow as chants increased in complexity. In fact,
the performance of psalms to harmonised chants did not for
long escape criticism for distorting both words and music.

For one critic, poor psalm-chanting was the worst feature of
cathedral music in 1728. He admitted that "when performed
decently, the organ presiding", even with the frequent
repetition of the first chord of each half of the chant, "the
harmony is exceeding good". But his experience in practice
was that a choir rarely maintained unanimity: even when sung
most deliberately, "the pronunciation is at best a huddle

____

* The notes "are intended to signify no exact Measure, onely the square
black notes (or Brieves) are put, where the syllables are to be sung slower
then the other". (Lowe)
". . . though the ordinary Tunes are done in Notes, yet they are not
intended to signifie any *exact time*, but to take notice that the *Minim* and
Semibrief, are only put where the syllables are to be sung slower and more
emphatically than the rest". (Clifford)

unintelligible, as if all strove to have done first". When sung unaccompanied (the organ "keeps the quire upright") "the chanting is scandalous, such a confused din as no one living not pre-instructed could guess what they were doing". But "considering how little (or rather no) care is taken of this noble part of the service . . . it is a wonder that . . . it is so well performed as it is".[9]

These strictures fell on deaf ears. Some years later it could still be said that "in our Cathedral *chanting* . . . some of the words are uttered with too much rapidity, while others at the *mediatio*, or half-close, and terminations, are protracted to an unreasonable length".[10] Yet, to be fair to the singers, a prolonged rallentando at the middle and end of each verse would have been unavoidable in some of the more elaborate eighteenth-century chants. To adapt them to a natural speech rhythm would have been beyond the capacity of the most proficient of choirs.

Another serious stumbling-block to fluent chanting was the absence of adequate systems of pointing. These were not introduced until the nineteenth century, and then only accepted with conservative caution.[11] Lacking pointed psalters, each choir had to manage as best it could with the minimal assistance of punctuation marks as given in the prayer book.[12]

What eventually forced the introduction of comprehensive methods of pointing was the acceptance of the sensible practice of singing different psalms to different chants. The anomalies of a lengthy sequence of verses, of mixed mood and character, sung to the same progression of harmonies repeated over and over again must have struck any sensitive person, but it was at least possible to manage the psalms for the day by rote when there was no change in the chant. Confusion would have arisen if a variety of chants were used without some guidance, and the suggestion that a "Cathedral Psalter" be compiled of a selection of the many chants then in use so as to provide a suitable one for each particular psalm[13] undoubtedly stimulated the invention of pointed psalters.

CANTICLES

In the order of Morning and Evening Prayer, where the lessons are such a central feature, the English church has traditionally stressed the canticles that follow those lessons. It can indeed be argued that as New Testament hymns their musical interpretation should be little different from that of the Old Testament psalms, and some might wish that the temporary expedient adopted at the Restoration of using the same music for both had become permanent.

But before then composers had welcomed the emphasis on the canticles, and responded with a fine series of settings that form one of the hallmarks of "Elizabethan" church music. These either, as in the "short" service, served a limited purpose of presenting the words in a terse yet dignified manner, or, as in the "verse" and "great" services, unashamedly interrupted the course of the office, elaborating, adorning and enriching their particular texts. The achievements in the latter type of Morley, Byrd, Weelkes, Gibbons, Ward and Tomkins, more than justify such licence.

After the Restoration there was less concern to uncover wealth of meaning in this way, and the emphasis on the canticles shifted, not through any doctrinal tack, nor through any immediate change in the ability of choirs to sing music of such complexity, but for the simple reason that the anthem assumed precedence. Those parts of the office that were performed daily were hurried through as quickly as possible to make way for a moment of relaxation. Lengthy setting of the canticles only delayed the time when the anthem could be enjoyed.

Anything as complex as the verse service became redundant; but one of its attributes was salvaged. Variety in vocal scoring became grafted on to short service brevity, resulting in a hybrid that flourished for many years without the addition of any new strains. Services such as Humfrey in E minor, Wise in E flat, Blow in G and Purcell in B flat held a delicate balance between compactness and diversity of expression. Earlier composers, with apparently effortless fluency, had compressed within terse paragraphs lively ingenuity in each vocal line, but Restoration writers favoured the contrast and interest obtainable from an adroit interplay of solo combinations and full choir. Purcell, when he so wished, drove his parts to progress against each other with obstinate individuality; Blow could turn a skilled hand writing cunning canonic Glorias; yet in the last resort, it is the interaction of differently scored sections that sustains the interest in their services.

Some later works achieved succinctness and variety, although services such as Croft in B minor and Nares in F do represent a tendency to rely on well-worn devices as a substitute for genuine originality. Only Greene in C retained the old vitality. Unfortunately its assumed complexity prevented it from being sung at all frequently. It was not published until thirty-five years after Greene's death, and its appearance then in Arnold's *Cathedral Music* (a collection that met with a very poor response) did not ensure its wide use, and even a century later it was still considered too intricate.

Blow wrote four sets of canticles in the short service style. Notable as these are, they consciously adopt an archaic manner of speech and instance a freakish late development of the early Stuart examples rather than a significant contribution in a continuing tradition. By the eighteenth century that idiom was obsolete; Greene could no more be expected to write like Gibbons than Johnson like Bacon.

Although the inner substance was lost, the outer shell remained intact, persisting in the services of King and other dull grub-street hacks. The tediousness of their efforts is due not so much to their lack of originality as to the fact that the singers who had to perform their music were so untalented. The slender ability those unfortunate "mechanics" possessed was gelded by the function of having to sing four canticles almost every day of the year. Slow to read music and unwilling to learn new, choirs were mollycoddled by the eighteenth-century mockery of the short service. Short became synonymous with easy; simplicity with unrelieved monotony. It would not have been so bad if this tasteless product had not become fodder for many succeeding generations of church musicians. It could still be said in 1891 that "the service in F is perhaps King's most felicitous effort. Few pieces of Church music have ever been so widely sung".[14]*

Eighteenth-century church music was not distinguished for its service writing. There were no successors to the fruitful industry of Blow and Child in this sphere until Stanford and Howells. Settings of the canticles continued to be written that fulfilled an undemanding function and yet were neatly designed and pleasingly melodious, such as those by Boyce in C, Arnold in A and Robert Cooke in G, but none of these stand comparison with the work of seventeenth-century composers.

ANTHEMS

It has already been indicated how the anthem furnished a primary attraction for the musical churchgoer. The popularity of the verse anthem in particular is reflected in the attention given to it by eighteenth-century composers, but the full anthem was by no means neglected. The simplest fare in the latter category, short little pieces, were very suitable for the less able choirs† and there are only a few worthwhile instances of

* To pick on King is unfair. He has himself to blame ("as little affected by the service as the organ-blower") but his services are not that much more ordinary than those by, say, Kelway. Travers in F beats them all for sheer monotony. The "melody" in the first fifteen bars of the Magnificat's Gloria uses only six notes—F, three times; G, six times; A, seven times; B flat, nine times; D, five times; and C, twenty-five times—outdone only by the inept subject for a canon which opens the Gloria of the Nunc dimittis.

† A cathedral organist noted in 1771 eight anthems that were especially useful for the long Morning Service "in a Cold Frosty Morning": Batten's *O praise the Lord all ye heathen* and *Deliver us O Lord our God*; Child's *O Lord grant the King a long life* and *Praise the Lord O my Soul*; Farrant's *Call to remembrance* and *Hide not thou thy face*; Creighton's *Lord thou art become gracious* and *I will arise . . .* "and such like Anthems, about a Minute and Half long, which are much used *at some Cathedrals*, even in Summer".[15]

this strictly functional type. Blow wrote fourteen short anthems[16] that in constraint and condensed thought are reputable successors to Tallis's *O Lord, give thy holy spirit*, or Richard Farrant's *Call to remembrance*. The burial sentences by Croft showed too what could be done in this idiom, while the supreme examples are Purcell's *Remember not, Lord, our offences* and *Thou knowest, Lord, the secrets of our hearts*.

In itself the miniature full anthem was not taken too seriously. In an expanded form it developed sizeable proportions which spread into a wide ternary plan (taking the hint from Weelkes's *Alleluia* and *Gloria in excelsis Deo*) with two sections for full choir flanking a central movement for solo voices. The contrasts in scoring were handled convincingly, but contra-puntal writing in the choruses was often artificial and academic. Counterpoint, in eighteenth-century English church music, no longer held the valid purpose that it had previously possessed when it had been treated like a conversation between many people, each individual speaking sound sense and yet collectively formulating an argument of compelling logic. With Boyce and his contemporaries the private statements were often meaning-less, only the composite result forming a rational synthesis. They could escape the stultifying respectability of fuguing in solo anthems; in their full anthems they were obliged to be well-mannered, to present an ecclesiastical character, by writing "solemn and grave musick", that is good, solid counterpoint. What Hanslick wrote of the use of fugue in the mid-nineteenth century could equally well apply: "it has more recently tended to become a mere form, but in Church music it remains the composer's solemn duty".

The first section of an anthem by Boyce, *Turn thee unto me, O Lord*,[17] achieves a characteristic individuality in its separate parts. A comparable full anthem by Croft, on the other hand, demonstrates an inclination to concentrate on the whole at the expense of the particular. *O Lord, rebuke me not*[18] is beautifully poised in its symmetry; the two full sections, related thema-ally, balance each other and are offset by the delicacy of the intervening trio. The progression of parts is always directed to upholding this design, moving towards moments of primarily harmonic interest. A closer look reveals cracks in the structure where the individual lines, instead of growing meaningfully, are stunted by their too frequent implications of tonic–dominant harmonies. Furthermore, rarely do all six parts seem inevitable and essential; apart from the sonorities their texture creates, three or four would often adequately demonstrate the argument.

Whereas an eighteenth-century composer may have been pushed against his inclination to wear a garment that did not fit, Purcell successfully trimmed the cloth to suit his taste. He evolved quite unaffectedly his own convincing style of part-writing. In some of his anthems, in order to follow the music's logic, the ear must switch from line to line as they all *together* trace a horizontal course; at the point where one seems to have lost its interest, it is only making way for the contour continued elsewhere. This kind of contrapuntal texture is represented in Greene's *Lord, let me know mine end*.[19] And here the stammering utterances of the text are also welded to a free-flowing thorough bass.

Rhythmical rather than melodic subtlety is often a distinctive feature in the Restoration composers' part-writing. Failure to

Ex. 3

Lord, let me know mine end   Greene

seek out this facet in performance can prevent their music from being fully appreciated. The technique of rubbing two voices against each other, and generating tension not so much by interplay of melodies as by a rhythmic counterpoint, is particularly apparent in some of the solo ensembles of anthems by Humfrey and Blow. Their music has many instances where latent rhythmical implications are disguised by triple-time barring, where cross rhythms give life to each line both individually and in combination with others.

The verse anthem possessed an aim different from that of the full anthem. Designed to entertain, it was not overmuch inhibited by ideas of what was proper and decent for church use. Composers, when they had observed their obligations with a due share of full anthems, felt at liberty to satisfy their own natural inclinations by writing verse anthems less restricted in style.

At the Restoration the verse anthem was already well established. The adoption of a figured-bass accompaniment gave it a new point of departure; the ever-increasing popularity of the solo singer encouraged its further development. This was continually being fed by international celebrities drawn to the royal court and London's musical life, and the trend reached an extravagant climax in the days of Handel's operas. Although the virtuosity of operatic singers far outstripped the capacity of the Gentlemen of the Chapel Royal, there was no shortage of able choirmen to delight the devout with their skilful performances of solo anthems.

By the eighteenth century the verse anthem, with its succession of aria-like movements, had reached cantata-type proportions. Owing much at first to the appeal of favourite voices, its popularity was later borne along by a general relish for music in church that was a match for the instrumental sonata and concerto grosso that had such prestige outside. Even at the beginning of our period, Locke's *Lord, let me know mine end*[20] is like a vocal concerto grosso. The choruses in much the same way as orchestral ritornelli punctuate the solo sections. The model, however, for the form of this piece is to be found in earlier seventeenth-century verse anthems whose pattern of a repeated sequence, solo—chorus, was used by many writers. This became diversified with the introduction of string "symphonies" and "ritornelli", playing an essential structural role and creating new possibilities for contrast between solo voices (in varying combinations) instruments and full choir. The latter's function was at times confined to that of longstop; by way of compensation, the play between the others was often extensive and skilful. Two instrumental anthems by Purcell (one early and one late composition)—*My beloved spake*[21] and *O sing unto the Lord*[22]—are a match for any in this genre, and together demon-

strate how Purcell learnt to make the most effective musical use
of the varied vocal and instrumental textures.*

The part played by the band of violins considerably extended
the sheer size of the verse anthem. When, later in the seventeenth
century, strings ceased to be used, although the available range
of colours was thereby reduced, the length and proportions
remained little affected. In fact, by the eighteenth century, the
verse anthem had grown into a lengthy succession of solo
movements and ensembles, with contributions from the full
choir which either completed it with a coda-like finale (as in
Nares's *The souls of the righteous*) or else punctuated its paragraphs by joining in the discussion with the solo voices (as in
Greene's *Arise, shine, O Sion*).[25] The fabric being no longer
laced together by symphonies and ritornelli, tonality then
offered a recognisably sure way to unity. With the whole
anthem firmly rooted in the home key, individual movements
could make prolonged excursions into related keys provided
they did not lose sight of the tonic.

Instruments were still included in anthems for special
occasions, but these anthems bore little relation to those for
daily use. Trumpets, oboes and strings could add grandeur, but
they could no longer reshape the liturgical anthem as King
Charles's band of violins had done. In any case these orchestral
anthems were uncomfortably "large" for certain churchmen.

---

* Blow's coronation anthem, *God spake sometime in visions*,[23] is a fine
example of formal mastery stretched over a large canvas and stimulated by
the resources used. Scored for four-part string orchestra, eight-part verse
and chorus (S.S.A.A.T.B.B.B.) it is in four clearly defined and yet inter-
locking sections: (i) an extended instrumental symphony and a chorus;
(ii) a verse, using various groupings of the eight voices, and a chorus; (iii) a
three-part verse and a chorus; (iv) a section using all the resources in turn
before a sonorous "hallelujah" finish.

An unpublished anthem by Blow, *O sing unto the Lord a new song, let the
congregation*,[24] although on not quite so ambitious a scale, displays equally
effective scoring and grasp of form. One section leads naturally into the
next, the instruments playing a vital binding role. Despite its superficial
diversity the whole is united, internally, by the repetition of various
passages and, overall, by a continuity of mood. A fine ten-part Gloria
concludes the anthem.

The Bishop of Chichester heard *The ways of Sion* by Handel at the funeral of Queen Caroline in 1737, and subsequently remarked: "after the service, there was a large Anthem, the words by the Sub-Dean of Westminster, the music set by Mr. Handel, and is reckoned to be as good a piece as he ever made". The Bishop, trapped as he was, could only comment dryly: "it was above fifty minutes in singing".

A churchgoer was quite accustomed to sitting out an hour-long sermon; a fifty-minute anthem was apparently too much.

English cathedral music had been resuscitated after the Commonwealth to be later gradually suffocated by philistinism and disinterestedness. Strength and vigour seeped away, and cathedral music slowly settled into complacency, lacking the energy essential for survival. Responsibility for this can be shared between the decline in status of the music and the musicians (reflected in the many commonplace services and anthems written in the eighteenth century) and the general musical developments of the late seventeenth century which drove expressive sonorities and vigorous angularities into much smoother idioms. The most highly prized qualities became elegance and symmetry. No more marked contrast can be found than that between the loaded dissonance of Purcell's *Man that is born of a woman*[26] and the mellifluous grace of Clarke's *How long wilt thou forget me.*[27]

7

"Cathedral Musick"

THE MUSICIANS

THE ORGANIST

During the seventeenth century there was little distinction between choirman and organist. The latter was often one of the choir who happened to be able to undertake the not very exacting organ duties. If he was also master of the choristers, then he assumed some pre-eminence. As well as training and looking after the boys he saw to the proper presentation of the daily music, but he did not necessarily organise the whole choir. Rehearsals were wisely left in his hands at the Chapel Royal, though even there the ultimate responsibility lay with the dean and sub-dean. Lesser choirs were in the charge of the precentor or (as with Aldrich at Christ Church, Oxford) the dean, and often, it seems, left to their own devices. As the master of the choristers gradually extended his capacity and authority to run his choir, he could not automatically expect much encouragement or anticipate immediate success. Apart from the slender talents of the choir members, the necessary discipline and organisation were often lacking. What chance was there of any constructive planning of the choral services when even the choice of music was hopelessly haphazard?

For someone who was only an organist, his tasks were less satisfying than those of the singers. Confined to playing accompaniments and the occasional voluntary, he had as yet neither recitals to develop any virtuosity nor outside interests to relieve repetitive routine.

It has been considered that Blow was being very magnanimous

when he made room for Purcell to become organist of Westminster Abbey. In fact, he was just handing over the least interesting of his duties to a bright pupil, as he later did to Clarke at St. Paul's Cathedral. That Blow subsequently came back to Westminster Abbey is understandable when seen as a move to consolidate his influence in London's church music world.

Plurality has been much vaunted as a characteristic of eighteenth-century church life. Widening a person's interests and professional activities, providing both kudos and extra income it was not uncommon amongst organists to take on more than one appointment. The plethora of posts held by Blow and Boyce can be explained not so much on grounds of financial ambition (although this would not have been neglected), as that this was the way they maintained their leading positions. Like the ordained ministers of the church, they thus gained great influence in their sphere, both earning prestige for themselves and dispensing patronage to their protégés.

Opportunities in London for ambitious musicians increased with the growth in the eighteenth century of the number of parishes that employed organists. They could often earn considerably more than their colleagues in the provinces by holding concurrently two or three comparatively lucrative posts. But plurality was not unknown outside the metropolis. John Pigott succeeded his father in 1704 as organist of the Temple Church where he continued to serve even after his later appointment to St. George's Chapel, Windsor. Finding the travelling irksome as he grew older, he changed the Temple for Eton College, still holding his employment at St. George's until he resigned in 1765. Most organists were obliged for financial reasons to remain in office till death, but Pigott managed to enjoy a few years' peaceful retirement. Not, it must be added, that he can have made much profit out of his two posts; a legacy provided him the wherewithal.[1]

Another, to us, irregular feature was the manner of election. This same John Pigott who had stepped into his father's shoes

E

at the Temple gained his place at Windsor (in competition with
the organist of Bristol Cathedral) through the active interest of
his uncle, who happened to be a canon of St. George's.

If you were not fortunate enough to have strategically placed
family connections, then you were well advised to weave your
own networks. An applicant for a new post of organist at
Christ Church, Spitalfields, set about this with extraordinary
thoroughness. And he was duly rewarded for his pains. Peter
Prelleu, when he had learned in 1735 that the parish was about
to acquire an organ for the church for the first time, and before
any mention had been made of appointing an organist, "made
an early interest for the place of organist, but was opposed by a
young man who lived in that neighbourhood: the contest was
carried on with such spirit by both parties, as was scarce ever
known, but in popular election to some great office".[2] Such
blatant pursuit of the main chance was so general that the
ex-organist of Lichfield Cathedral (he was then organist of two
parish churches in the locality, Sutton Coldfield and Tamworth)
could boast, as though it were unusual, "that of the five
Organist's Places which I have had, in the Space of four and
thirty Years, (two of which I now possess,) I was always elected,
at every one of them, without being personally known to, or
soliciting the Interest of, any individual Person".[3]

One London church, St. George's, Hanover Square, when
appointing its first organist in 1725 refused to be "teazed by the
solicitations of candidates of mean abilities", and took the
sensible step of setting up a panel of eminent advisers. Handel,
Pepusch, Greene and Galliard had to audition the candidates
and "determine their degree of merit". In this open competition
the gifted player Thomas Roseingrave defeated his rivals on
the extraordinary quality of his improvising, was recommended,
and appointed. But whether St. George's, as they became
familiar with their organist, appreciated his originality, is much
less likely. They bore with him for twelve years. Then, in 1736,
Roseingrave "was sent away from St. George's Church on
account of his mad fits".

Revealing certifiable insanity or mere eccentricity, Roseingrave's music and behaviour clearly did not conform to the norm expected by a respectable London congregation. Endearing foibles like his practice of papering the walls of his room with the music of Palestrina were harmless enough, but the St. George's parishioners would have been made to feel most uncomfortable by the nervous-sounding harmonic progressions that feature in some of his organ voluntaries. Similarly, they could not indefinitely endure their organist acting in this manner: "If, during his performance on the organ at church, any one near him coughed, sneezed, or blew his nose with violence, he would instantly quit the instrument and run out of church, seemingly in the greatest pain and terror". Whether fairly or not, the root cause of such behaviour was attributed to a woman: Roseingrave's peace of mind had been shattered when he had been jilted by a "lady of no dove-like constancy". "After this misfortune poor Roseingrave was never able to bear any kind of noise, without great emotion."[4]*

In the last resort, in whatever way appointments were gained, organists who were sane, able and of good character successfully reached high office. Croft, it was admitted, "seems to have gone through life in one even tenor of professional activity and propriety of conduct. We hear of no illiberal traits of envy, malevolence, or insolence." Another writer added that he "was a grave and decent man". Applicable as much to his church music as to his character, the "universal respect" that both gained for him was expressed during his lifetime when he was twice eulogised (unusually for a musician) in dedications

---

* Thomas Roseingrave (1690–1766). Toured Italy in 1710, where he became influenced by the playing of Domenico Scarlatti and the music of Palestrina; appointed the first organist of St. George's, Hanover Square, in 1725 but later moved to Ireland, living with his nephew.

Modern editions of his keyboard music are published by Stainer and Bell (*Ten Organ Pieces*, edited by Peter Williams) and the Pennsylvania State University Press (*Compositions for Organ and Harpsichord*, edited by Denis Stevens).

from two separate preachers: "So great an ornament to Your Profession" ... "The Master of the Song in our Israel".*

Boyce was another musician who, in his day, earned admiration and sincere affection. In a biography written shortly after his death it was shown how, despite an exceptionally busy and successful professional life, he had yet retained that rare virtue, modesty.

> Dr. Boyce's merit consisted in the union in his own person and character, of the various excellencies of former church musicians. . . . He was endowed with the qualities of truth, justice, and integrity, was mild and gentle in his deportment, above all resentment against such as envied his reputation, communicative of his knowledge, sedulous and punctual in the discharge of the duties of his several employments, particularly those that regarded the performance of divine service, and in every relation of life a worthy man.[6]†

So revered was Boyce that he was honoured with a stately funeral in St. Paul's Cathedral (even though he had not been an organist there) accompanied by the grandest panoply that the church and the three London choirs could provide. That it was not solely a formal occasion can be seen from the effect it had on the singers taking part who were so moved that they were unable to do full justice to the anthem (Boyce's own setting of *If we believe*). It was noted that the performance was "not in the most correct manner, for the whole Choir were so overcome by their Tears and Sobs, that the very fine Effect of the Music

* "... who, by joining to an happy genius, constant study and application, have equal'd to any of your Predecessors, Tallis, Bird, Gibbons, Child, Blow, Purcel, great names in the Profession, with whom I should join Aldrich, did he not stand in an higher Class."[5] The author goes on to wish Croft a long life. The next year, however, Croft died.

† The interest shown by Boyce in Samuel Wesley's youthful compositions was not forgotten. "He told my Father to let me run on my own way without check of rules, or Masters", and thus encouraged, the precocious boy Wesley sent him a gift of an oratorio he had written (at the age of eight). Boyce's reply was typical: "Doctor Boyce's Compliments and Thanks to his very ingenious Brother Composer."[7]

was considerably diminished".[8] What it lacked in technical polish, it must have gained in sincerity and spirit!

The acclaim these two musicians received offsets the more lurid information that has become attached to other members of their calling and, at the same time, indicates the respect that their profession as a whole was beginning to achieve. With the examples of relatively blameless lives of men like Croft and Boyce, church musicians could no longer be heedlessly dismissed as sports.

Respect of a different nature came from another quarter. By the eighteenth century English audiences were somewhat belatedly becoming aware of the attractions of that venerable instrument, the organ, and some organists were earning a novel celebrity as virtuoso players. Father Smith's vox humanas and Renatus Harris's cornets tickled the ears of those who, tiring of castrati and foreign fiddlers, were seeking new sensations. The charms of players and their organs were enjoyed and compared; "organ hunters" ran about "from one Parish Church to another, to hear the best Masters".

Church organs ceased to be the only sources of attraction when the pleasure gardens at Vauxhall and Ranelagh started to provide light organ music for the delectation of their customers. Finger-happy players who there found a platform to display their skill generated a vogue for facile voluntaries, popularity for the organ, and notoriety for themselves. Yet, however much this raised the status of London organists, for a cathedral organist there was neither gain nor glamour.

Certainly this was Alcock's experience at Lichfield. He had little spare time at his disposal. In fact, he affirmed that, as a student, "I had more leisure in one Day, than I have had since in a Week, or Fortnight; besides the Advantage of hearing fine Music, and the best Performances, which I never had after I left London". He was tied by having to teach the boys and attend services twice daily throughout the year, and he was granted only two days' absence in every two or three weeks in which to teach out-of-town private pupils. Thus prevented from cultivating a large enough teaching practice adequately to supplement his cathedral wages, he found it hard to maintain his large family. He was particularly resentful when his salary was reduced on the occasions when his son deputised at a service for him. And he could not allow this duty to go by default; he was required to play an organ voluntary at every service throughout the year, "even in the severest cold Weather, when, very often, there was only one Vicar, who read the Service, and an old Woman at Church, besides the Choristers". Consequently, his health suffered. This "not only brought, but fix'd the Rheumatism so strongly upon me, that I am seldom free from Pain, and sometimes confin'd to my Bed".

No wonder Alcock was jealous of his predecessors whom he supposed to have been "possessed of very advantageous Places, living at Ease, in plentiful Times".[9]

Some cathedrals expected their organist not only to play for all services but also to sing with the choir in unaccompanied music. The organist of Chester Cathedral would not have been alone in possessing neither willingness nor ability to fulfil such double duty, yet in 1737 he was severely admonished for refusing to sing in an anthem. There had, indeed, been days when organists excelled as singers. Cooke was famous as a singer in the Italian manner—"without doubt he hath the best manner of singing in the world", Locke styled himself a bass, and Purcell (though this has been doubted) is reputed to have sung one of his more difficult counter-tenor solos at a public performance "with incredible Graces".* But by the eighteenth century such versatility was rare. Then it could be dryly noted:

> It hath bin a misfortune, that most of our great masters of musick have wanted good voices, where-by it is become proverbiall to say any one sings like an organist.[12]

---

* Cooke was heard by Pepys on 27th July, 1662.
On a manuscript copy of Locke's music at Oxford is written "made, prickt, and sunge, at the musick Schoole . . . by Mr. Lock . . . and sung the Base then himself: and Mr. Blagrave the countertenor".[10]
Purcell's solo, "Tis Nature's voice", appeared in his 1692 *St. Cecilia Ode*.[11]

The combined post of master of the choristers and organist was no sinecure, as Alcock found to his cost. Some churches allowed an assistant, and not all were so mean as to deduct pay as apparently Lichfield had done. In 1685 when Child was in his eightieth year the Windsor authorities, realising he might need a little help, appointed an ex-chorister to "assist the organist upon all necessary occasions and diligently instruct the Choristers in the art of singing", and a few years later gave this deputy, John Golding, the place and pay of a lay-clerk. He made such a success of his task that in 1691 (he must by then have been doing most of the work) a bonus of £5 was awarded for the "extraordinary pains that Mr. Golding hath taken in instructing the choir in the past year". On Child's death, Golding was appointed in his place.[13]*

Wise, on account of his connections with the Chapel Royal, was frequently absent from Salisbury. But he was not so fortunate in his deputies as Child had been at Windsor. Stephen Jeffries' subsequent career suggests that Salisbury would not have been sorry when he ceased to assist Wise to become organist of Gloucester Cathedral in 1682. On Thanksgiving Day in 1688 he expressed his political views (this was the third year of the Roman Catholic King James's reign) by playing on the organ after Morning Service a "common ballad" with strong Protestant associations in the presence of "fifteen hundred or two thousand people, to the great scandal of religion, prophanation of the Church, and grievous offence of all good Christians". Jeffries was immediately reprimanded, and then boldly repeated the offence after Evensong.

Insomuch that the young gentlewomen invited one another to

* Senility was not the only reason for having an assistant. Another was an attack of gout. Burney, when he could scarcely accompany a psalm, found himself helping out at Chester for such a cause. "The first Music he learned was of Mr. Baker the Organist of the Cathedral, who being distressed for an assistant during a fit of the Gout, taught him to play a Chant on the organ before he knew his Gammut or the names of the keys. And this single Chant . . . was all that he was able to play to the Choir during his master's first fit of the Gout."[14]

dance, the strangers cryed it were better that the organs were pulled down than they should be so used, and all sorts declared that the Dean and Chapter could never remove the scandal if they did not immediately turn away so insolent and profane a person out of the Church.[15]

Jeffries remained in office long enough to build up a colourful reputation.* His escapades, after all, were fairly harmless; yet there were limits. One organist was dismissed because he had made advances to a young lady pupil of his, of noble parentage, "by kissing, courting and the like dalliance". Conscious of his error in trying to make a match beyond his station, he apologised and was subsequently reinstated. But seven years later, realising he would have had no second chance, he had already fled before being formally expelled by his Dean and Chapter for "many very great misdemeanors and enormities by him committed, and whereas a bastard child hath been lately filiated upon him".[16]

It is not difficult to find other instances of irregular behaviour, of organists and singers who brawled amongst themselves, who were imprisoned for debt, and even some who took their own lives.† Such conduct can be understood when measured

* It is easy to imagine how the lay-clerks of Gloucester relished telling these two stories to the gullible Hawkins when he was collecting material for his *History*. "The choirmen of Gloucester relate that, to cure him [Jeffries] of a habit of staying late at the tavern, his wife drest up a fellow in a winding-sheet, with directions to meet him with a lanthorn and candle in the cloisters through which he was to pass on his way home; but that, on attempting to terrify him, Jeffries expressed his wonder only by saying, 'I thought all you Spirits had been abed before this time'."

"A singer from a distant church, with a good voice, had been requested and had undertaken to sing a solo anthem in Gloucester Cathedral, and for that purpose took his station at the elbow of the organist in the organ-loft. Jeffries, who found him trip in the performance, instead of palliating his mistake and setting him right, immediately rose from his seat, and leaning over the gallery, called out aloud to the choir and the whole congregation, 'He can't sing it'."

† On the one hand, an organist at Gloucester was criticised for "beating and wounding one of the singing men", on the other, a choirman at Windsor for giving the organist "uncivill and rude language" while he was

against the standards of the society in which those musicians lived, and their own inferior position within it; improvement of character was hardly encouraged by an age that hid beneath its elegant veneer a raw, unpolished coarseness. Certain misdemeanours, however reprehensible, were felt to be neither unusual nor, least of all, detrimental to the misdoer's ability as an artist. It was a later generation that by its stricter moral code criticised what it considered to be the unconventional and improper lives of some musicians, and in consequence tended to belittle their music. If Wise, at scarcely forty years of age, chose to be knocked cold by a nightwatchman for swearing and molesting, that was his concern. Two centuries later a successor of his could live until ninety, and then die by his bedside saying his prayers. This has no bearing on a fair assessment of the compositions of either organist, but the Victorians did not hesitate to link what they thought was the best music with the more blameless life.

ORGAN MUSIC

In seventeenth-century England neither the development of the organ as a musical instrument nor its humble functions encouraged the composition of organ music to any great extent. Besides, many organists relied on their ability to extemporise and there was little need for them to notate their fancies. The few extant pieces by Purcell have the appearance of brilliant improvisations, and indicate that, having great skill in this art

playing the organ during a service, and because he later "did trip up his heeles and when down did inhumanely beat him".

"Mr. Silvester the organist being forc'd to abscond from debt they allowed him to be absent from the services of the church till Lady [Day] next to give him an opportunity in the mean time to make his peace with his creditors."

Jeremiah Clarke: "he unfortunately put an End to his Existence by his own hands; his mind was naturally of a melancholy cast".

Read of New College, Oxford: "a young hot-head, ript up his owne belly upon some discontent".[17]

E*

and with his busy life, it was too time-consuming to write out set pieces. A longer-lived artist like Blow took the trouble to make available some organ versets and voluntaries and, fortunately, a sufficient number have survived to provide a contribution of real value to English organ music.[18]

Even after a new interest in organ music in the eighteenth century had created a demand for published sets of voluntaries, improvisation continued to be given pride of place, whether it was Handel charming his audiences during the performance of his organ concertos, or Roseingrave convincing his assessors of his suitability for the post at St. George's, Hanover Square. "Voluntary [i.e. extempore playing] upon an Organ is the consummate office of a musitian. It is air, melody, harmony, humour, imitation, and what not."[19] Inevitably, abuses of the art crept into church services in which context improvisations became criticised both for their poor quality, "incompetent doodlings", and for "imitating common songs or Airs". Whether this was true or not we cannot tell, but we have ample evidence of the type of organ music that was popular in the eighteenth century. Even so, the pieces that did appear in print were published for commercial reasons, or at least to hinder plagiarism, and they do not include all styles. The "versets" so well suited to liturgical purposes that Blow wrote,* and the type of "solemn" voluntary liked by Boyce never reached print. They were considered too dull for general consumption. Boyce himself was said to have seldom used any tone but that of the Stopped Diapason (though he may have had in mind registration for accompanying from a figured bass) and to have preferred a three- or four-part texture to the popular two-part idiom of the solo voluntaries.[21]

Interesting as much of the organ music of the period can be, it hardly deserves being given too much prominence. In church, at any rate, it always remained subordinate to the anthem.

* One who knew Blow testified that he "was reckon'd the greatest Master in the world, for playing most gravely and seriously in his Voluntaries".[20]

A congregation may have welcomed anything up to a quarter of an hour's organ music between the psalms and the first lesson[22] as a sop for struggling through the former and a spur to better concentration on the latter, but they were not as a rule likely to have given an outgoing voluntary their serious attention.

Differences of style in seventeenth-century keyboard music between pieces written for liturgical or secular use, or for the organ or harpsichord, later became much less clearly marked. The London church organists with their feet treading firmly in the ways of secular music were largely responsible, as is shown by this observation made in 1712:

> A great many of our church musicians being related to the theatre, they have, in imitation of these epilogues, introduced in their farewell voluntaries a sort of music quite foreign to that of church services.[23]

Along with the infiltrations of a secular style went an intermingling of the idioms of organ and harpsichord music. To play a suite by Blow on the organ, or a verse on the harpsichord, would be a crass anachronism, yet Greene and Handel published their fugues and voluntaries as apt for either instrument.*

Those for whom such a development was not acceptable made attempts to preserve the autonomy of both organ and harpsichord, emphasising that the former expressed "the grand or solemn Stile, the latter, those lively or trickling Movements which thrill in the Ear". Even so, conservative fugues that were solid, respectable and intellectually undemanding, though not uncommon in the organ music of Greene, Stanley and Handel, did not finally gain favour until later in the eighteenth century,

---

* It was said of Greene: "He was an excellent organist and not only perfectly understood the nature of the instrument, but was a great master of fugue. He affected in his voluntaries that kind of practice on single stops, the cornet and the vox-humana for instance, which puts the instrument almost on a level with the harpsichord; a voluntary of this kind being in fact little more than a solo for a single instrument, with the accompaniment of a bass."[24]

and the solo stop voluntaries, once they had respectfully introduced themselves with slow, chordal diapason music, continued for some time to delight their audiences with light and airy tunes interspersed with ear-titillating figurations.

John Robinson was said to have been the first organist to play this type of voluntary in church.* His imitators provoked one writer to complain that they merely vaunted a "brilliant finger", and to "lament that the idea of a voluntary on the organ is lost in those Capriccios on a single stop, which, as well in our parochial as cathedral service, follow the psalms", where previously there had been "a slow solemn movement"; but this did not prevent the most obscure talents from parading their technical virtuosity to good effect. Obadiah Shuttleworth, organist of St. Michael's, Cornhill, for one, was a bigger attraction than the preacher. "Celebrated for his fine finger on the organ", he "drew numbers to hear him, especially at the Temple Church, where he would frequently play near an hour after evening service".[26]

The solo voluntaries of Stanley and Walond were justly admired and enjoyed, although in the long run it was Handel (as might be expected) who displayed the "true organ style".

> A fine and delicate touch, a volant finger, and a ready delivery of passages the most difficult, are the praise of inferior artists: they were not noticed in Handel, whose excellencies were of a far superior kind; and his amazing command of the instrument, the fullness of his harmony, the grandeur and dignity of his style, the copiousness of his imagination, and the fertility of his invention were qualities that absorbed every inferior attainment. When he gave a concerto, his method in general was to introduce it with a voluntary movement on the diapasons, which stole on the ear in a slow and solemn progression; the harmony close wrought, and as full as could possibly be expressed; the passages concatenated with stupendous art, the whole at the same time being

---

* John Robinson (1682–1762). Organist of St. Lawrence Jewry (1710) and of St. Magnus, London Bridge (1713). He succeeded Croft in 1727 as organist of Westminster Abbey.[25]

perfectly intelligible, and carrying the appearance of great simplicity. This kind of prelude was succeeded by the concerto itself, which he executed with a degree of spirit and firmness that no one ever pretended to equal.[27]

One other form of organ music scarcely deserves even passing reference. The most a twentieth-century congregation has to endure in the accompaniment of their hymns are occasional "varied" harmonies, but these are harmless in comparison with the eighteenth-century procedure of ornamenting a tune out of existence and further disguising it with florid eruptions at the end of every line. Despite constant warnings that they should be kept brief and restrained, the interludes that were played between the lines and verses of metrical psalms could add as many as five minutes to their performance, and men of taste for long disavowed this practice. For those players who still persisted in it, the example of Stanley and Kelway was recommended:* at the end of a phrase make "an easy Transition of about three Notes, with a Shake so disposed as shall naturally lead into the first Note of the *following* Line"; between verses play "just enough to give the Congregation a little Respite".[29]

THE SINGER

The popularity of the more famous singers in the early part of

---

* John Stanley (1713-1786). A pupil of Greene. Organist of All Hallows, Bread Street (1724), St. Andrew's, Holborn (1726) and the Temple Church (1734). Master of the King's Band (1779). "This extraordinary musician . . . not only a most neat, pleasing and accurate performer, but a natural and agreeable composer." He and other organists "adhered to Handel's concertos, or composed for themselves in that style".

Joseph Kelway. Organist of St. Michael's, Cornhill (c. 1730-1736), St. Martin's-in-the-Fields (1736). A pupil of Geminiani and an exponent of Domenico Scarlatti's keyboard music. "He had, in his voluntaries on the organ, a masterly wildness, and long supported the character of a great player, in a style quite his own, bold, rapid, and fanciful."[28]

the eighteenth century was unrivalled. The notes that flowed from their "agile gullets" were eagerly devoured, and secured for them a dominant position that even the great conductors or avant-garde composers of today would envy.

Italian opera stars who dominated much of London's musical life (eventually toppling Handel into bankruptcy and nervous collapse) received no competition from the Chapel Royal singers who were consequently, perhaps fortunately, left to cultivate their art in the carefully nurtured ground of the King's Music, delighting royalty and at the same time reaching a wider audience in public performances of St. Cecilia odes, commemorative anthems, and oratorios.

The adulation of the human voice (expressed in the opinion that it was "superior to all Sounds in *Musick*" because it possessed "such a Delicacy in the Expression") was bound to leave its mark on music written for the church's services. Yet this was tempered, as can be seen when the relative restraint in solo sections of verse anthems is compared with the operatic arias, by the beneficial effects of a continuing tradition in English singing, never lacking worthy exponents.

Two members of the Chapel Royal in particular achieved a fruitful working relationship with their fellow composers, encouraging the composition of anthems demonstrating their vocal skill. John Gostling, born at East Malling, Kent (*c.* 1650), became a bass at Canterbury Cathedral and was admitted gentleman extraordinary of the Chapel Royal Choir in February 1678. Gostling was described as "that stupendous bass" with a voice of great range, and Purcell wrote a number of anthems for him.[30] More important for his welfare, he became a favourite singer of Charles II whom he twice accompanied to Windsor, entertaining him with choice songs. The King expressed his appreciation in a rare gratuity when he presented to him, with some humour, a silver egg filled with guineas, saying that he had heard "eggs were good for the voice".

Gostling became a minor-canon of Canterbury and sub-dean

of St. Paul's Cathedral, besides being a priest of the Chapel Royal. By the end of his long life (he was over eighty when he died) he had ceased to sing in the latter choir, living then at Canterbury until his death there in 1733.

A younger singer at the Chapel Royal, Richard Elford, possessed a counter-tenor voice of such quality and character as to inspire both Croft and Weldon to compose for him. Croft in the preface to his anthems published in 1724 acknowledged his debt in writing them to "the great Skill and fine Voices with which they have been performed", especially Elford's. "A bright Example of this kind, excelling all (as far as is known) that ever went before him, and fit to be imitated by all that come after him." Elford was unique in Croft's experience for the way he gave "due Energy and proper Emphasis to the Words of his Musick", such careful articulation and sensitive interpretation being essential in any worthy performance of church music.

Brought up in cathedral choirs, at Lincoln and then Durham, Elford subsequently came to London to try a career in the theatre. Thwarted in this, he joined the Chapel Royal where he gained such favour that a special place was created for him in 1702. He must have prospered, as in addition to being a lay-clerk at Westminster Abbey and at St. Paul's Cathedral he was also awarded an extra £100 a year to his salary at the Chapel Royal "on account of the uncommon excellence of his voice". (An admirable way of securing and retaining the best singers.) Unfortunately, Elford did not live long enough to enjoy his wealth. He died in 1714.

There is some reason in selecting a bass and a counter-tenor as instances of two popular singers. The tenor took long to live down the reputation of being "an ordinary voice", and the counter-tenor, whose range it closely resembled, was reckoned far superior. Handel followed Purcell in accompanying counter-tenor solos with a trumpet obbligato, and composers of such sensitivity would not have matched with that instrument a voice which had not comparable strength and clarity. Anthems with organ accompaniment often displayed a trumpet stop in similar scoring.*

In solo trios in Restoration verse anthems the counter-tenor and tenor parts frequently lie close to each other, with a distance of rarely more than a fourth at each extreme of the compass, and combine in close harmony to pitch themselves against the bass. There are some very telling instances of such scoring in Humfrey's anthem O Lord my God,[32] although Locke had already used the voices in this manner. The modern notion of "cathedral altos squawking in falsetto"[33] obviously does not apply to the type of voice that these and later composers were familiar with; and if the evidence from their music is not felt to be sufficient, there is the fact that at times a counter-tenor and tenor were considered interchangeable, judging by the appointment at the Chapel Royal of one in the place of the other.[34]

Nonetheless, by the middle of the eighteenth century, counter-tenor parts in some anthems written in that period suggest a less glorious voice and one with a more limited compass than Purcell utilised. It was Tudway's experience that in 1717 there were fewer counter-tenors than basses or tenors, and by the time Burney wrote his history later in the century the voice was scarce, and good singers "in that part of the scale" rarer still.†

The Chapel Royal may have attracted the ablest singers, but not all cathedral choirs were as deprived of talent as critics such

---

* "The fife and all the harmony of war" from Purcell's 1692 St. Cecilia Ode, and the opening to Handel's Birthday Ode for Queen Anne, 1713 (written for Elford) are examples of counter-tenor solos with trumpet obbligato.

Francis Hughes, a gentleman of the Chapel Royal in the reign of George I ("who had a very strong counter-tenor voice, could with ease break a drinking glass in this manner"—i.e. by setting up sympathetic vibrations) was named as the soloist in a "Trumpet Stop" movement in an anthem Croft composed for the opening of an organ at Finedon, Northamptonshire, Praise God in his sanctuary.[31]

† Burney also wrote of William Turner: "a counter-tenor singer, his voice settling to that pitch; a circumstance which so seldom happens, naturally, that if it be cultivated, the possessor is sure of employment".

as Mace and Hayes would have us believe. Their repertoire did not consist entirely of short and easy anthems; solo passages in elaborate verse anthems required more than a modicum of skill in their execution, and singers who could present these to good effect were in demand for oratorio performances and festivals.

A cathedral choirman shared with the organist many of the features and conditions of his life, for better or worse. Like him, he kept his place—which, after all, was only retained of necessity in lieu of a pension—till death. This would not have had such a bad effect on performances as might be supposed, the average span of life being shorter then than it is now, and in any case advanced age must have prevented attendance before vocal deterioration became too apparent. This kind of absence plus the uselessness of some vicars-choral must have reduced the effective strength of many choirs that look, on paper, bottom-heavy with generally twice as many men as boys.

The benefits of plurality, where obtainable, were received gratefully. A member of one of the London choirs often held a place in either of the other two and, at Cambridge, an organist of St. John's College managed also to be in the choirs of King's and Trinity Colleges.[35] Those who had no such opportunities for happy fraternisation had to accept the lowly status of church musicians already described, and ran the usual risks that went with their position in society. They did not escape accusations of being riotous or mealy-mouthed.*

Yet, despite all their defects, rough and ready as they were,

---

* e.g.: John Cave, a gentleman of the Chapel Royal attacked by a Scots-man on his way home in the evening, and "run through the body of which wound he departed this life".

The Rev. Mr. Powell, vicar-choral of Salisbury, being imitated by a chorister, swore at him and said, "God, I'le order you".

Thomas Kelway senior, vicar-choral of Chichester, accused in 1720 of being "notoriously guilty of divers imprecations and profane oaths" and of speaking certain "odious expressions" against a canon of the cathedral (namely, that the said canon should practise the utmost, lewd obsequious-ness: "I desire no better sport than to have the handling of that fellow").[36]

the impression is quite clearly created that the singers as a whole were jovial, hospitable and friendly. After evensong at St. Paul's Handel is said to have happily adjourned with some of the choir to the Queen's Arms near-by; and a stranger who visited Gloucester Cathedral in 1668, as a lover of cathedral music, found he did not for long lack good company: "afterwards wee went to the taverne with one or two of the choire, drank a glass of wine and had a song". Although singing in taverns is now legally restricted, in other respects the years have seen little change.

8

"Parochial Musick"

"ONE GRAND SCREAM OF TREBLE VOICES"

Respecting the Performance of parochial Service:—often considered by the Vicar or Rector an expensive noise, and [who]
assumes *supreme* authority over the Organist exacting from him
passive obedience and *non-resistance*.

    A Troop of *Girls* and Boys is appointed and stationed to sing
Tate and Brady's version of the Psalms in *Unison*. In this Vocifera-
tion the Congregation take no Part; render no Assistance, so that
the whole *Psalmody* consists merely of *one grand* scream of *Treble
Voices*.[1]

Ever since the re-establishment of the Church of England in
1660 "parochial music" has increasingly received the attention
of critics and reformers, and so disparaging a comment as the
above, made in the early part of the nineteenth century, is not
exceptional; nor is it likely to have been entirely unfounded.

    The disparity in type, standards and purpose between
cathedral and parish church music was clear enough in 1720
to one writer, for whom "Church music" had but a single
interpretation: "artful music, compos'd and performed with
great exactness to time, or measure, by a choir of voices". He
would have deplored the trend to bring "artful music" within
the province of parish churches and opposed subsequent attitudes which, instead of viewing the two as distinct yet complementary facets of a united activity, upgraded the music in
parish churches and apologised for that in cathedrals. In
minimising the differences, too little positive attempt has been
made to define the twin functions of parish and cathedral music,
honestly recognising the purpose and limits of the one, and with

vision constructing new possibilities for the other. Criticism has been supercilious or shallow, whether of metrical psalms and lengthy eighteenth-century anthems, or of their counterparts, hymns and the "musical delights" of sacred concerts and festivals.*

John Wesley, with characteristic zeal, tried to ensure when ordering the public worship of the new Methodist societies that their members sang praise to God, however imperfectly, "with the spirit and with the understanding also . . . in psalms and hymns which are both sense and poetry, such as would sooner provoke a critic to turn Christian than a Christian to turn critic". The music would be both "a proper continuation of the spiritual and reasonable service", and also an outlet to praise God "lustily and with a good courage". The ways of the established church he placed in sharp contrast: "the screaming of boys who bawl out what they neither feel nor understand, . . . the unseasonable and unmeaning impertinence of a voluntary on the organ, . . . the miserable scandalous doggerel of Hopkins and Sternhold", the congregation "lolling at ease, or in the indecent posture of sitting, drawling out one word after another".[2]

In Wesley's day parish church music was still struggling to leave behind the earlier seventeenth-century unaccompanied unison singing led by the parish clerk and his pitch-pipe, and had not yet reached the fully chanted service and surpliced choir aping cathedral practice. In between these two extremes it was evolving a refreshing variety of performances with the help of a mixed collection of musicians and instruments. Whether clerks or societies of singers, organs or village bands, all made their contribution. The problems that were experienced and the

---

* It is interesting to see how the fashion for festivals began in earnest in the eighteenth century. The anthem having already reached a maximum tolerable length and unable to take up a larger share of time in the church service, festivals such as those for the Sons of the Clergy at St. Paul's Cathedral, and the Three Choirs at Gloucester, Hereford and Worcester provided wide scope for musical entertainment. Furthermore, they were closely linked to charitable purposes and, thus made respectable, they prospered.

criticisms or solutions that were offered have a familiar ring today; but it is of particular interest to us to see the singers, often with many teething troubles, gradually form a recognisable prototype for the modern parish church choir.

One writer, deploring the general condition of parochial music in 1676, proposed the use of simple and familiar words and tunes for the "common–poor–ignorant–people" that formed the congregation, and recommended an organ to lead the singing or, failing this, a choir. Considering it was worth the expense of engaging the local schoolmaster to give children of the parish daily singing lessons, he assured his readers that thus "will your Quiresters increase even into Swarms like your Bees in your Gardens".[3] But country churches being perhaps a little nervous of this prospect, such advice did not have immediate effect. Later writers were frequently driven to complain of the "decay of psalmody", which was due, apparently, as much to inadequate performance as to the low esteem in which it was held, being "treated with the greatest Contempt by many who affect Politeness, and who think it beneath the dignity of a Person of Fashion to join in". Although they may have been heard taking part in responses and reading psalms, the "Quality and Gentry" were struck dumb by metrical psalmody, leaving the singing of this to their inferiors.

One of the first tasks then for that ardent reformer of church music, the Rev. Arthur Bedford, was to improve the standing of parish church music. In 1711 he had to start at the bottom rung by affirming that "in Churches where Psalms are best and oftenest sung, those Churches are always best fill'd". To effect this laudable aim members of the parish had to be taught "to sing Psalms in Consort", and this in turn would supposedly lead to a better understanding of the church's discipline, a reduction in illiteracy, a better relationship between clergy and people, and an improvement in morals. By giving the youth of the parish "that us'd to loiter in the Church-yard" something worthwhile to do in their vacant hours, "such who before

spent the Lord's Day idly, or in Taverns and Ale-houses, have
piously join'd together in the Church after Evening Service,
and spent a considerable Part of the Day in so heavenly an
Exercise", that is in singing metrical psalms.

Bedford had learnt from the experience of a fellow clergyman, who had found that forming a choir of singers in his
parish brought young people to church and gave him a point
of contact with them, that the choir were the most regular
members of his congregation, were largely instrumental in
removing parochial squabbles, and (last but not least) encouraged the parishioners to pay their tithes cheerfully. "Happy are
those", exclaimed another preacher, who help "the Poor, the
Destitute, the Orphan, the whole perishing Tribe, from the
Dunghil, and tune their pleasant youthful voices to Gratitude
to God". Bedford did not foresee to what extent the singers
would abuse such encouragement. Twenty-two years later he
had to emphasise strongly the importance of the *whole* congregation taking a full part in the singing, at the same time
admonishing the choirs for assuming an independent role with
a firm reminder that, although they could sing whatever they
liked before or after a service, their primary duty was to lead
the congregation.[4]

Itinerant singing masters, "those illiterate and conceited
fellows", who had discovered a novel way of making a living
going round the countryside purveying their little knowledge
to enthusiastic choirs, had encouraged parishioners to form
themselves into "societies of singers". These had spread
through the country and formed a new ingredient in parish
church music. With apparently limitless enthusiasm and much
less skill they sang not only psalmody but anthems, avidly
devouring any music they could tackle.

Although the better activities of these singing societies
formed that tradition of devoted service which is such a
backbone of strength in the present-day parish church choir,
congregations were for a time silenced into passive submission.
The "Scandal and just Offence" their practices gave to "sober

and well-disposed persons" was more than the typical resistance
of country churches to new-fangled ways.

An instance of a vigorous reaction provoked by an over-
enthusiastic choir and organist is recorded in events at the
Wiltshire parish of Calne. In 1736 the Dean of Salisbury had to
write to the minister and churchwardens there:

> Whereas Complaint has been made to us that several Irregulari-
> ties and Innovations have been lately introduced into the Church
> of Calne during Divine Service, to the great Scandal and Offence
> of the general part of the Inhabitants, by some persons pretending
> to sing Anthems and Services instead of Plain Psalm Tunes,
> which the congregation have been customarily used to do; And
> likewise by playing on the Organ light gay Tunes, highly improper
> and indecent to be play'd in the House of God. . . .
>
> We do strictly enjoyn the said Minister, etc., for the future not
> to permit anyone to play on the Organ during Divine Service,
> but the Organist himself; and not to suffer him to play any thing
> more than a grave voluntary after the Reading Psalms; And two
> plain Psalm Tunes in the Morning Service. One after the Littany,
> the other before the Sermon. And in the afternoon, one Psalm
> after the Prayers are ended and another after the Sermon—as the
> Minister shall direct—Something like this—or any thing you
> shall think more proper.

This was insufficient, apparently, as in the following year the
organist was again admonished for playing his "light gay
Airs", and the minister held directly responsible to the dean for
the choice of psalms.[5]

Town as well as country parishes suffered from the activities
of the singers. In 1763 the Vicar of Newcastle, though praising
the best aspects of parochial music, spoke not only of the
"confusion and dissonance" resulting from trying to sing too-
ambitious music in country churches, but also of the disastrous
results in towns "when a Company of illiterate People form
themselves into a *Choir* distinct from the Congregation. Here

Devotion is lost, between the impotent Vanity of those who *sing*, and the ignorant *Wonder* of those who listen."[6]

In criticism of parish church music, a choir was an obvious subject for attack. Another target was "the disgusting dulness of Sternhold and his companions", on account of both the inherent weaknesses in their clumsy paraphrases and the tedious-ness of the average performance which dragged out a psalm to twice its proper length in order to accommodate the organist's whims and fancies for ornamentation. Attempts were made to have the music performed "in alla breve time" as in cathedrals (as "swift as the common Chymes upon Bells") and to en-courage the organist to keep the music moving; but whatever was gained here was lost in the customary interludes. Not surprisingly the number of metrical psalms sung at a service had to be reduced, and verses omitted.[7]

The Book of Common Prayer had never made provision for metrical psalms in its daily services, only custom sanctioning their being sung before and after Morning and Evening Prayer, and also before and after sermons. Custom solidified into immovable tradition, and no one thought of discarding psalmody altogether even when its performance reached interminable lengths. Brightening tunes with grace-notes and ornaments may have made them more endurable, but eventually the tradition was rescued by the fresh and invigorat-ing words of hymns written by Isaac Watts for the Congre-gationalists and Charles Wesley for the Methodists. By the nineteenth century, in the established church, hymns had almost entirely replaced metrical psalms.

That hymns took so long to become generally used was due to the conservative attitude that would brook no change, however urgently necessary. Psalmody then was as sacred to some as hymns are now. The arguments against the introduc-tion of hymns read strangely like those more recently used against the efforts of the twentieth-century Church Light Music Group. No truck was had with the secular melodies of the Methodists, or their "frothy Way of Singing"; on no account had the Church of England to follow the example of "these frantic Enthusiasts".

The melodic elaboration of the following hymn tune is indebted to the gayer practice of the Methodists, giving the melody a distinctive character which we can now appreciate from our present position of detachment from the worst excesses of the eighteenth century. The additional hypothetical reduction to the bare bones of the tune will serve to indicate the formula that was later arrived at for a hymn tune purged of all extras and clipped to the simplest shape.★

Ex. 5

Parochial music was not entirely beyond the attention of higher authority. The Bishop of London, in issuing directions to the clergy of his diocese in 1724, considered psalmody of

★ This tune, *Bishopthorpe*, appears in late-eighteenth-century collections. See the *Historical Companion to Hymns Ancient and Modern* (1962), the invaluable introduction to which (by W. H. Frere and W. K. Lowther Clarke) provides a compact history of psalmody and hymns.

little importance in comparison with the more weighty matters he had to expound, yet even so he found space to give some helpful counsel. Metrical psalms should be used to divide the three parts of the Morning Service (Matins, Litany and Ante-Communion) and they should be chosen by the minister and not, as was customary, by the parish clerk. The people and especially the youth of the parish should be rehearsed in the singing of some tunes, the "most plain and easy, and of most common Use",* though this was not intended to encourage "those idle Instructors, who of late Years have gone about the several counties to teach Tunes uncommon and out of the way".

In 1741 Bishop Secker instructed his clergy on much the same lines, adding the realistic advice to encourage the youth of a parish to learn psalmody, "if there be need, with some little reward". The "preposterous shame of religious performances with which the present age is so fatally tainted", the Bishop continued, would be laid aside if the whole congregation were to be persuaded not just to hear but to bear a part in the singing, there being little to equal the grand harmony of "a general chorus, in which any lesser dissonances are quite lost". Thus psalmody (the old idea of music as an aural lubricant) would "diversify long services".[9]

Exhortation and advice had some effect. Not all comments were disparaging and Lady Alice Harblon, for one, found the "manner of singing Psalms" at Welford, Berkshire, in 1770 "particularly pleasing. The tunes are solemn but exceedingly melodious. Mr. Archer's Steward, honest John Heath leads the

---

* The Bishop had in mind only half a dozen melodies.[8]

Despite the many books of psalmody published in the eighteenth century, it does seem that frequent repetition of tunes was the rule rather than the exception. For example, A Small Collection of Psalms published in 1761 for the use of Chichester charity children gives thirteen tunes and thirty-nine "portions of some of the most useful Parts of the Psalms: If three Psalms be allowed to each Sunday, the Collection will be sung through once in a Quarter." The publication of more impressive collections does not necessarily imply that a wider range was used throughout the year. Congregations have always been notoriously conservative in their taste.

set, with as agreeable a voice as I ever heard. The game keeper plays upon the Hautboy, and the gardener upon the Bassoon, and these, joined to eight or ten voices, form a Harmony that strikes the attention most amazingly." In 1751 an Irish bishop was pleased to discover that at Selby Abbey "they chant all their service", and that they "sing well not only the psalms but anthems".[10]

The use of anthems had by then become quite widespread in parish churches, introduced to some by the journeyman singing master. Earlier publications of simple sacred pieces and new psalm tunes had provided honest fare,* but the singers' societies who wished to extend their repertoire beyond psalmody turned to the less wholesome products of the self-styled teachers of psalmody. Enterprising publishers have subsequently ensured that there has been no shortage of material for parish choirs.

When Trusley church, Derbyshire, was rebuilt in 1713 it was opened in grand style. "We had both vocall and instrumental musick, the service read as at Cathedrals, an Anthem very well performed".[11] But this was extraordinary. Much more often a congregation was subjected to mawkish anthems, "ill-constructed fugues", meanly presented by singers whose taste led them to know, or like, nothing better.

Somewhat tardily, awareness of this state of affairs began to concern the better placed musicians. James Nares, master of the choristers at the Chapel Royal, had written in 1783 of his personal experience of appalling standards. His remedy was to compose a few pieces easy enough for the humble capacity of

---

* In 1711 Bedford referred to the Psalms of Child (1639) and the Lawes brothers (1648), Dering's *Cantica Sacra* (1662), *Cantica Sacra* published by John Playford (1674), and pieces by Blow and Purcell in *Harmonica Sacra* (1688 and 1693). No other comparable collection had been published between then and 1711 apart from *The Divine Companion* (assembled by Henry Playford in 1701) which, as Bedford says, consisted of "easy Hymns and Anthems for the use of the Country".

A thorough and much needed study of anthems and other music in parish churches has been undertaken by Nicholas M. Temperley, and the publication of the results of his researches is planned in the near future under the title *The Music of the English Parish Church*, 1660–1880.

the performers and "not wholly unworthy the attention of the more enlightened part of the congregation". Nares stated:

> Having often been an auditor in country churches, where what they called Anthems were sung in parts, I own I have been usually mortified by the performance, though at the same time I pitied the performers; who had against them not only their own inexperience, but the badness of the music. Nor could I help observing that the same time and pains bestowed upon some early music, composed in a good style, would have produced an effect much more creditable to the singers, as well as more pleasing to the audience.[12]

Anthems, however much relished by the singers, never replaced psalmody or hymns as the essential musical feature of the parish church service. The unchanging parts, responses and prose psalms (or "reading psalms" as they were called) were either spoken antiphonally or, following ancient practice, intoned to the simplest form of plainsong. In the former method members of the congregation, many of whom would have been unable to read, either listened to the minister and parish clerk, as to a lesson, or else spoke the words after them line by line. This practice of "lining out", though accepted, was never popular; preference was given to singing the psalms, if only on a monotone with simple inflexions, when it was something of an achievement if the people sang reasonably well together and in tune.

The difficulties in performance were greatly increased when singing to Anglican chants, as in cathedrals, eventually superseded simpler methods. The individual skill and collective discipline necessary for an adequate musical rendering of prose psalms is achieved only with intensive training and frequent rehearsal. No composer in his right mind scores lengthy recitatives for chorus. Centuries of congregational psalm-singing have exposed manifest obstacles, and no amount of circumnavigation has prevented disastrous shipwrecks. Many parish churches may have been better advised to leave the chanting of psalms to the more able choirs or to have at least confined it to being a private exercise.*

The defects of the worship in eighteenth-century churches were, to a sensitive man of taste, abhorrent, to a stranger to English ways, mystifying. The one was driven to exclaim, "why is the *whole* congregation to *sing* any more than preach, or read prayers?"; the other, a German pastor to the Lutheran church in London, to draw an unflattering comparison with the confused mumbling in a Jewish synagogue. In trying to describe the Anglican church service to his fellow-countrymen he said:

> Whoever has not been brought up in the English church will not think himself much edified, when he attends in it for the first time divine service. The Common-Prayer book contains some very excellent prayers: but as they are read all the year round, and frequently without much devotion in a hasty manner, with a voice not always sufficiently loud and intelligible, it is no wonder that the congregation should appear rather tired, and without many signs of fervent devotion. The alternative reading verses of the Psalms, by the clergyman and the congregation, the loud repeating of the Litany, the Creed and other parts of the service by the latter, makes it rather resemble a Jewish synagogue....
>
> The singing is generally not very harmonious; that recitation of some parts of the service, which . . . is divided between the clergyman and the congregation, is done in a manner that betrays rather carelessness than attention; the perpetual motion of kneeling and rising again, that monotony which prevails, and that inanimated manner in which the sermons are commonly delivered, have, in my opinion, nothing of solemnity in them, and can hardly promote edification and devotion.[13]

---

* William Law in his popular manual, *A Serious Call*, insisted on beginning all personal devotion with a psalm, and that not merely read but sung: "a psalm only read is very much like a prayer that is only looked over". He accepted no excuse for ignoring this beneficial discipline, not even that of being tone deaf. "It is singing, and not artful fine singing, that is a required way of praising God."

THE "MUSICKERS"

Criticism might have been tempered with a fuller understanding of the limitations of many parishes, especially rural ones,
and a better appreciation of the honest and well-meaning
efforts of those who tried their best to sing God's praises,
whatever the conditions. At first it was not so much the
choir-man—such as the one who wrote this in his singing-
book:

> John Caplin
> His Hand and Pen,
> He will be good
> But God no when

—as the much maligned parish clerk who bore at once the
brunt of leading the public worship and ridicule for its
imperfections.[14]

Unlearned he may have been, but he was still the vicar's
right-hand man, loyally performing with him the divine
offices at all times of the year. In a small village parish, even in
the depth of winter, the parson could rely on having the clerk,
if few other members of the congregation, to make the responses together and say the psalms. And this was worth the
price of having one who, when the congregation was larger,
fell often into confusion trying to lead the singing of the
metrical psalms. These the clerk had to choose, announce and
perform clearly enough for others to follow. Nature may have
endowed him with a powerful voice if not a particularly elegant
one (the old clerk who had served Buxted parish church for
forty-three years received an obituary in 1666 that might have
served his calling as a whole: "whose melody warbled forth
as if he had been thumped on the back by a stone") but he
would have possessed only a primitive knowledge of liturgical
propriety and less of music. Liable to choose unsuitable tunes,
which would as often as not be bowdlerised by his imperfect

memory, he might, worse still, begin the melody wildly off-key if he did not first give himself the note on a pitch-pipe.

> The People, rather than sing in Pain, will sometimes leave off in the Middle of a Verse, and let the Clerk go through the Remainder as well as he can by himself, who, being out of Breath, and quite hoarse with straining, does it with great Difficulty, and is then obliged to begin the next Verse either higher or lower.

No wonder organs became popular; however many ornaments and interludes were introduced into psalmody by their players, they were at least confined to set keys and could prevail by sheer volume.

> The greatest blessing to lovers of Music in a parish church, is to have an organ in it sufficiently powerful to render the voices of the clerk, and of those who join in his *out-cry*, wholly inaudible.

In time the organ and choir assumed the lead in the singing, and the parson accepted the responsibility of choosing the hymns. The clerk became verger or sacristan. As one put it, "first vicar he called me clerk; then another came, and he called me virgin; the last vicar said I was the christian". The office in the eighteenth century (with its small perquisites) was either given to the curate (the "clerk-in-orders") to supplement his meagre salary, or else to a "decayed Inhabitant" to ease the burden on parish poor relief.

In better days the clerks had supported a thriving Worshipful Company in the City of London. At the Restoration they had equipped their hall with an organ to help improve their singing, meeting one evening a week for regular rehearsal. But no efforts of a Worshipful Company seemed able to maintain the honour the profession may once have possessed. If the clerk had not become superfluous he would have been laughed out of court by such as Pepys, who found it "mighty sport" to hear one at his church sing out of tune, and derided by others into insignificance.*

The invective that had been hurled at the clerk was redirected to the choir when it replaced his guidance of the congregation's singing. Choirs of reasonable ability distracted the congregation with their anthems, and those that limited themselves to giving a lusty lead to the singing fell victim to criticisms of lacking finesse and of being "shrill-toned". Yet, even when accused of excessive bellowing and goatish bleating, they still made conscientious efforts to ground their work on a well organised basis.

At Cuckfield parish church, for instance, at the end of the seventeenth century a gallery for the singers was erected, and those who had borne the cost agreed on rules for "the better order of those that sitt and sing in it". The parishioners who had assembled together to learn and practise psalmody were to be the sole occupants of this gallery, and none could join them there till approved "Good or Competent Singers by the major part of the Quire". There was a rigid demarcation of pews in the gallery; all had to take their allotted places "without murmuring". Seats in the front were apportioned by voice, rank, and the size of the contribution to the cost of the gallery's construction. The vicar was an active supporter, being in fact the one who purchased the necessary faculty from the Bishop. Wisely, the latter had granted this on condition that the singers from time to time disposed themselves "in the congregation to assist others to sing".

Although choirs occasionally had to be brought down to ground-level with such a proviso, they continued to perch in their west-end galleries for well over a century. The musical advantages of this position were recognised, as at Welford, Berkshire, where permission was given to the singers in 1719

* Richard Steele in *The Spectator* related with relish and some humour the fictitious predicament of a parish clerk disastrously distracted from the performance of his duties, and the cunning ruse with which he overcame the cause of his troubles. This tale along with other similar anecdotes can be read in The Everyman Library edition (25th January, 1712; 7th October, 1712; 9th July, 1711, etc.).

Plate 1

A chorister of the Chapel Royal, *c.* 1690 (reputed to be a portrait of Croft).

By courtesy of the National Portrait Gallery

The Sacred Choire

Plate 2

Frontispiece to Weldon's *Divine Harmony* [1716], printed for
I. Walsh. An imaginary representation of a service in the Chapel
Royal attended by choir, instrumentalists and congregation.

By courtesy of the Trustees of the British Museum

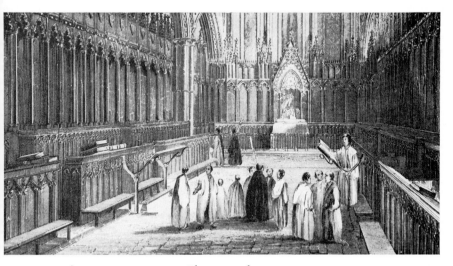

Plates 3 and 4

The choirs of Oxford and Ely Cathedrals respectively, from engravings by B. Winkles (1837).

Plates 5 and 6

Procession of musicians of the Chapel Royal and Westminster Abbey represented in Sandford's *The History of the Coronation of James II* (1687).

By courtesy of the Trustees of the British Museum

Plate 7

Prospectus Londinensis; the City at the beginning of the eighteenth century dominated by churches and St. Paul's cathedral.

By courtesy of the Guildhall Library

Grand Chorus Before and after the Song.

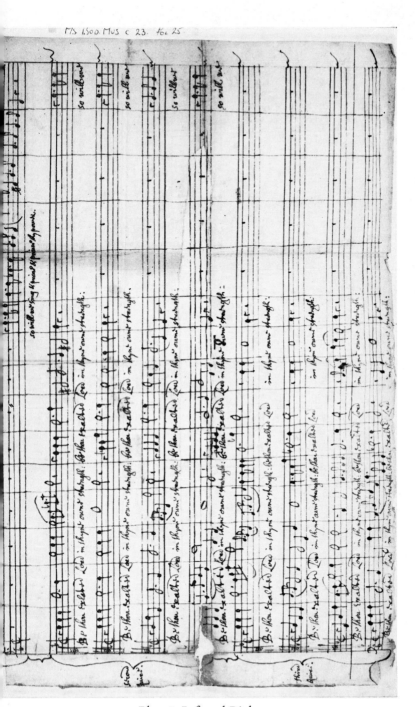

Plate 8, Left and Right

The opening page of Locke's copy of his anthem *The King shall rejoice*, "A song of thanksgiving for his Majesties Victory over the Dutch on St. James His Day 1666".

By courtesy of the Bodleian Library

Plate 9

Monument to Robert Pierrepont (died 1669) by (?) Bushell in
St. Mary's old church, West Dean. The visual equivalent of
Locke's anthem illustrated in plate 8.

Plate 10

Monument to Sir John Evelyn (died 1685) in St. Mary's old church, West Dean. The visual equivalent of Daniel Purcell's anthem illustrated in plate 11.

Plate 11, Left and Right

A solo movement from Daniel Purcell's anthem *Bow down thine ear, O Lord*, reputedly in the composer's hand.

Plate 12

The Renatus Harris organ in St. John's, Wolverhampton; part of the instrument that lost the "battle of the organs", at the Temple (1687/8).

to build themselves seats at the west end, "it being upon triall, the most advantageious Place for the singing of Psalmes, and the most commodious for Rendering the Congregation Regular and uniform". Those who paid for these seats "shall sing or endeavour to sing [sic!] at all Costomary times of singing of Psalms".[15]

The occupants of the singing galleries had often to be reminded that it was their duty at times to "disperse themselves into the body of the Church for the direction and assistance of such persons as shall have a pious intention of learning to sing". Raised above the heads of the congregation (who had to turn to face them in the psalms) they felt they were superior. Not surprisingly, it came about that those "who are distinguished by the Appellation of THE SINGERS, who, being placed in a Gallery or pew, engross this Part of the Public Worship [i.e. psalmody] to themselves", either made the congregation mute or left them to their own unharmonious devices. The nineteenth-century novelist Thomas Hardy compared the effects of this to the confused chatter at a dinner party—"just as the west end of a church is sometimes persistently found to sing out of time and tune with the leading spirits in the chancel".

No amount of well-meant advice on the ordering of choirs*

* One set of "useful Instructions for ordering a Society"[16] listed six practical points:
  1. Establish the right pitch. Once the tenor and bass parts know their notes, "the Boys may very easily perform the two upper Parts".
  2. The Tenor should lead "the whole Tune in true Time".
  3. Let there "be but one Leader to each Part".
  4. A "Pitch Pipe is very useful to learn by".
  5. The choir should be directed by a singing master, or else by "the head singer".
  6. In the gallery, basses should stand in the front row, with their backs to the congregation, and face the altos, flanked on either side by tenors and trebles respectively.
As regards the second injunction, the relative advantages of having the tunes in either the tenor or the treble part were frequently discussed. Generally it was felt that children's voices could not give a strong enough lead and there were time-honoured precedents for placing the melody in the tenor part. Archbishop Parker had done this in his *Psalter* (*c.* 1567) adding: "The Tenor of these partes be for the people when they will syng alone, the other partes, put for greater queers."

F

prevented the incidents at Castle Cary that parson Woodforde related in his diary. Beginning with a squabble over the use of the singers' gallery, the first signs of real trouble appeared on 26th February, 1769. "The Thirty-Sixth Psalm★ was sung this afternoon in Cary Church by the Singers. Done out of Pique to old William Burge. Old Mr. Burge concerns himself too much with the Singers."

Later in the year Woodforde, too, became the victim of the choir's peculiar form of pique.

> I was disturbed this morning at Cary Church by the Singers. I sent my Clerk sometime back to the Cary Singers, to desire that they would not sing the Responses in the Communion Service, which they complied with for several Sundays, but this morning after the first Commandment they had the Impudence to sing the Response, and therefore I spoke to them out of my desk, to say and not sing the Responses which they did.

Although the vicar had won the first round, a fortnight later the choir hit back. "I read Prayer and Preached this morning at Castle Cary Church. N.B. No singing this morning, the Singers not being at Church, they be highly affronted with me at what I lately had done."

When the singers' sulks had passed, they could not refrain from voicing, through the words of their psalms, some lightly veiled slander. "The Singers at Cary did not please me this afternoon by singing the Twelfth Psalm New Version,†

★ "The wicked by his works unjust, doth thus persuade his heart,
That in the Lord he hath no trust, his fear is set apart.

Yet doth he joy in his estate, to walk as he began,
So long till he deserves the hate of God as well as man.

His words are wicked, vile and naught, his tongue no truth doth tell:
Yet at no hand will he be taught which way he may do well."

etc.

† "Help, Lord, for good and godly men do perish and decay:
And faith and truth from worldly men is parted clean away.

Whoso doth with his neighbour talk, 'tis all but vanity:
For every man bethinketh how to speak deceitfully."

etc.

reflecting upon some People." But such rancour was not allowed to continue for long, and by Christmas a combination of cajolery and bribery had closed the dispute. "To Cary Singers this evening being Xmas Eve at Parsonage after giving them a Lecture concerning their late behaviour in Church on promise of amendment gave £0. 2. 0."

The last we hear of this choir is their being called, while a service was in progress, "a Pack of Whoresbirds" by "one Thomas Speed [who] came into the Church quite drunk and crazy".

Woodforde must have missed so lively a body when he was later transferred to another parish. However erratic their behaviour had been, their singing had spoilt him for a church musically less well equipped. On arrival at his new parish in 1775 the diarist wrote: "my clerk is a shocking Hand. The worst singing I ever heard in a Church, only the Clerk and one man, and both intolerably bad."[17]

Not all Societies of Singers were unworthy members of their parish church, though some had as little to do with its services as bellringers. Like modern campanologists, they toured from church to church trying out new venues and fresh ale, as is indicated by the churchwarden's accounts for Caddington, Bedfordshire, in 1779—"Paid for Beear gave to the Luton Psalm Singers". In course of time, more emphasis came to be placed on forming a choir of children. The "charity children", after all, were more manageable than the independent and unruly Singing Societies. Although hard at first to persuade children of the "Pay-Schools" to be taught psalmody, their poorer brothers and sisters formed in many churches the nucleus of a choir and, when well taught, made some contribution to raising the standards of parish church music. A writer who styled himself the "Principal Teacher of Psalmody to the Charity Schools" in the London area affirmed that, by the children's example, "many Persons, who before used to esteem Parochial Singing a trifling Concern, have been induced to bear a Part in this Angelic Exercise".

Parish church music owes as much to the eighteenth-century singers' societies and children's choirs as to the Oxford Movement in the nineteenth century; modern choirs with their origins in the two earlier bodies have everything to gain by being aware of the best traditions of both, however much later decorum and discipline has regulated the earlier liveliness and imperfect skills.

Generally it was only the larger town parishes and the London churches that could both afford an organ and secure an organist to assist the singing and bring relief to lengthy services with interludes and voluntaries. Where this was appreciated, an organist could find his appointment a relatively lucrative basis for a musical career, his not-too-onerous duties leaving him time to teach or compose.

The start of Charles Burney's career as a parish church organist shows what could be achieved in this capacity by someone of his drive and ambition. Beginning when he was thirteen as a temporary and far from competent assistant at Chester Cathedral, and later at St. Mary's, Shrewsbury, he then first acquired the interest in music that in his maturer years led to the writing of his mammoth four-volume *General History of Music*. When he moved to London in 1744 (at the age of eighteen) he became an apprentice to Arne; but this he terminated, learning more of music by self-study than from his master. In 1749, helped by influential friends and members of the vestry, he gained an appointment as organist of St. Dionis's, Backchurch, which, with its salary of £30 per annum, gave him the security and leisure to develop both a private teaching practice and a reputation for himself as a musician. Two years later this promising opening was interrupted by a severe illness.

At that time, fortunately for Burney, the Corporation of King's Lynn, Norfolk, was offering great inducements to attract a competent organist for St. Margaret's Church. The annual salary of £20 had been increased by subscription to the considerable sum of £100 "as an encouragement [to] a regular bred musician of some character to come down from the capital to instruct the children of the principal families in the town and Neighbourhood in Music".

Burney did not miss this opportunity. He moved to King's Lynn. But, enjoying fashionable London life, he did not take kindly to the provinces and, irritated both by an inferior instrument and ignorant audiences, he tried to resign after three years. The original inducement, the £100 subscription, had by then expired. Nonetheless, he stayed on for a few more years, perhaps persuaded by an enlightened town council who awarded a £20 increment to his salary—"paid by the Mayor and Burgesses to Mr. Charles Burney, Organist, as an encouragement for him to remain and teach Musick in this Town".

By 1760 Burney was back in London. Quickly picking up the threads, he secured enough pupils to make it no longer necessary for him to be a church organist, and embarked on his work as a musical historian which eventually brought him such eminence.[18]

Although Burney and others like him laid the foundations of their fame as organists in the larger parish churches, there were some in the same occupation who achieved notoriety of a different sort. One author painted the moral for all would-be organists when he related the biography of John James, organist first of St. Olave's, Southwark, and later of St. George's, Middlesex. He became celebrated for his style of performance, which was "learned and sublime". But he neglected one thing. "He paid very little attention to his interest, and was so totally devoid of all solicitude to advance himself in his profession, as to prefer the company and conversation of the lowest of mankind to that of the most celebrated of his own profession." Mixing with "butchers and bailiffs", he gained the character of a "blackguard". Worse still, "he indulged an inclination to spirituous liquors of the coarsest kind, such as are the ordinary means of ebriety in the lowest of the people; and this kind of intemperance he would indulge even while attending his duty at church".[19]

The success or failure of the London organists was not matched in the lives of musicians in country churches. In any case the organ was of little use in remote parishes where it was well-nigh impossible to find anybody to play it, and other ways had to be found of accompanying the congregation. The west-gallery bands provided one solution, the barrel-organ another.

The Sunday worship of many parishes was marked by no particular finesse or gentility; the rustic character became reinforced when the "musickers" joined the singers in their west-end galleries. Forming a mixed consort, they played anything on which they could tolerably pass muster, from stringed to all kinds of wind instruments, from "gran'mother fiddle" to serpents and bassoons. Their hey-day was at the turn of the eighteenth century; whether or not their playing had assisted the congregation's singing, by the middle of the nineteenth century they had almost ceased to exist. Certainly village life lost one of its more colourful activities when the Victorians pulled down the galleries and made the "musickers" homeless by displacing them from their natural habitat.

The problems of controlling the players and their playing may have made the barrel-organ a preferable alternative and eventually a serious rival to the village bands. It was easy to manipulate and, once installed, caused little expense or trouble. Although the barrel-organ was not fully developed until the early years of the nineteenth century, one is known to have been used at Peak Forest, Derbyshire, in 1700 and another at Hartfield, Sussex, in 1726.[20] Towards the end of the century the Precentor of York could openly state a preference for "the Mechanical assistance of a cylindrical or barrel-organ to the fingers of the best parochial organist".

The most distinctive feature of eighteenth-century parochial music was this glittering variety. When more uniform ways were later adopted, it is questionable whether the achievement of a better regulated worship was worth the loss of such lively individuality. "One grand scream" or "confused mumbling", "tarrible fine playin' " or "incompetent doodling" it may have been, but it was all a natural part of parish life and an honest endeavour to express, in whatever manner best suited their talents, the congregation's praises.

The Organ in Church

"A DANGEROUS AND ANTICHRISTIAN MACHINE"

The organ as developed by many European builders in the seventeenth century became an instrument of great versatility, and its musical possibilities were realised to the full by leading composers of the time. In Germany in particular there was established a tradition of organ-building that culminated in the masterpieces of Arp Schnitger and the Silbermann brothers, and that received its finest compliment in Bach's organ music. But in England, over a similar period, there was nothing to compare with such achievement.

The Civil War has often been blamed. Much has been made of the destruction done by the Puritan soldiery, spoiling organs and pawning pipes for pots of ale. Yet, harassing though this must have been, there is another basic reason beneath the English inability to match the skills that were acquired in France, the Low Countries and Germany. In short, antagonism to the organ in church. For many it might have been tolerated in taverns; in church it was an abomination to be abhorred as much as the red robes of the great whore of Babylon.

In England after the Restoration the organ was rarely found outside cathedrals and churches with musical establishments, and the Puritan influence was so strong from Elizabeth's reign onwards that relatively few parishes dared to possess such an instrument. One church (Holy Trinity, Coventry) that did in fact have an organ built in 1632 had it taken down and sold after less than ten years. As will be seen later, the battle to have the organ accepted as a desirable encouragement to congregational singing was a long one, and was only gradually won during the century following the end of the Commonwealth.

Before this the official ordinance of 1644 that prohibited organ playing in church services and commanded "the speedy demolishing of all organs, images and all matters of superstitious monuments" only gave formal expression to a widespread feeling, and legalised the destruction that had already been inflicted by the over-enthusiastic Roundheads.

That the Puritans should so object to organs as to link them with images and superstitious monuments seems due not only to the fact that they were considered expensive extras (a familiar enough argument) nor solely on account of their secular connections, but chiefly because they were thought to distract from simple and thoughtful worship, to aid and abet "curious singing". Anything that obstructed the presentation of God's word had to be forcibly rooted out; the attention of the congregation must not be diverted by artifice or confused by inessentials.

Many Puritans must at least have felt uneasy about indiscriminate destruction perpetrated during the Civil War, though few would have failed to share John Vicars's delight that in 1649 organ music and elaborate singing were no longer heard in Westminster Abbey, being replaced by a daily sermon:

> ... the most rare and strange alteration of things in the *Cathedral Church of Westminster*. Namely, that whereas there was wont to be heard nothing almost but *Roaring*-Boyes, tooting and squeaking *Organ Pipes*, and the Cathedral catches of Morley, and I know not what trash; now the Popish Altar is quite taken away, the *bellowing organs* are demolisht and pull'd down, the *treble* or rather *trouble* and base singers, Chanters or Inchanters driven out; and instead thereof, there is now a most blessed Orthodox Preaching Ministry, even every morning throughout the weeke, and every Weeke throughout the whole yeare a Sermon Preached, by the most learned grave and godly Ministers.[1]

Whatever the fate of church organs and choirs, domestic music making continued during the Commonwealth. "Many chose rather to fidle at home, than to goe out, and be knockt on the head abroad." The singing of holy songs privately, with or without instruments, was a flourishing and fashionable recreation, and even organs were tolerated as long as they were confined to taverns and the home. The poet Milton possessed his own instrument and, in 1641, unreservedly expressed his delight in organ music—"while the skilful *Organist* plies his grave and fancied descant, in lofty fugues, or the whole symphony with artful and unimaginable touches adorn and grace the well studied chords of some choice composer". The Protector himself had both an organ and an official player, John Hingston. Given the right time and place, Cromwell enjoyed a little instrumental music as much as anyone, and in fact for the wedding of one of his daughters in 1657 he generously hired as many as forty-eight violins and fifty trumpets.[2]

At the Restoration organs were quickly brought back to their former places. For a time they must have had a novelty value, attracting people to church in the way sermons had done fifteen years earlier. On 30th December, 1660, Pepys went to Westminster Abbey "and walked there, seeing the great confusion of people that come there to hear the Organs".* Anthony Wood wrote about conditions at a similar time in Oxford:

> And that they might draw the vulgar from the aforesaid praying and preaching which was still exercised in some churches and houses, they restored the organs at Christ Church, Magdalen, New, and St. John's College, together with the singing of prayers after the most antient way: to which places the resort of people (more out of novelty I suppose than devotion) was infinitely great.[3]

It was, however, to take some time before organs found their way into churches where they did not sing prayers "after the

---

* Pepys had already on 4th November heard the organ there: "I went to the Abbey, when the first time that ever I heard the organs in a Cathedral".

most antient way" (i.e. the fully choral service). The attitude to organs in church dominant during the Commonwealth could not be changed overnight; and now added to this was the somewhat dubious associations the instrument had acquired as a result of being driven underground for so many years.

The authorities at cathedrals and similar places did not stop to think about this. So eager was their desire to restore everything just as it had been before the Civil War that they quickly replaced or rebuilt their organs. This could not always have been easily managed as it is known that at least nine had been destroyed, though admittedly due as much to high-spirited soldiers billeted in the churches as to the official order of 1644. The prospects of such hooliganism had been foreseen at a number of places, and precautions had been taken against it. At Cambridge the organ in Jesus College Chapel which had been built for £200 in 1635 was taken down in 1642, and rebuilt at the Restoration by Robert Dallam; that at Christ's College was safely stored and returned to the chapel in 1660; and those at Trinity and St. John's Colleges were re-erected in 1660 and 1661 respectively. A brand-new organ built by Robert Dallam in 1640 for Gloucester Cathedral was sold to one Yate the sheriff, and replaced in 1661. Thomas Harris set up the organ (which had been kept intact) in its former place at Salisbury Cathedral. At Magdalen College, Oxford, the organ was still in 1654 not only *in situ* but also in use; it was later moved to Hampton Court for Cromwell's benefit, but returned in 1660. At Ely Cathedral the organ was neither removed nor apparently damaged. Organs at Durham, Lincoln, St. Paul's and York also evidently escaped harm. Canterbury Cathedral could use enough of its organ at the Restoration until a new one was built in 1662 by Lancelot Pease. By 10th April, 1661, Rochester had repaired their damage, and Pepys "there saw the Cathedrall, which is fitting for use, and the organ then a-tuning".

"NEAT, RICH, AND MELODIOUS ORGANS"

When the cathedrals and chapels had equipped themselves with new or rebuilt organs, parish churches began to follow suit. The organ-building trade expanded, and the development of the instrument, which had been so stunted by the attitudes and events of the first half of the seventeenth century, at last forged ahead under the example of such builders as Bernard Smith and Renatus Harris. These two craftsmen used their skill and the valuable experience they had gained abroad to amplify existing types into musical instruments able to accompany the grandest psalmody or the most delicate anthem, as well as to play a wide variety of solo music.

Amongst organs built earlier in the century only the largest had two manuals, the chorus ranged in octave pitches from open diapason to twenty-second with few mutations, and there was frequent doubling at unison pitch. The pre-Commonwealth organ at Magdalen College, Oxford, contained (on the Great) one open and one stopped diapason, two principals, fifteenths and twenty-seconds, and (on the second manual) one stopped diapason, two principals, one recorder and one fifteenth.* A typical single-manual specification for St. John's College, Cambridge, built in 1634 by Robert Dallam, consisted of five ranks: diapason, principal, recorder, fifteenth and twenty-second. Even the same builder's larger two-manual organ at York Minster had a very similar scheme with some extra ranks on the Great, including a twelfth. The fact that this scheme shows little change on that adopted by Dallam's father at Worcester Cathedral twenty years earlier

* See this extract from "The Proposals of Renatus Harris to the Reverend the President and Fellows of Magdalen College in Oxford, for repairing and making several alterations in their organ, 17 July, 1686: . . . finding by experience that when two unisons are together in an organ as two principals, two fifteenths, etc., that they never agree well together in tune, and one stop of each sort is in a manner as loud as two of the same name; . . . so that I propose to make your eight stops to consist of these following, one open diapason, one stopped diapason, one principal, one great twelfth, one fifteenth, one tiers, one furniture of two or three ranks. . . ."

demonstrates the static condition of organ design at that time.

In 1662 Lancelot Pease had begun to develop the Great in a new organ for Canterbury Cathedral. Its thirteen ranks included both a "small and great twelfth", and a tierce. By 1674 Thomas Thamar had included at Pembroke College, Cambridge, amongst the eight stops not only a twelfth but also a sesquialtera, cornet and trumpet. The scheme for Smith's organ for Christ Church Cathedral, Oxford, built six years later, was almost identical to this with the addition of a tierce on the Great, and a small, four-rank second manual.

Smith's greatest opportunity came just afterwards when, in 1683, he was awarded the contract for a new organ for the Temple Church, though his instrument was not accepted until 1688. During that time it had to compete with a rival one erected in the same building by Harris, and the Benchers of the Temple, being unable to agree on which organ to have, only finally settled in Smith's favour after a four-year long argument. This must have brought welcome publicity to both builders, and must also have done much to unfold the possibilities of the organ as a musical instrument. The impact on the musical public of the day would have been at least as decisive as that of the Festival Hall organ 270 years later. In size alone the Temple organ surpassed any previous instrument: ten stops on the Great, six on the Chair, and seven on the Echo organ. This innovation of a third manual was in fact the immediate predecessor of the modern Swell. All the pipes were enclosed in a box, thus reducing their volume and giving them a distant sound which "echoed" the other manuals. At least five of the ranks were wholly or partly made of wood, and the specification embraced such new solo stops as "A Violl and Violin", and a "Voice Humane". Both the Echo and Great organs had cornet, sesquialtera and trumpet stops; and the Great had a mixture as well. Most of the ranks on the Echo organ, as a solo department, played only in the treble octaves, but the range of the Great and Chair embraced sixty-one notes, including quarter notes for G sharp/A flat and D sharp/E flat.

The Temple Church example undoubtedly influenced the organ-building activity that was now increasing all the time. For instance, St. Mary-at-Hill, Billingsgate, acquired in 1693 a two-manual instrument (although the church was small) with eleven stops in the Great including a three-rank mixture, five-rank cornet, a trumpet and a "Vox-humane". It even went to the luxury of having a "Trimeloe" stop.[4] Smith was fortunate enough to secure the contract for the new St. Paul's Cathedral, and built there between 1695 and 1697 a large three-manual organ of twenty-seven stops. The superb workmanship in this instrument ensured its doing good service with little alteration for very many years. It was not dismantled for renovation for over a century and remained in use until the choir screen was removed in 1860.

In 1710 Harris built for Salisbury Cathedral the first four-manual organ. He himself hinted in a pamphlet printed shortly afterwards that its scheme originated in ideas he had conceived for an extra organ for the west end of St. Paul's Cathedral. He obviously relished the idea of another Temple-type confrontation with Smith, and already went so far as to describe his organ as having "more Varieties express'd thereon than by all the organs in England, were their several Excellencies united". The fourth manual at Salisbury was not an independent department but a borrowed Great; Harris provided the extra keyboard operating the majority of the stops of the Great organ "by communication", a system he had invented to enable the player to have greater command of the stops. There were, however, other more important features. The size of the Great, fifteen stops dominating a seven-rank Chair, was matched by a similar Echo organ, though this was never intended as a second chorus as it operated only the upper half of the complete compass and its pipes were placed inside a box. The mixture ranks, sesquialtera and cornet, were on the Great; and both the Great and Echo had separate mutations, a twelfth, tierce and larigot on either manual. Most striking was the number of reed stops: a trumpet, vox humana and crumhorn on the Great and

Echo, with in addition a clarion on the Great, and a bassoon
on the Chair.

Harris was to include a french horn stop in his last organ for
St. Dionis, Backchurch. Other stops such as the hautboy and
Snetzler's celebrated dulcianas were to appear later. But
Harris's work at Salisbury represents a culminating point in the
development of the English organ, after which there was no
great alteration in the general scheme for many years. Traditions
established by Smith and Harris were continued by such as
John Harris, who carried on his father Renatus's good work in
partnership with Byfield, and Byfield's son, who in turn worked
with Jordan and Bridge. Schreider and Schwarbrook were
other eminent builders. But it was Snetzler who exceeded them
all in sheer productivity during the forty years or so that he
lived in England after coming from Switzerland in the 1740s.
The largest organs of the time generally had three manuals,
though rarely more than thirty stops. The Great had the
monopoly of a full chorus, including two or three mixture
stops, but the Choir remained small and must have been
limited to the function of accompanying either voices or solo
stops. Echo or Swell manuals* were usually of limited compass,
and provided the imitative sounds of which eighteenth-
century audiences never tired.

Picturesque spellings and descriptions in seventeenth-
century specifications are more informative than many modern
stereotyped equivalents, though they cannot take the place of
first-hand knowledge. Such pipework as survives can tell us a
little of the original tonal quality, but often, for the sound of a
complete chorus, we have to accept a conjectural reconstruction.
Nonetheless, the imagination is stimulated to hear sparkling
mutations in a "Simbale in 2 stopse ringing throu in 5's", and
silvery tones in "Tribles to the Tierce", or a "sifflet 1 fut longe".
Experience of some song recitals makes it not difficult to envisage a "Voice humane" in conjunction with a "shaking

* By the eighteenth century the nomenclature "Chair" and "Echo" was
being replaced by "Choir" and "Swell".

stopp", and turn with relief to the aristocratic sound of a
"Gedackt of wainescott". It is hard to conceive how as coarse a
reed as "Sagbot" could share the same bellows, but he never
appeared again until disguised as a bassoon or contra fagotto.
The majestic sonorities of the lower registers are clear enough
in the pompous description of "One open diapason of tynn the
biggest pipe containing thirteene foote in length with his
bigness according to the monicords". An even greater double
diapason of 20 feet in length could only be described by the
Honourable Roger North in terms of the capacity of a vast
tankard, "contents of the speaking part, 3 hogsheads, 8
gallons".

More exact descriptions are found in Sir John Sutton's
A Short Account of Organs, written in 1847 when many eighteenth-
century and some seventeenth-century instruments were still
intact. The chorus of a Smith organ was specified as being "very
fine and very brilliant in effect, though not quite so much so as
the Chorus afterwards introduced by Snetzler in his Organs
which, though extremely brilliant, is almost too shrill, and
when heard in a small building rings unpleasantly in the ears".
Sir John was a great admirer of Smith's work, but he had to
admit that Harris's

> Diapasons are both sweet and rich and his chorus is vivacious
> and ringing, even more so than Schmidt's, and his reed stops . . .
> are also superior to his. In many respects, there is a resemblance
> between the organs of these two workmen; and though Harris's
> wooden pipes are excellent, they never possess that peculiar reedy
> and brilliant tone which is so charming in all Schmidts.

Despite some criticism of Snetzler, it was emphasised that

> his instruments are remarkable for the purity of their tone, and
> the extreme brilliancy of their Chorus-Stops, which in this
> respect surpassed any thing that had been heard before in this
> country, and which have never since been equalled. His reed
> stops were also much better than those built before his time. His
> Organs though they are more brilliant than their predecessors,

fall short of that fulness of tone which characterized those of
Schmidt, Harris, Schreider, etc. . . .

Burney, who was familiar with continental organs, praised
highly the tone of English instruments:

> Most of the organs I have met with on the Continent seem to
> be inferior to ours by Father Smith, Byfield, or Snetzler, in
> everything but size. As the churches there are often immense, so
> are the organs; the tone is indeed somewhat softened and refined
> by space and distance; but when heard near, it is intolerably coarse
> and noisy. . . . In our organs not only the touch and tone, but the
> imitative stops, are greatly superior to those of any other organs
> I have met with.[5]

The late seventeenth-century English organ must have been
a musical instrument of some subtlety. With all its upperwork
it aimed for brilliance, and achieved clarity rather than shrill-
ness; its well-developed Great chorus was colourful and not
necessarily loud; and contrasting with this were the charming
and distinctive solo stops. Sheer noise and power were much
later characteristics, and the relative gentleness and delicacy of
the tone of a "Father" Smith organ provided the perfect
vehicle for the rich and dissonant idiom of much of Blow's and
Purcell's music.

Subsequent builders accepted as standard the basic features
established by Smith and Harris, developing various subsidiary
ones. The cornet stop, for instance, was to become as popular
in the eighteenth as the tuba in the twentieth century. This is
apparent not only from the fact that it was an indispensable
item in any worthwhile specification, but also from the amount
of music specially scored for this stop. Consisting of five ranks
playing from middle C upwards (the unison, octave, twelfth,
fifteenth, seventeenth) it provided a blended, composite sound,
ideal for the sprightly and mannered melodies in voluntaries of
the period. These voluntaries, apart from a slow introduction
in chordal style for diapasons, usually consisted of movements

in two parts which deliberately eschewed a heavy contrapuntal style in favour of a tuneful, singable idiom using phrases that could be easily grasped, delighted the ear with their sparkling figurations, and did not weary the mind with clever development or lengthy construction. Music of this nature needed the cornet and, in addition, reed stops such as the vox humana, crumhorn and trumpet. These latter, however popular, presented practical problems of tuning. Roger North did not like them for this reason and for the fact that he found them slow of speech—"the basses will always snore". Even in 1749 Handel, approving a specification of a small one-manual organ, preferred to do without reeds "because they are continually wanting to be tuned, which in this country is very inconvenient".

Another way of providing varied solo colours was devised in the Echo organ. A series of ranks reflecting some of those in the Great but reduced in volume by being placed inside a box, this department became common on all large organs. Its expressive possibilities were realised when a mechanism was invented for opening and shutting the box, and Jordan advertised just this with some pride in the *Spectator* of 8th February, 1712, for the public opening of a new organ in St. Magnus's Church, London Bridge, "consisting of four sets of keys, one of which is adapted to the art of emitting sounds by swelling the notes, which never was in any organ before". Harris and Byfield fourteen years later referred to "The Ecchoes, which are made to Swell or express Passion" on their new organ at St. Mary Redcliffe, Bristol; and gradually the Swell organ became established as a permanent feature.

With such inventiveness and originality amongst builders, it may seem strange that a part of the instrument we now consider essential should have been almost entirely ignored; that is, the pedal organ. It could hardly be that the existence of pedals on continental organs was unknown. Robert Dallam and Thomas Harris spent about eighteen years in France before the Restoration building organs. Renatus Harris was born there during this time. Bernard Smith, whatever his original nationality, was certainly abroad during the years of the Commonwealth. Both Schreider and Schwarbrook were German craftsmen, and Snetzler had lived for over thirty years abroad when he came to England. Even Handel apparently made no attempt to encourage the use of pedals.

The first suggestion of pedals came from Renatus Harris in the pamphlet published between 1710 and 1712 containing proposals for a grand organ for St. Paul's Cathedral. Harris advertised a "double double Diapason of Profundity" (40 feet long and 2 feet in diameter) and said: the organ "shall consist of Six entire sets of keys for the hands, besides Pedals for the Feet". St. Paul's eventually had pedals, of a sort, in 1721, as there is an account of that date showing that Schreider was paid £36 "for Adding six large Trumpet Pipes down to 16 foot tone to be used with a pedal or without", and £20 "for the Pedal and its movements". The first authentic instance of pedals was in Harris and Byfield's organ built for St. Mary Redcliffe, Bristol, in 1726, which had "Pedals to the lower Octave". Much later, in 1757, Snetzler built a three-manual instrument for the German Lutheran Chapel in the Savoy with a pedal organ of nineteen notes. Such an addition was still quite rare for some time after Snetzler. If as late as 1860 a cathedral organist could turn his back on pedals to the extent of telling a builder "you may put them there but I shall never use them", it is hardly surprising to find no demand for them in the eighteenth century.

Hostility to pedals arose not so much from an attitude that would have nothing to do with the added complexity of an organ played with the feet as well as the hands, as from the fact that English composers and performers preferred a style characterised by lightness and clarity rather than by great sonorities. Cleanness of articulation and neat phrasing of melodies on varying registrations accompanied by distinct, florid and wide-ranging bass parts left no room for pedal organs of limited compass, inadequate size, and doubtful

efficiency. In any case the manual compass of so many
organs, extending lower than today's standard bottom C,*
gave the player ample opportunity to provide a firm bass when
required.

No hard-and-fast rule was accepted on the ideal position for
an organ in church, though in cathedrals and buildings of
similar size there was a definite preference for organs on the
choir screen, where the advantages can be both musical and
visual. The older position on the north choir wall was less
frequently used. Pease placed his organ there at Canterbury
Cathedral in 1662. Thamar did the same at Winchester in 1685,
and a hundred years later a visitor could still note that "the
organ is, as it should be, on one side". A rare instance of an
organ entirely out of sight, at Windsor, drew one appreciative
comment: "I like the contrivance of the unseen organ behind
the altar".[7]

In most parish churches the organ followed the singers to
their west-end gallery. Three faculties issued in close succession
in the Salisbury diocese illustrate this: one permitted the
building of a gallery and organ at the west end of Potterne
Parish Church; another agreed to an organ for St. Helen's,
Abingdon, "to be built without any charge to the parishioners
. . . and sett up in the Gallery over the doorway . . . on the
West side of the Church"; and the third allowed St. Thomas's,
Salisbury, "to erect and build by a voluntary subscription a
Gallery with a staircase and an Organ at the West End of the
Middle Isle".[8]

It is impossible to be precise about the actual pitch of organs.
It has been shown that church pitch at the beginning of the
seventeenth century was over a tone higher than it is today,
and it is clear that from the middle of the century this was

---

* The largest pipes in organs at Wells (1662), Winchester (1665) and
Exeter (1665) Cathedrals, and at the Temple Church (1684) were 12½ ft.,
13 ft., 20½ ft. and 12 ft. respectively.

This extensive lower range gives good reason for using pedals where
appropriate in modern performances of seventeenth- and eighteenth-
century music.[6]

gradually lowered to secular pitch, and by the eighteenth century approximated to modern standards. Furthermore there was no set standard of pitch as there is today, which might have varied between church and concert hall, and from place to place. The general tendency after 1660 was for organ builders to accept a lower pitch than that which had been previously current in English church organs. Robert Dallam in 1661 was asked about building an organ for New College, Oxford, "half a note lower than Christ Church organ". Also at Oxford, Harris agreed in 1690 with Magdalen College to "alter the pitch of the said organs half a note lower than they now are". Between 1689 and 1691 Gerard Smith rebuilt the organ at Ely Cathedral, but James Hawkins, who was organist during this time until 1729, had to transpose the music he played there because, as he said, "the organ here is 3 quarters of a note higher than the pitch of the organs are now".*

Too rigid an approach to this problem is therefore unwise. In general terms, some anthems and services written in the years immediately following the Restoration might more suitably be performed higher than the original notation now indicates, but this becomes less likely to be necessary in the eighteenth century. The main criterion should be to secure the most effective and convincing performance, being ready to transpose in order to find a pitch appropriate for the music.

"THE LAWFULNESS AND USE OF ORGANS"

The technical and musical development of the organ was disturbed to some extent by a ground-swell of controversy

---

* Good authority gives the exact pitch of a Smith organ at Hampton Court Palace (1690): a′=442 c.p.s.. Also that used by Harris at the same time, and by Green a century later: a′=428 c.p.s. (present Standard International a′=440 c.p.s.)

Many organs during this period were tuned to mean-tone temperament, and present equal temperament did not become general until the nineteenth century, though Snetzler had tuned his first English organs in this way.[9]

about its suitability in church. At the Restoration few parish churches, as distinct from cathedral and collegiate establishments, retained any tradition of using instrumental accompaniment in their services. In 1667, for instance, an organ at Hackney was such a rarity as to induce Pepys to hear it (though this was not the only attraction for him):

> To Hackney Church. . . . That which we went chiefly to see was the young ladies of the school, whereof there is great store, very pretty; and also the organ, which is handsome, and tunes the psalms, and plays with the people; which is mighty pretty, and makes me mighty earnest to have a pair at our church.[10]

Not all churchmen were as enthusiastic as Pepys, and for the best part of a century much indifference and antagonism had to be overcome before organs in parish churches became at all common.

Thomas Mace in 1676 championed the usefulness of an organ, and offered advice on how to find somebody to play the instrument. The "most *Excellent-large-plump-lusty-full-speaking-organ*" at York Minster had greatly impressed Mace during the Civil War, and he was equally fond of a chamber organ in domestic music-making. Yet he saw how something in between these two extremes could help the singing in parish churches. Realising that there were many who "take *Boggle* at the very *Name* of an *Organ*", he prudently counselled how to secure a reasonable standard of singing without instrumental support; but his experience was that even the best voice combined with the best ear found it very difficult to sing a psalm unaccompanied and remain in tune. " 'Tis sad to hear what *whining, toting, yelling* or *screeking* there is in many *Country Congregations*" where there is no organ. To rectify this, and because accompanied psalmody "be the most *glorious, magnificent,* and a *stately-steady way*", he strongly urged the use of an organ. Mace considered it not difficult to raise necessary funds to buy an instrument adequate for most small churches (between £30 and £60) though he did foresee problems in obtaining an organist. Even these could be solved. Any music master would be glad of an opportunity to teach a parish clerk to *"pulse or strike most of our common Psalm-Tunes . . . for a trifle (viz. 20, 30, or 40 shillings;)"*. Then the clerk, having gained a basic ability on the organ, could in turn earn his share by teaching the same to the brighter youth of the parish. This would give them something worthwhile to learn and do, and in no time the parish would *"swarm or abound with Organists"*.[11]

Two interesting publications appeared in 1696 marking the opening of organs in London and in Devon.[12] The Rev. Dr. Towerson preached a sermon at the official opening of a new instrument for St. Andrew's, Undershaft, in the course of which he admitted that since the Restoration there had been a change in attitude towards vocal music in church ("there are not many, that are Enemies to that Musick") but that there was still opposition to using the organ. He knew too well that "the Affections of the generality of Man are, and will be dull", and he had such little faith in the power of a sermon to rouse men from their stupor as to suggest this was something the organ might do. Besides, from the solely practical point of view, the average worshipper had so little "skill in Singing, as to carry them with any tolerable *concent* through the Psalms, or Hymns" that their worship was not only inadequately performed, but kept others away from church. The answer was plain. "The *Organ*, in particular, both by the *Lowdness*, and the *Harmoniousness* thereof doth, with a kind of grateful Violence, carry the Voices of Men along with it."

A more subtle approach was that of the Rev. John Newte. At Tiverton, Devon, he succeeded after some struggle in overcoming the opposition in the parish to an organ, and had one built by Gerard Smith which was opened on 13th September, 1696, and which he claimed was the first in his diocese outside Exeter since the Commonwealth. He still, however, felt it necessary to publish a pamphlet explaining his actions to his bishop in the Dedication: "My Lord, We have at last . . .

Erected an Organ in our Parish-Church. A thing which I have almost these Ten years endeavoured to do." That the project had taken so long to come to fruition was due to it being hindered by "want of sincerity in some, or a vigorous Prosecution in others, under the Everlasting Pretence of the Badness of the Times". He gave a number of reasons for having an organ in church, two similar to those used by Towerson, and three more besides:

It will regulate the untunable Voices of the Multitude, and make the Singing in the Church more orderly and harmonious.

It will stir up the Affection of Men, and make them the fitter for Devotion.

It will compose their Thoughts, and drive away Evil Suggestions from their Minds.

It will prepare them for the being better Edified in the Divine Service they are about.

Lastly, It will make the whole service of God to be the more Solemn and August, and the People more Serious and Reverential.

For the last purpose Newte perhaps had in mind that the organ would calm, or at least cover, such noises as he mentioned later, like the opening and shutting of pew doors, and "the nauseous Rawkings, and unnecessary Coughing and Spitting, which is made by the People".*

Although much later the organ in church could still be dubbed by its critics as a "dangerous and antichristian Machine,

---

* Newte mentioned three specific places where the organ should be used in a service besides the "several Times when the *Psalms* are sung". First, a voluntary before the service, to put the congregation into a serious frame of mind. Secondly, between the psalms and first lesson, to "melt us into a fit Temper to receive the best Impressions from the Word of God". Lastly, an outgoing voluntary, to "take off some little whispering Disturbances . . . and to drown that ungrateful rushing Murmur" of people going out of church.

Another writer explained that the Tiverton instrument had not been a burden on the parish rates, having been paid for by voluntary subscription. Even the organist's salary of £30 per annum had been supplied out of "certain rents and dues belonging to the church".[13]

invented by the Scarlet-Whore", the need arose not so much to put a cogent case for its use as to admonish against its misuse. Organists who attempted "by the gaiety of their performances to dissipate that drowsy disposition into which good Christians are apt to sink" were corrected by the Rev. Arthur Bedford in 1711. Worried as he was by the invasion of secular elements into sacred music, he wanted to place the church organ in quarantine free from contamination by the "lewd and profane songs" of the theatre. The organist too frequently set out to divert his listeners, putting aside the "solid grave Harmony" of a sacred idiom in preference for light-hearted jingles. "Every thing which is serious, is call'd in Derision, The old Cow Path, and presented as dull and heavy." Improvisations were even more despicable ("extempore Maggots" Bedford called them) there being few organists outside cathedrals having any knowledge of this art.

Bedford, admitting that organs "are lawful in the Worship of God", proceeded to propound various reforms. First and foremost, the organist must be a good Christian. Secondly, the voluntaries he plays must be "grave and serious". Thirdly, in psalmody, the tunes must be announced "as plain as possible, that the meanest Capacity may know what the Tune is", accompanied simply without "any Graces or Flourishes", and the interludes between lines must be exact and give clear indication to the congregation when to begin the next phrase. Otherwise "the singers mistrust that they are out of Tune, and not the Organ; this discourages them in the Worship of God, and they who sung before the Organ was erected, then lay it aside". Fourthly, "it would be very convenient in Parochial Churches, that the Organist did not play so loud whilst the Congregation is singing. The full Organ is generally too loud for a Congregation, and drowns the Voices that they are not heard". Fifthly, the organist ought to "avoid all extempore Fancies". Lastly, the organist ought to free himself of all secular musical activities so as to devote his mind and talents to divine music.[14]

However quick he may have been to criticise new-fangled developments, Bedford supported music in church that did not offend his conservative tastes. The fact that he felt free to criticise and admonish indicates the relatively secure footing that music had achieved in the eighteenth-century parish church. That organs were considered no longer merely desirable but indispensable in some parishes is clear from a comparison of the disposition of instruments built or attended to by Smith and Harris with those of Snetzler later. The immediate task for Smith and Harris had been to refurbish cathedrals and college chapels and to supply organs to those London churches which were quick to appreciate their usefulness. By far the largest proportion of Snetzler's work, on the other hand, was carried out in provincial parish churches.*

Although the vogue for an organ in every parish, however small, belongs to the Victorian period, in the latter part of the eighteenth century the instrument had become almost a status symbol for the wealthier town churches.

> The use of the organ in parish churches . . . within this last century has increased to so great a degree, that in most of the cities and great towns in the Kingdom it is a sign of great poverty in a parish for a church to be without one.[15]

Parishes that had been organless for more than a century remedied the deficiency,† and no longer were obliged to apologise for their action. Those who had taken "Boggle at the Very Name of an Organ" had been silenced, and congregations willingly succumbed to having their voices carried along, "with

*Organs built or attended to by	Cathedrals, colleges and royal chapels	London churches	Other churches
Smith	25	20	19
Harris	18	20	9
Snetzler	11	10	68

† It took a church in Salisbury 125 years to replace an instrument demolished during the Interregnum. "St. Martin's, New Sarum. A Gallery was erected on the screen leading into the Chancel, and the Organ then introduced, placed on it. Previous to this there had been no Organ since 1653 when it was demolished and sold for ten shillings."[16]

a kind of grateful Violence", by the organ's "lowdness and harmoniousness".

Let the last word come from a German minister who said in 1786:

> The church-music of the English is but indifferent, when compared to that in many parts of the continent. The Dissenters have not even so much as organs, and they often sing their psalms not in very pleasing melodies. In episcopal churches organs are generally to be found; though many in the country, nay, even some churches in London, are without them. Sometimes a set of people, a little instructed in singing, make up the want of an organ on Sundays.

Possibly he thought English musical talents were diverted to bell-ringing, as he added:

> As the English are very fond of ringing bells, the churches are frequently furnished with a set of them, that may be rung in some musical manner; which, though it makes an intolerable noise, is nevertheless, thought by many highly entertaining. . . . I once lived near a church-yard in London, where there is, what they call an excellent set of bells; and I would, from my own experience, advise those who love quietness or study, to keep at a good distance from churches.[17]

Ex. 6

Chimes at Gloucester Cathedral [18]   William Hayes

List of Composers

Being not so much part of the body of the book as a swollen appendix to the previous chapters, the following pages are chiefly for those who need to refer to biographical details of composers and to their church music.

These notes on the lives of the composers summarise the facts that are known about them as given in standard reference books.[1] There is a need for original research to amplify or correct existing information, and for a thorough survey of the music. But, although the notes are brief and the list incomplete, no composer of significance is omitted. In fact many minor composers are included; the supply of music for eighteenth-century cathedrals, whatever its quality, flowed freely. Most cathedrals enjoyed the home brew provided by their own organists, but this, however fresh it may originally have tasted, deteriorated with keeping and soon went stale. A less intoxicating spirit was offered by the parish church organists who found for their psalmody and easy anthems a gullible market in the rising number of societies of singers.

To discuss in detail every relatively important piece of church music would stretch this book beyond reasonable limits. Closer attention is given to the work of two composers for good reason: Humfrey, for both the significance and the intrinsic worth of his music (the one has been recognised, the other undeservedly ignored) and Handel, whose English church music, surprisingly, has often been overlooked. Purcell has the benefit of a valuable study by Westrup, a modern complete edition, and an analytical catalogue, and aspects of Blow's music have been discussed in a number of articles by Watkins Shaw. A fresh assessment of the church music of Boyce and, especially, Greene is long overdue.

No mention is made in this summary of the many sacred songs that were written for domestic use. A long tradition of singing "divine hymns" in the home was maintained right through the seventeenth century, for which most leading composers supplied their "choice psalms", solo airs and dialogues. Continued in the following century in the private practice of psalmody, the tradition still survives today in the passive pursuit of watching hymn singing on television—"Songs of Praise" is by far the most popular programme in religious broadcasting.

Eighteenth-century church music was written usually as a direct response to supply a specific demand and rarely just to express personal experience. Byrd may have composed the motets in his *Gradualia* for clandestine liturgical performance, but he openly revealed one reason why these Latin pieces have such enduring quality:

> There is a certain hidden power, as I learnt by experience, in the thoughts underlying the words themselves; so that, as one meditates upon the sacred words and constantly and seriously considers them, the right notes, in some inexplicable manner, suggest themselves quite spontaneously.[2]

Composers after the Restoration were motivated by less lofty impulses. In the canticles the aim was to proceed through the text in the shortest possible time, and scope for variety was limited to simple contrasts between solo voices and chorus, and the antiphonal use of the choir. The anthems could be more expansive, but only if they entertained the congregation seeking relief in a lengthy service or anxious to observe the prowess of a favourite singer.

This lack of serious purpose, as we see it, mitigates against the acceptance today of many late-seventeenth-century and eighteenth-century anthems. There are other obstacles. The frequent inability to capture an appropriate style, heavy-pressure organs doing duty for their delicately voiced predecessors or for a string group, choirs lacking solo voices of adequate calibre, ignorance of performance conventions, all these present formidable hurdles to be overcome.

To achieve the best effect, late-seventeenth-century verse anthems must be treated as chamber music, intimately scored for solo ensembles of voices and strings or continuo. Increasingly, in later music, the underlying motive of vocal display must be expressed more prominently, though always with tact and good taste. The difficulties of presentation are not so much technical as requiring a discerning understanding of style and a soundly based knowledge of relevant musical conventions.

Fortunately in recent years there has been no lack of thought and discussion applied to the problems of performing seventeenth- and eighteenth-century music.[3] All that is necessary here is to supplement this with some comments of interest in our particular field.

Although we can never exactly reconstruct the sound of choirs in Purcell's or Boyce's day, we can at least discover the ideals they were striving for. "Clearness, brilliancy, neatness, expression, embellishment, intonation, firmness, modulation, smoothness and elegance"—these have a general relevance.* More precise is the comparison with certain instrumental timbres: "nothing comes so near, or rather imitates so much, an excellent voice, as a cornet pipe". That may have been agreed in the seventeenth century, but later the model changed from sweetness to flexibility and clarity. In the eighteenth century it was the stringed instruments that were reckoned to "shew their nearest Approach to the Perfection of the Human Voice".[5] There is a close interrelation between instrumental and vocal idioms in music of these periods and this needs to be

---

* In fact they are attributes that were applied satirically to the eighteenth-century Italian castrati, but they are nonetheless indicative of desirable qualities in singing.[4]

made apparent in performance. The characteristic sounds of a consort of viols—a clear yet homogeneous texture, delicate expression—must be sought after in many of Purcell's full anthems so that they become vocal equivalents to his Fantasias for viols; just as much as the violin's brilliance and vitality has to be captured in many solos in eighteenth-century verse anthems, with singers taking the role of ripieno players in a concerto grosso.

Whatever the manner of singing, standards vary little. A woman who sings "like a mouse in a cheese, scarce to be heard, and for the most part her teeth shut" is no uniquely eighteenth-century phenomenon. Nor is bad blend in choirs: "the Reason why so many grand Chorus's . . . are so miserably torn and shattered, is from the great Number of indifferent Performers, (commonly inter-mixed with fine Voices) who by their bawling and straining so overpower the others, the Delicacy of the good Performer is lost". Principles such as "a *good Ear*, is better than a fine *Voice*, and a *bad Ear*", and the precept "take pains to take no pains", are always relevant to singing and hardly need restating. Of the many pieces of advice that were offered, this from Burney will serve as a summary:

> *Good singing* requires a clear, sweet, even, and flexible voice, equally free from nasal and guttural defects. It is but by the tone of voice and articulation of words that a vocal performance is superior to an instrumental. If in swelling a note the voice trembles or varies its pitch, or the intonations are false, ignorance and science are equally offended; and if a perfect shake, good taste in embellishment, and a touching expression be wanting, the singer's reputation will make no great progress among true judges. If in rapid divisions the passages are not executed with neatness and articulation; or in adagios, if light and shade, pathos, and variety of colouring and expression are wanting, the singer may have merit of certain kinds, but is still distant from perfection.[6]

Preoccupation with stylistic accuracy can too easily allow the expression of the music to be neglected. "You will do well to

Remember . . . to *Play Loud,* and *Soft,* sometimes *Briskly,* and sometimes *Gently,* and *Smoothly,* here and there, as your *Fancy* will (no doubt) *Prompt you unto."*[7] This, written in 1676, is a useful reminder that modern presentations of seventeenth-century music do not have to be arid and dull; it need not be enlarged on here. But a few comments will not be out of place on the particular problems of performing services and anthems of our period.

The organ was used extensively in vocal pieces; it was even considered essential for those that ostensibly are complete in themselves. With an instrument tuned to mean-tone temperament there would have been fewer problems than is now the case where a well-tuned choir is often at loggerheads with a well-tempered organ. Yet in contrapuntal music by Purcell, and more so in that by Croft, the organ is necessary to bind the texture together and assist continuity as the lines progress from one part to another. Accompaniments in full anthems should be judiciously managed so as to interfere as little as possible with the chording and internal balance of the choir, not slavishly following the voice parts but rather discreetly and lightly reinforcing their argument, perhaps in one place emphasising the real bass, in another by octave transposition going above the treble. A thicker texture and block chords can then be reserved for special effect when demanded by the music.

It is legitimate practice to vary dynamics with skilful registration. Writing "of soft and lowd"—"this conduceth much to the delight of musick"—Roger North admitted that the organ could not so well "soften by degrees" as the voice, "but with a skillful hand and variety of stops, performes it tolerably".[8] Further contrast can be achieved by making good use of the different departments of the organ. Boyce (in the same place where he said verses should be sung less briskly than full passages) suggested that "where the music is alternately sung by the different Sides of the Choir, it is recommended to the Organist to play the Full Choir-Organ and to use the great organ only when all the Voices sing together".[9] Specific directions for organ registration appear in eighteenth-century music (accompanying the more widespread use of the organ) though there is little guidance in seventeenth-century manuscripts. There is, however, a Blow autograph of three anthems which is particularly explicit, and worth instancing here.[10]

Ex. 7

Blessed be the Lord my strength   Blow

It is in the realisation of a figured bass that the keyboard player has the greatest opportunity to exercise his taste and sensitivity. How he manages this can make or mar an otherwise fine anthem. Generally we must rely upon an editor's efforts (Vincent Novello's editions of eighteenth-century anthems provide little more than a filling in of the harmonies, but they bear a heavy responsibility for showing what not to do) or else such expert guidance as is given in Arnold's *The Art of Accom-*

G

paniment from a Thorough Bass. The nature of the realisation will depend on whether it is accompanying the full choir or solo voices, but in the latter case it is especially true that a melodic rather than chordal texture is the goal. "The Accompanyments in the Thorough-Bass should never be struck in Chords with the Right-Hand, as upon the Harpsichord." Avison was here speaking of the continuo in organ concertos, but the point has a wider application. A later writer was referring particularly to anthems when he disparaged a method "which is, when the *Bass* rests, and only the *Treble,* and *Contra-Tenor,* are going on, or, perhaps, the *Tenor* Part is singing with them, of keeping a continual Roaring upon the *Full-Organ,* by striking Chords, or, at least, *Octaves,* with the Left-hand, to every Note . . . nothing can be more absurd".[11]

These opening two bars of a solo movement in an anthem by Croft were published with only a figured-bass part for organ. A late-eighteenth-century owner of the volume in which this appeared pencilled in this upper part, and so indicated, if not the most perfect solution, at least the appropriate style.

Ex. 8
Lord, thou hast searched me out   Croft
Slow

In every case the style of the realisation should be as close as possible to that of the composer. A similar maxim, though harder to put into effect, should apply to such optional embellishments as ornaments. Fashions in this art changed as much between the seventeenth and eighteenth centuries as did styles of composition, and a decision on how many or how few ornaments are to be added can only be answered from a full knowledge of contemporary practice, a knowledge guided by innate artistic taste. "Let him alone, said Mr. Purcell; he will grace it more naturally than you, or I, can teach him."

But while the enrichment and decoration of both vocal and organ music was taken for granted as being an indispensable ingredient especially in eighteenth-century music, there is a danger of pursuing this with too much enthusiasm. Ornaments must not only be interpreted in contemporary style but also be suited to the nature of a particular piece.

A comment by Burney on some of Weldon's anthems reflects both changing tastes in gracing and, in our present view, a lack of due respect for period.

> But now, let who will execute them, they must appear feeble and old-fashioned, unless the embellishments of George the First's time are changed for those in present use.[12]

Perhaps a late-eighteenth-century scribe was thus encouraged to add ornaments profusely to his copy of Wise's anthem *The ways of Sion*, but though such treatment may have suited music of his day, it was quite out of keeping with the simplicity of expression in the original.[13]

Ex. 9
The ways of Sion   Wise

for these things I   weep,   I   weep, mine   eyes   runneth down____ with wa-ter.

for ·these__ things I___   weep,__   I   weep,__   mine   eyes   run - neth

down _____ with   wa - ter.

Finally it is worth noting that a singer adding graces requires greater sensitivity than an organist. For the latter ornaments have a rhythmical rather than an expressive function. In addition, whereas it is more difficult to notate vocal embellishments, the organist is disciplined by his instrument to be more precise. Many manuscripts and published organ pieces exist to indicate eighteenth-century practice and there is no need to do more here than give one further instance from the Blow autograph already referred to.

Ex. 10

Let the righteous be glad   Blow

BENJAMIN ROGERS, 1614 (Windsor)–1696 (Oxford).

Chorister and lay-clerk at St. George's, Windsor. Organist of Christ Church, Dublin (1639–1641). Returned to Windsor in 1641 and taught music there during the Commonwealth. Organist of Eton College at the Restoration. Lay-clerk at St. George's, Windsor (October 1662). Organist and master of the choristers at Magdalen College, Oxford (July 1664). Doctor of music, Oxford (July 1669). In January 1685 he was removed from his place at Magdalen College "on account of irregularities" but was granted an annuity of £30.

Rogers wrote some glees and instrumental compositions, including organ pieces, and much church music of a conservative nature. His services and anthems were for long in cathedral repertoires, perhaps on account of their harmless nature. The evening canticles in "A re" and of the "Sharp Service" have modern editions (O.U.P. and Novello respectively).

CHRISTOPHER GIBBONS, 1615 (London)–20th October, 1676 (London).

One of Orlando Gibbons's three sons. Chorister at the Chapel Royal. Organist of Winchester Cathedral (1638). After the Restoration he became an organist of the Chapel Royal, private organist to Charles II, and organist of Westminster Abbey. Doctor of music, Oxford (1663).

Christopher Gibbons wrote a large number of string fantasias and some anthems, and collaborated with Locke in writing the music for Shirley's masque *Cupid and Death* (1653).

HENRY COOKE, *c.* 1616 (?Lichfield)–1672 (Hampton Court).

His father was probably John Cooke, a bass from Lichfield, who was "pisteler" of the Chapel Royal in 1623. Chorister at the Chapel Royal. A lieutenant in the Civil War, later made captain. He taught music during the Commonwealth, and perhaps went to Italy. A bass in the Chapel Royal at the Restoration and master of the children. Assistant to the Corporation of Musicians (1662) and later marshal (1670), resigning his office in 1672 "by reason of sickness". Moved to Hampton Court in 1669.

Cooke composed music for Charles II's coronation, various songs, some thirty anthems, and contributed (along with Henry Lawes, Locke and others) to D'Avenant's production of *The Siege of Rhodes* (1656).[14]

Of the older generation of Chapel Royal musicians active at the Restoration, Cooke exercised the greatest influence, not only as a singer and choir-trainer whose example and discipline set the Chapel Royal music on a well-organised basis after the Interregnum, but also through his guidance of the younger composers. His choristers, Humfrey, Wise, Blow, Turner and Purcell would all have been open to assimilate Italian styles through the example of his own music. The anthems by Cooke that survive show him to be a forward-looking composer who, if he was not entirely successful in handling new idioms and resources, at least prepared the ground for his pupils.

Eleven of Cooke's anthems in his own hand, "fowle originalls" used as rough drafts for making fair copies for performance, have survived in a composite volume at the library of the Barber Institute.[15] One of these is a setting of the funeral sentences, three are for voices alone, and the remaining seven are with strings. It is these latter which are of the greatest interest (though primarily historical rather than musical) being apparently the earliest verse anthems with violins and continuo.

Behold, O God, our defender, written for the coronation of Charles II in 1661, is a forerunner of later instrumental anthems, both in its general lay-out and in certain idiomatic features. Scored for four-part (S.A.T.B.) verse and chorus and four-part strings, its various sections, apart from the opening symphony, are all limited in scope and undeveloped, yet they balance each other in compact proportions. The strings open the anthem with a twenty-three bar common-time "symphony", and introduce the final "alleluia" section with a shorter "prelude", interspersing between chorus and verse phrases two brief "ritornelli". In contrast to the antiphonal effects of this final section, the opening verse is more continuous, and its last phrase is taken up by the chorus. The over-all plan ((1) symphony-verse-chorus: (2) a combination of instruments, verses and chorus) and the disposition of the strings and voices form a blue-print for the Restoration anthem.

We will rejoice in thy salvation may have been written for a special occasion, a thanksgiving service for a victory, judging by its text and by the fact that it is scored for four-part strings (the remaining anthems are for three-part strings). In fact the strings are used only once outside the opening symphony (an extended triple movement in two sections), the rest of the anthem being set for four- and five-part verses, and a six-part chorus. This final movement is here given in full as foreshadowing those majestic sonorities that Blow was later to cultivate so effectively in his large-scale works.

One of the longer anthems, *Come let us pray, and God will hear*, shows Cooke trying, not very successfully, to create a

Ex. 11

We will rejoice in thy salvation

Cooke

larger unit. Although each half of the anthem is encompassed by a string prelude (à 3) and a chorus, the intervening sections are stretched beyond the limits justified by their musical content. The bass line lacks a sense of direction, standing merely as a support to the voice and hardly maintaining any independent significance, and the frequent and repetitive cadences (thirty in the tonic, twelve in the relative major) perpetually interrupt the flow, showing a preoccupation with this device for its own sake, regardless of the stop–go effect. A shorter anthem for similar forces, *We have sinned and committed iniquity*, suffers less

Ex. 12

We have sinned and committed iniquity   Cooke

from this defect, and the sections following on each other in quick succession never have a chance to pall. This anthem shows not only Cooke's use of the strings, the formal framework of two halves each preceded by an instrumental prelude, but also such characteristic features of the Restoration anthem as solos in semi-recitative (example 12) or in arioso style (example 13) and a chorus of simplicity and charm (example 14)—a model of the similar homophonic choruses that composers such as Wise and Turner wrote to conclude their anthems.

Ex. 13

Ex. 14

ALBERTUS BRYNE (Albert Bryan), *c.* 1621–?1668 (London).

Organist of St. Paul's Cathedral from *c.* 1638 until the Commonwealth, and immediately afterwards. Organist of Westminster Abbey from 1667 until succeeded by Blow in 1668.

Although a service in C and some anthems survive in manuscript, Bryne is known only for his service in G. Written in the traditional short service style, the morning canticles are dull; but the Magnificat and Nunc dimittis possess sufficient interest to have justified their continued use.

GEORGE JEFFREYS, died 1685.

It has been stated that Jeffreys was a member of the Chapel Royal before 1643, in which year he was appointed joint organist with John Wilson to Charles I at Oxford. After the siege of Oxford in 1646 Jeffreys became steward to Lord Hatton at Kirby Hall, Northants, and remained there until his death in 1685.

Apart from some early string fancies (*c.* 1629), music for plays and masques (1631), dialogues, Italian songs and a cantata, his compositions are all settings of sacred texts, both Latin and English. Jeffreys wrote thirty-five English anthems and sacred songs, over twice as many Latin motets and sacred songs, a morning and evening service, a Gloria and responses to the Commandments.

Jeffreys attracts attention as a mid-seventeenth-century English composer who quickly accepted the example of early Italian baroque composers, and as a writer of a considerable amount of sacred music who yet remained outside the establishment. Claims are now made for the importance of this previously neglected composer, whetting the appetite for further knowledge of his music.*

WILLIAM TUCKER, died 1679 (London).

A minor-canon and precentor of Westminster Abbey, a gentleman of the Chapel Royal, and a composer of some services and anthems. That as many as eleven of the latter were added to the Chapel Royal books between 1670 and 1676 might be due to his having been a copyist there.

MATTHEW LOCKE, 1622 (Exeter)–August, 1677 (London).

Chorister at Exeter Cathedral under Edward Gibbons (1638–1641). Visited the Low Countries in 1648. Composer in the

* Four pieces are now available in modern editions: a two-part sacred song, *Erit gloria Domini* (O.U.P.), an anthem for S.A.T.B. and organ, *He beheld the city*, and two Latin motets, *O Domine Deus* and *O Deus meus* (Novello). See also an article by Peter Aston on George Jeffreys in the *Musical Times*, July 1969, p. 772.

King's private music (1660), and a little later "composer for the violins". At an unknown date he also became organist in the Queen's Roman chapel at Somerset House.

Locke contributed music for various stage productions: Shirley's masque *Cupid and Death* (1653), D'Avenant's *Siege of Rhodes* (1656), Shadwell's version of *The Tempest* (1674), and the same author's *Psyche* (1675). His music "for the King's sagbutts and cornets" was performed during Charles II's progress from the Tower to Whitehall on the day before the coronation. Locke also wrote consort music, and some keyboard pieces were published in *Melothesia* (1673). His church music includes pieces for both English and Latin services: thirty anthems (six with instruments) and some sacred songs, twelve Latin motets and songs (six with instruments), six psalms, and a Kyrie and Creed in F. A setting of Magnificat and Nunc dimittis in D minor has been attributed to him.[16]

Locke also found time to become involved in two controversies which were recorded in 1666 and 1672. The first was written in answer to criticism of his setting of the responses to the Commandments and a Creed which had occasioned "confusion in the Service by its ill Performance". The singers had been caught out by Locke's original music, and he later admitted: "I have been noon of the fortunatest that way." ("Modern *Church Musick* Pre-accus'd, Censur'd, and Obstructed in its Performance before His *Majesty*, April 1, 1666. Vindicated by the Author Matt. Lock.") For the second controversy Locke wrote "Observations on an Essay" (1672) against T. Salmon, and produced a year later the sequel "The Present Practice of Musick Vindicated".

Locke is the most original of the senior generation of Restoration composers whose music had a widespread influence on his younger contemporaries, but which also, necessarily, shows signs of struggling to come to grips with new idioms while still bound to past conventions. His Anglican and Latin church music deserves to be better known than at present by one or two anthems. *Lord, let me know mine end* is in form

related to the verse anthems of the earlier part of the seventeenth
century, with each solo section completed with a chorus; but in
style it is forward-looking (*e.g.* the expressive treatment of the
two voices at the words "like as it were a moth fretting a
garment", and the free, open-ended counterpoint of the final
section). Another English anthem that has been published,
When the Son of Man, is more unusual in its form, and has
instruments (in the idiom of viols) in the solo passages, though
with no independent symphonies.

Locke was happiest when writing on a grand scale, and the
fourteen short male-voice anthems written for Rickmansworth
parish church (where Locke was organist for a time) can be
dismissed as quaint, often dull exercises. More successful is the
five-part *Turn thy face from my sins*. Its construction anticipates
the full anthems of Purcell (chorus–verse–chorus), while the

Ex. 15

Turn thy face from my sins   Locke

traditional idiom of the opening chorus links it with earlier writing. Locke's transitional position is often expressed in nervous-sounding harmonic progressions, shown here in a few bars from the verse section of this anthem, and in the instrumental prelude to *I will hear what the Lord*.

Ex. 16
I will hear what the Lord   Locke

The larger scale of *Not unto us, O Lord*, one piece that is known to have been in the Chapel Royal repertoire during the composer's lifetime, enables Locke to alternate, with good effect, eight-part choral writing with verses for counter-tenor, tenor and bass. A feature in many of Locke's cadences is their richness of sound, and the particularly sonorous conclusion to this anthem is worth noting.

Ex. 17

Not unto us, O Lord

Locke

It is not surprising to find so forward-looking a composer experimenting in his anthems with vocal and instrumental scoring. *I will hear what the Lord* (voices in six parts and instruments in three) and *O be joyful* (four-part voices, two violins, counter-tenor and bass viols) are interesting, but a little disjointed, showing that Locke had not gained the ability to hold the sections together that Humfrey later achieved. *The*

Ex. 18

Sing unto the Lord, all ye saints   Locke

Lord hear thee (five-part voices, four-part instruments) is more closely knit, and also well varied in its scoring for instruments, solo voices and chorus. But it is two big thanksgiving anthems that are Locke's finest achievement. In these, mastery of handling unusually large forces is matched by rich invention and musical interest. *Sing unto the Lord, all ye saints* is scored for four-part (S.A.T.B.) chorus, verse (A.T.B.B.) and a five-part instrumental accompaniment of strings, oboes and flutes. The instruments play an integrated part and are not confined to independent symphonies and ritornelli, combining, for instance, in the opening verse with the four voices to form a rich counterpoint. There is none of the scrappiness apparent in some anthems, and in the verse sections the voice parts expand in a natural and expressive way. The strength of some of the vocal lines and the chromatic touches are of a kind usually associated with Purcell (example 18).

On an even larger scale is *The King shall rejoice*, written to celebrate a victory over the Dutch in 1666. It opens and concludes with a tutti chorus for three four-part choirs, five-part strings and a consort of viols. In between, these resources are used in a variety of combinations with the voices in small groups or in effective antiphonal scoring. Even with two typical Restoration-style tripla sections, the work maintains a spaciousness and sense of drama. If there is any one anthem by Locke that deserves to be published, it is this.

Of the Latin music, four motets have instrumental accompaniment; but two of special charm are duets with continuo, published in Dering's *Cantica Sacra II* (1674): *Cantate Domino* and *O Domine Jesu Christe*. The latter is brief, written in a sensitively expressive style. *Cantate Domino* is more extensive, yet still retains a natural simplicity and ease of manner. They both demonstrate to what extent Locke had assimilated Italian idioms, and how he in turn provided a model for the younger Restoration composers. These two extracts are the opening bars of *Cantate Domino*, and of the second part of a companion piece, *Omnes Gentes.*

Ex. 19

Cantate Domino

Locke

Ex. 20

Omnes Gentes

Locke

ROBERT CREIGHTON, *c.* 1639 (Cambridge)–17th February, 1734 (Wells).

Precentor of Wells Cathedral from 1674 until his death.

His music that at one time enjoyed some vogue is monotonously correct and inoffensive.

PELHAM HUMFREY, 1647–14th July, 1674 (Windsor).

A chorister at the Chapel Royal (1660–1664). Five of his anthems were included in the second edition of Clifford's *Divine Services and Anthems* (1664). From 1664 to 1666 he was granted a total of £450 from the Secret Service money "to defray the charge of his journey into France and Italy". He was back in England by October 1667. "Musician for the Lute in the Royal Band" (1666), gentleman of the Chapel Royal (1667), master of the children in succession to Cooke, and composer in ordinary for the violins (1672).

During this short life he wrote music for the stage, three odes, songs, a service and several anthems, sixteen of the seventeen that have survived in various manuscripts having string symphonies.

It would be likely that Cooke, who favoured an advanced style in his church music, recommended his brightest pupil amongst the first set of choristers at the Restoration to study abroad. If so, Cooke could hardly have been disappointed. Humfrey soon developed a novel manner of writing, and gained such repute that at the age of twenty-five he was awarded his father-in-law's responsible post as master of the children.*

Pelham Humfrey's church music was, however, too advanced

---

* It appears that Humfrey had difficulty in maintaining the respect and discipline gained by Cooke. He was, after all, only twenty-five, and earlier, indiscreet criticism of the Master of the Music, Grabu, could not have helped. One of three orders made in the summer of 1672 stipulated: "Whereas his Majesty is displeased that the violins neglect their duty in attending in his Chappell Royall, it is ordered that if any of the violins shall neglect to attend, either to practise or wayte in the Chappell, whensoever they have received notice from Mr. [Thomas] Purcell or Mr. Humphryes, that for such fault they shall be suspended their places."[17]

for some tastes. Even Pepys at first took exception to a
particular anthem:

> . . . and so I to chapel . . . and heard a fine anthem, made by
> Pelham (who is come over) in France, of which there was great
> expectation, and indeed is a very good piece of musique, but still
> I cannot call the Anthem anything but instrumental musique with
> the voice, for nothing is made of the words at all.

A fortnight later Pepys invited Pelham Humfrey to his home.
Though he might by then grudgingly have admired his music,
he was far from impressed by his manner:

> . . . an absolute Monsieur, as full of form, and confidence, and
> vanity, and disparages everything, and everybody's skill but his
> own. The truth is, every body says he is very able, but to hear
> how he laughs at all the King's musick here, as Blagrave and others,
> that they cannot keep time or tune, nor understand anything; and
> that Grabus, the Frenchman, the King's master of the musick, how
> he understands nothing, nor can play on any instrument, and so
> cannot compose, and that he will give him a lift out of his place;
> and that he and the King are might great! and that he hath already
> spoke to the King of Grabus would make a man piss.[18]

Pepys did not take kindly to this upstart teenager. But this
had no relevance to the crucial influence that Humfrey's music
was to have on the development of the English anthem.
Adding to the innovations of Cooke the expertise he had gained
abroad, Humfrey established in his anthems a model for Blow
and Purcell of the use of strings, principles of construction, and
the expressive treatment of voices. The use in verse anthems of
violins and a figured bass was an innovation that Humfrey
most successfully exploited. Whereas previously the organ or
viols had with the voices been part of an integrated texture,
Humfrey gave the strings both independent significance and
also an essential formal role. His symphonies are often compact
miniatures of great beauty, but their placing within an anthem

(and more particularly the linking ritornelli) provides a scaffolding for the whole structure. Humfrey thus relieved himself of the necessity of securing formal unity by means of a continuously evolving contrapuntal texture, and was free to explore to the full the expressive possibilities of the words in settings for solo voices (singly or in combination) over an independent bass. Well-placed cadences and modulations punctuated these paragraphs. As individual and mature voices could best interpret the text, either in melodic phrases or recitative-type passages, the full choir with trebles was used sparingly, generally only at the end of the main periods.

Many of Humfrey's anthems possess a clear pattern: symphony (common-time, followed in some anthems by a triple-time section)—verses (sometimes with interlinking ritornelli)—short chorus. The longer anthems have a second half of similar design. The principle behind this of contrasted textures in balanced porportions, linked by the repetition of certain passages and united by a purposeful use of tonality, was adopted by the other Restoration composers. If it seems that their instrumental anthems occasionally peter out or end inconclusively, this was no conscious fault of the composers. The final "hallelujah" was never intended to have the status of the last movement of a Romantic symphony, and the idea of an ultimate climax was foreign to late-seventeenth-century writers. They chose, like the Biblical ruler of the feast, to offer the best wine at the beginning.

Stylistic traits in Humfrey's anthems are not as novel as they may seem at first sight. Senior composers such as the Lawes brothers, Child, Porter and Locke had already explored current Italian methods and the monodic style. Humfrey added his own distinctive idiom and delivered it in a recognisably French accent. In fact his thorough-going acceptance of continental influences made it all the easier for Purcell to do likewise naturally and unselfconsciously, at the same time using the best of native traditions.

One readily accessible anthem by Humfrey, *O Lord my God*,

why hast thou forsaken me, displays many typical features: preoccupation with a contrite text (from Psalm 22), a minor tonality, string writing of nice intensity, expressive lines for men's solo voices (A.T.B.) that capture the spirit of the words, succinct choruses, and balanced proportions. Although this work can be divided into ten sections, they need not cause any disunity, progressing as they do without break, linked thematically and by a consistently maintained mood. The tonic key predominates but there is sufficient modulation for contrast and although the pulse varies little, the interplay of common and triple-time measures prevents tediousness. The repetition of the string and chorus sections anchors the whole work, and enables the solo passages each to be treated in a distinctive and diverse manner.

Like as the hart has many similarities with *O Lord my God*, and also achieves a variety of texture within a unified approach to the temper of the text. *Thou art my King, O God* gains its cohesion in a more obvious way, by the repetition in rondo fashion of various sections: the opening symphony at the end of the first half, a string ritornello three times between verses, the opening quartet before the final chorus. This rondo treatment is used even more strikingly in *Rejoice in the Lord, O ye righteous* (an unusual excursion into continuous gaiety and ebullience) where the return of the opening quartet for men's voices and string ritornello after the succeeding two sections drives the anthem forward with cheerful momentum.

In both these last two instances the ritornelli fulfil a vital formal function. In one anthem where strings are not used, *Have mercy upon me, O God*, the balance is maintained by the disposition of the voices in ensemble and solo passages, the two choruses and the two trios having a similar place in the structure as symphonies and ritornelli. A complete extract of one of the solos will serve to demonstrate the smoothness of idiom acquired by Humfrey in arioso sections: an elegant melody divided into well-proportioned phrases which are marked by various cadences and modulations. The bass is an

Ex. 21

Have mercy upon me, O God.   Humfrey

equal partner but it has sufficient rhythmical independence to
prevent the section from being too four-square.

Three somewhat longer anthems with strings are undeserving

Ex. 22

By the waters of Babylon   Humfrey

of their present oblivion—none of them have been printed. Of these, *O praise the Lord, O give thanks unto the Lord* and *By the waters of Babylon*, the latter is the most effective. The nature of its text seems to suit Humfrey's manner, but there are signs in the music that this could be one of his later anthems. At one place the chorus is used with dramatic effect, and the alternating solo trio has lost some of the French polish of other anthems, admittedly encouraged by the words "How shall we sing the Lord's song in a strange land?" (example 22.)

The strings play an even more integrated part than usual (the opening bass solo is accompanied by a violin obbligato); and the solo voices are used imaginatively, as in the following introduction to a three-part verse where the lower range of the tenor is contrasted with the bass in his higher register. The final chorus, taking up an expressive motif from the preceding verse, is long enough to seal the work convincingly and yet, by its comparative restraint, never exceeds the scale of the whole anthem.

O give thanks unto the Lord may well have been written for a special occasion (the words from Psalm 118 are associated with the Easter festival). The opening symphony has about it the breadth of some by Purcell, and the chorus has a more significant and extensive role than usual, in places being used antiphonally with the verse singers and the strings. The brighter arrangement of solos for two counter-tenors and tenor (in place of counter-tenor, tenor and bass) and the more extrovert character of the music also reveal a festive origin for the anthem.

A short setting of the collect for the feast of the Circumcision, *Almighty God, who madest thy blessed Son* is unusual in that it has verses for two trebles as well as counter-tenor and bass. This has moments of delicate beauty and is both compact and well-proportioned: symphony-verse-symphony-verse-short chorus.

The service in E minor also has verse sections for trebles. This *Service in E la mi*, a complete setting of the morning and evening canticles (Te Deum, Jubilate, Kyrie, Credo, Sanctus,

Ex. 23

By the waters of Babylon   Humfrey

Gloria, Magnificat and Nunc dimittis) has much in common
with other early-Restoration settings such as those by Wise and
Purcell. But Humfrey's, in some respects, is the most interesting. The texture of the verse passages are varied (S.A.T.–S.S.T.–
A.A.T.B. in the Magnificat) and never overrule the surround-
ing full-choir sections. Being intended for repertoire use it is as
terse as the traditional "short" service, and largely of a homophonic character. Yet this is given a sense of direction in the
progression through different keys, and relieved by brief, well-

placed "points". The part writing is rarely dull, even though, as
in the following bars from the Nunc dimittis Gloria, it can be
a little over-fanciful. But the music has a subtle unity, and it is
surprising that at least the evening canticles have not found an
established place in cathedral repertoires.

Ex. 24.

Nunc dimittis in E minor   Humfrey

HENRY ALDRICH, 1648 (London)–14th December, 1710 (Oxford).
Student at Christ Church, Oxford. Canon of the cathedral
(1681) and dean (1689). He collected many music manuscripts
which now form a valuable part of the Christ Church library.
A man of many abilities—scholar, antiquarian and architect,
theologian and also musician.[19] His skill in this latter respect
found its main outlet in adapting and arranging the works of
earlier composers, but his own compositions show a little
originality. His complete service in G is, within its limitations,
a successful exercise in the traditional short service style; and
there is a setting of some interest, in a more advanced idiom, of
the evening canticles in E minor.

Aldrich's main influence on church music lay in his cultured
and active patronage. As Henry Playford respectfully put it in
his dedication to the Dean of his second book of *Harmonia
Sacra* (1693):

In Addresses of this kind, Men are usually so far from suiting the
Subject of their Treatises to the Qualifications of the Person they
Apply to, that we may shortly expect to see *Musick* Dedicated to
the Deaf, as well as *Poetry* to Aldermen, and *Prayer-Books* to

Atheists; and tho generally it is a difficult Matter to find a *Worthy Patron* for any One of these Excellencies, yet we happily find them all lodg'd in your self.

MICHAEL WISE, *c.* 1648 (probably at Salisbury)–24th August, 1687.

One of the first choristers at the Chapel Royal under Cooke. He was a lay-clerk at St. George's Chapel, Windsor, in 1666, and became organist and master of the choristers of Salisbury Cathedral in 1668. Gentleman of the Chapel Royal (6th January, 1676) where he was described as a "counter-tenor from Salisbury". Suspended at the time of the coronation in 1685. Almoner and master of the choristers of St. Paul's Cathedral (27th January, 1687). He died later in the same year (in lurid circumstances, according to one tradition). He composed at least thirty-six anthems and a number of services.

Wise, for all his acceptance of the verse anthem form of the Restoration composers, was in many ways a conservative composer. Even in anthems such as *Blessed is he that considereth* or *By the waters of Babylon* he retains the older pattern of a sequence of ensemble verse passages followed by choruses. Perhaps, caught between a basic sympathy for traditional idioms as developed through the music of Lawes and Child and a desire to accommodate the innovations of his time, he fell between two stools. He achieves moments of fine inspiration, but these are often surrounded by much dull music. Whether of choice or necessity, his vocal writing is generally of no great difficulty—possibly one reason why his music enjoyed such popularity in the eighteenth century (Boyce published as many as six anthems by Wise). This often seems to limit the effectiveness of his music, although at times it results in moments of simple expressiveness. An anthem such as *Thou, O God, art praised in Sion* proceeds monotonously, albeit briskly, in triple time throughout with writing of no originality. Yet in *The Lord is my shepherd* such ingenuousness can approach a charming innocency, emphasised by the scoring for treble duet.

With the encouragement of melancholy texts and a minor key Wise writes passages of rare beauty, all the more effective for the simplicity of the idiom. In *How are the mighty fallen* (much altered by Aldrich and retitled *Thy beauty O Israel*) a treble solo leads into this final trio where the impact of the words is conveyed with the utmost economy (example 26).

The chorus sections in Wise's anthems are, as in those of his contemporaries, brief. The verses, generally, are not very expansive either, and Wise has a preference for duets and trios rather than solos. Yet for all the peremptoriness of some

Ex. 26

How are the mighty fallen   Wise

anthems, he often achieves a fine balance and proportion between sections. In the two halves of *Open me the gates of righteousness*, the first, in G minor (consisting of a trio for two trebles and bass, a treble solo and a short chorus) is matched by the second part in G major (a trio in triple time leading into common time, and into the final chorus). In the better-known *Awake; put on thy strength*, key contrasts and delicate changes of mood are united within a consistent idiom and the well-placed repetition of some of the material. The chorus, though with little more to sing than "hallelujah", has an integrated part to play.

A feature in Wise's anthems is the absence of passages for strings. It is feasible that in some cases he wrote orchestral

Ex. 27 ·

Blessed is the man that hath not walked   Wise

symphonies and ritornelli, and that the surviving manuscripts replaced these with a few bars for continuo alone. One of the eleven anthems that are known to have been used at the Chapel Royal,[20] *O praise God in his holiness*, has a slender trace of this in the opening two bars of the organ part which, marked "Symphony", could possibly represent a reduced prelude for strings.

Perhaps Wise did not appreciate the talents of his fellow gentlemen of the Chapel Royal, but to an exceptional degree amongst the Restoration composers he scored his solos for treble voices. One anthem, "The prodigall" (*I will arise*), is set exclusively for treble verses with a solo, duet and trio in sequence. But even when adult voices are used, the trebles often steal the limelight, as in the echo effects of the duet ("And the voice said, cry") in *Prepare ye the way of the Lord*. *Blessed is the man that hath not walked* is unusually scored for the lower voices (tenor and two basses), but in this way, together with a three-flat key, Wise is searching for a sombre effect. The central verse section of this anthem has particularly appropriate word-setting (example 27).

It is, however, Wise's best known anthem, *The ways of Sion do mourn*, that most satisfyingly captures sensitivity of expression and the spirit of the text.* This is due not merely to the effective use of bass and treble soloists but also to the masterly way the plaintive character is sustained through long periods with subtle variations in mood and scoring. As in many anthems by Humfrey, only the most sensitive and skilful performance, restrained and withdrawn, can realise the passionate intensity of this piece.

JOHN BLOW, February, 1649 (Newark)—1st October, 1708 (London).

A chorister at the restored Chapel Royal under Cooke until

---

* Probably a work of Wise's later years, it was not amongst those anthems of his that were transcribed into the Chapel Royal books between 1670 and 1676.

1664. Three of his anthems were included in the second edition of Clifford's *Divine Services and Anthems* (1664). Studied under Christopher Gibbons, probably John Hingston, as well as Cooke. Organist of Westminster Abbey in succession to Bryne (Michaelmas, 1668–1679). "Musician for the virginals" in the King's music (January, 1669). Gentleman of the Chapel Royal (March, 1674). Master of the children of the Chapel Royal (July, 1674–1708). He also succeeded Humfrey as composer for voices in the King's private music and, at an unknown date, was later one of the three organists of the Chapel Royal (possibly succeeding Christopher Gibbons in 1676). The Dean and Chapter of Canterbury conferred on him the degree of doctor of music in December, 1677. Almoner and master of the choristers of St. Paul's Cathedral (September, 1687). Later, in 1703, this post at St. Paul's was granted to his ex-pupil Jeremiah Clarke (who had been organist there since 1699). He returned to Westminster Abbey as organist again in 1695, after Purcell's death. Appointed to a newly created post of composer for the Chapel Royal (1699). Having attained a position of influence in London's three leading choirs, he was apparently content, as no subsequent appointments have been recorded. Blow left £100 to his housekeeper, £50 each to his sister and niece and the residue to his three surviving daughters. He had invested considerably in property during his life: at his death he held leases in three messuages in Great Sanctuary, two in Orchard Street, and three in Duck Lane, all in the City of Westminster, and a copyhold estate at Hampton Town.

Blow composed twenty-four odes for various occasions, an important masque (*Venus and Adonis*), some instrumental music including a fine corpus of organ pieces, various vocal chamber music, and a great quantity of church music—ninety-six anthems (at least twenty-eight with orchestral symphonies), eleven Latin motets, nine complete services and a number of other canticle settings.[21]

When Blow in 1700 dedicated his collection of secular vocal

H

music, *Amphion Anglicus*, to the Princess Anne he stated that he was preparing a similar volume of his sacred pieces:

> To those, in truth, I have even more especially consecrated the Thoughts of my whole Life. . . . With them I began my first Youthful Raptures in this Art: With them, I hope calmly and comfortably to finish my days.

Church music remained for Blow throughout his life a primary interest, an interest that was not diverted (as in Purcell's case) to other spheres. Although Blow did not live to fulfil his plans to publish his sacred pieces, he left behind him a large number of manuscript services and anthems which in bulk alone outstrip the work of any of his contemporaries in this field. Considering the importance that Blow himself attached to his church music, it has received scant recognition. In fact, were it not for the tireless research of Watkins Shaw,* we might still be regarding Blow as no more than a quaint contemporary of Purcell.

A true evaluation has been hindered by the placing of these two composers in the same stable. It is hardly fair to Blow to compare his music on similar terms with that of Purcell, and it can too easily lead to an underestimation of the former's significance. Blow's music may be inferior, but it certainly forms an important contribution to English church music in the latter part of the seventeenth century. Unfortunately, it has also been made a scapegoat for what has been viewed as the follies and foibles of its period. To eighteenth-century taste the music of the Restoration composers was embarrassing in its waywardness and lack of polish. What was then considered rude now exercises a certain fascination. But whether Blow's "crudities" were deliberate or due to incompetence,† they are

---

* See this writer's article, "John Blow's Anthems" (*Music and Letters*, XIX, p. 429) and "The Autographs of John Blow" (*The Music Review*, XXV, p. 85). *Musica Britanica* has devoted one volume (1953) to Blow's coronation anthems and three instrumental anthems.

† In a discussion of two Blow manuscripts on music theory Watkins Shaw deduced that Blow was not particularly systematic, and that he was "a little scornful of theoretical niceties and skill".[22]

a feature of his writing and must not be allowed to divert us from an overall view of his music. It has, for instance, been considered that on account of his striking harmony, Blow was a bold innovator, but Watkins Shaw has convincingly argued that, on the contrary, he was a traditional composer who chose deliberately to disregard many of the stylistic developments in late-seventeenth-century music.

Blow's position in the musical life of his day was unrivalled, and there is a need now for a fresh investigation of his music in order to discover the justification for such eminent status.

The earliest dated composition (1670) is the verse anthem *O Lord I have sinned*. Its diminished intervals and chromatic phrases add expressive touches characteristic of the period, but in its general approach and treatment of the verse passages it is much more traditional than the music of many of Blow's contemporaries. An early full anthem, *Save me O God*, is similarly expressive and more closely woven with the verses playing a subsidiary part to the chorus, anticipating the three-section form (chorus–verse–chorus) of the eight-part *God is our hope* and *O Lord God of my salvation*. Of these two, the latter (1680/2) is less traditional in idiom, evolving the kind of thick sonorities that Purcell enjoyed writing so much at this time. But in Blow's case the search for this richness of sound seems to take precedence over the invention of melodic lines that are both interesting and inevitable. To use a scientific analogy, the attempt to create violent nuclear collisions results in the fundamental particles being broken open into their constituent quarks.

A later full anthem, *My God, my God, look upon me* (1697), is less frenetic. Although it may lack a certain spontaneity, it possesses a symmetry outlining the dramatic scope of the piece. The opening entries are not only repeated at the end, but also serve to introduce the middle two sections leading up to a climax with the choir singing in block chords. This symmetry is apparent on a smaller scale in the short coronation anthem *Let thy hand be strengthened* where the homophonic style is given a

new look by the balancing of phrases each neatly rounded off
with their cadences in various keys. It is not surprising then to
find that in the larger instrumental anthems Blow displays a
rare mastery of form, resulting in these being amongst his finest
sacred compositions. Even an early anthem like *O sing unto the
Lord a new song*, written before 1673, handles the various forces
(three-part strings, four-part verses and eight-part chorus) in

Ex. 28

O sing unto the Lord a new song   Blow

such a skilful way that the diverse material never disintegrates into meaningless fragments. Its five overlapping sections consist of a symphony, tenor solo with a four-part chorus, four-part verse with chorus, bass solo with four-part verse, four-part verse with a splendid extended eight-part chorus (and strings) setting of the Gloria. Example 28 above demonstrates typical texture in a verse section, and the equally characteristic fluidity of harmony and rhythm.

I said in the cutting off of my days adopts the outline of Humfrey's anthems: symphony (with the opening solo placed within it), verses with ritornelli, chorus; then a second part beginning with a triple-time symphony, solo recitative, verse and repeat of the chorus. Even one of the less thrilling anthems, *And I heard a great voice*, despite its length maintains an inner unity, unfolding through the various sections of the text naturally, and without the scrappiness of some early Restoration anthems. Its form, in modern terms, could be categorised as A–B–A varied–C (using material from A). *Lord, who shall dwell in thy tabernacle*, interestingly scored for four-part strings, two flutes and bass flute, begins with an impressive symphony and ends with a short chorus. The intervening succession of verses and ritornelli introduce one by one the virtues named in the text (Psalm 15). The effect is cumulative as the sections progressively decrease in length, capped finally by a change to D major after the predominant D minor. A greater variety of mood is found in *Blessed is the man that hath not walked* (in C) where a vigorous opening symphony containing a three-part verse leads into a gentler four-part verse. A more lively section with the chorus, strings and verse singers in antiphonal groups is conclusively finished with a jubilant "hallelujah" on a ground bass. The opening counter-tenor solo will serve to illustrate the flowing melodic lines that Blow was capable of writing (example 29).

By far the finest published instrumental anthem is one written for the cornonation of King James II in 1685, *God spake sometime in visions*, for four-part strings, verses and chorus

Ex. 29

Blessed is the man that hath not walked   Blow

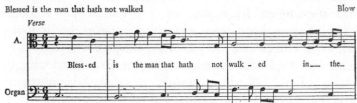

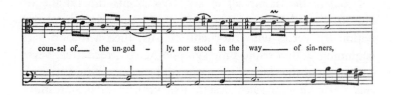

(S.S.A.A.T.B.B.B.). Not only is this a masterpiece of construction with its command of varied material and textures over a large span, but it also reveals Blow's imaginative powers at their peak.

In contrast to this is a series of short full anthems (some have been published by O.U.P.). Despite the fact that most of these contain verse ensembles their style is archaic, as though they were deliberately intended to imitate and supplement such useful repertoire pieces as Richard Farrant's *Hide not thou thy face*. Neat and concise, with brief points contrasting with chordal phrases, they are not without interest, although the writing in places can be viewed as illustrating either Blow's originality or incompetence. Fair examples of the general character of this series can be found in *Bow down thine ear*, *In the time of trouble*, and *My days are gone like a shadow*.

Comparable with these short anthems are the four Short Services, settings of the morning and evening canticles in D minor, G minor, A minor and F major. A successful attempt to follow the model (and idiom) of the Elizabethan and early-Stuart short service, they have a unique place in late-seventeenth-century canticle settings. More than any of his contemporaries Blow devoted a considerable amount of attention to this aspect of liturgical music, and with his sympathy for traditional styles was well equipped to meet its demands. Yet, however conservative his writing may be in this genre, he frequently adds distinctive touches and an almost obstinate individuality, as in the following passage from the G major setting, a service nearly as comprehensive as Purcell's later one in B flat. In fact he maintains independent interest in all the parts even when the texture is homophonic, with the verse passages providing contrast in scoring rather than in idiom. Whether or not it was Blow who set the fashion for canonic Glorias he frequently used this device not only with cunning but also to good musical effect. Another idea he adopted was the use of a "motto" theme to introduce different canticles within the same series.

Ex. 30

Magnificat in G

Blow

Eleven Latin motets for solo voices are early pieces and, with the brilliant exception of the five-part *Salvator mundi*, worth little attention. The other five-part work, *Gloria Patri qui creavit nos*, can bear no comparison to this supremely expressive motet, but there is a duet over a ground bass, *Paratum cor meus Deus*, which could make a pleasing and useful anthem for trebles.

DANIEL ROSEINGRAVE, *c.* 1650–May, 1727 (Dublin).

Said to have been a chorister at the Chapel Royal. Organist of Gloucester Cathedral (1679–1681), Winchester (1682-1692), Salisbury (1692–1698). Organist and vicar-choral of St. Patrick's Cathedral, Dublin, and organist and stipendiary of Christ Church, Dublin (1698); he remained at the former cathedral until 1719, and at the latter until his death in 1727.

Daniel's youngest son, Ralph Roseingrave (*c.* 1695–1747) succeeded him at both cathedrals in Dublin, where (at Christ Church) two services and eight anthems by him are preserved.

Both Burney and Hawkins spoke well of Daniel Roseingrave as a composer, but little of his church music now survives (two anthems, *Lord, thou art become gracious* and *Haste thee, O Lord,* are at Oxford in the libraries of Christ Church and the Bodleian respectively). *Lord, thou art become gracious* deserves occasional performance. A five-part verse anthem comparable with many by Blow, it displays both an original style (*e.g.* the chromatic twists in the example below, of a sort so relished by Daniel's second son, Thomas) and a mastery of form. The opening five-part verse in D minor is followed by a short chorus, a bass solo

Ex. 31

Lord, thou art become gracious   Roseingrave

leads into an expressive solo quartet, and finally a more extensive and vigorous treble solo, with a concluding chorus, brings the anthem to the tonic major and a confident finish.

THOMAS TUDWAY, *c*. 1650–23rd November, 1726 (Cambridge). Chorister at the Chapel Royal in or soon after 1660. Organist of King's College, Cambridge (1670) and master of the choristers (1679–1680). Also organist of Pembroke College. In 1705 he was made professor of music at Cambridge and gained his doctorate. From 1714 to 1720 he was at work on the six-volume collection of cathedral music for Robert, Lord Harley, later Earl of Oxford, which includes an evening service, eighteen anthems and a Latin motet by Tudway. This did not succeed in popularising his church music, and Boyce would seem to have shown some discernment in not adding any of Tudway's pieces to his collection.

Tudway's six manuscript volumes (British Museum, Harley MSS 7337–42) are both of great importance for the music they contain (from the time of the Reformation to Tudway's own day) and also of considerable interest on account of the introductions he wrote to certain volumes. That to the first volume merely states his aim of "rescuing from the dust, and oblivion, our Ancient Compositions of church Musick; at this time so much mistaken, and despised". The second is an essay on the state of church music following the Restoration. The third is brief and of no particular interest. The fourth promotes the suitability of the style of earlier music, as against more modern secular idioms, for performance in church. The fifth introduces the contents of the last two volumes, all by composers contemporary with Tudway. And the final volume relates a history of the music of antiquity and the development of church music in relatively recent times to, in Tudway's view, its decadence in his own day. He bemoans the fact that church music is "so little regarded in an Age when music is come to such a height of improvement", and also that "when there was never so learned a Clergy, nor learning at so great a hight, Religion itself should

H*

be so boldly attacked, and orthodoxy, in belief, and worship, so impudently repugn'd".

WILLIAM TURNER, 1651 (Oxford)–13th January, 1740 (London).

Chorister at Christ Church Oxford, under Edward Lowe, and later at the Chapel Royal. A counter-tenor as well as a composer, he sang in the choirs of Lincoln Cathedral, the Chapel Royal (1669), St. Paul's Cathedral and Westminster Abbey. Doctor of music, Cambridge (1696).

Turner wrote a number of odes and occasional pieces including St. Cecilia odes for 1685 and 1697, a birthday ode for Princess Anne (1698), and a coronation anthem for Queen Anne, *The Queen shall rejoice* (1702). He also wrote many songs, some anthems and two services.

Boyce included in his collection only one anthem by Turner whose slender claim to fame as a composer has rested on the fact that he collaborated with his fellow choristers Humfrey and Blow in writing the "Club Anthem". Turner was active in church music throughout his long life, but his anthems (many with strings) are now accessible only in manuscript collections. The controlled pathos of one that has been published, *Lord, thou hast been our refuge* (probably written shortly after he became a gentleman of the Chapel Royal in 1669), shows Turner to be deserving of more attention than he has yet received. Admittedly his music shows no great gift for melody, and often he failed to sustain the interest right through a piece, yet there are a number of anthems which evince a sure grasp of form and, in the string symphonies especially, a lively rhythmic sense. In fact the string passages often hold the greatest interest, and this particular instance from *Hold not thy tongue, O God* compares not unfavourably with Purcell's writing.

In common with his contemporaries, Turner used the full choir sparingly. In his choruses traditional idioms are apparent, and the conclusion, for instance, of the early anthem *Lord, what is man* shows that, for all the novelty of their writing for solo voices and for strings, the Restoration composers did not lose

Ex. 32

Hold not thy tongue, O God   Turner

touch with their predecessors. But, as might be expected from a composer who lived well into the eighteenth century, Turner was far from being retrogressive, as can be demonstrated by these opening bars of the symphony to *God sheweth me his goodness*, and by the bass ostinato accompaniment to a counter-tenor solo in *O praise the Lord* (examples 33 and 34).

Behold now praise the Lord is an unusual anthem in that it is constructed on a ground bass throughout. By this means it achieves both unity and a sure sense of progression to the final

Ex. 33

God sheweth me his goodness   Turner

Ex. 34

O praise the Lord   Turner

cadence. The ground is stated twice in the opening string symphony (in four parts), and continues through the following verse for counter-tenor and tenor with violin obbligato, a string ritornello, and a further verse for counter-tenor and two tenors. At this stage the ground flows into a triple-measure string ritornello before the final chorus, a note by note setting (though in an imitative style) of the Gloria.

HENRY HALL, *c*. 1655–30th March, 1707 (Hereford).

Chorister at the Chapel Royal under Cooke. Organist of Exeter Cathedral (1674–1677), vicar-choral of Hereford Cathedral (1679) and organist there from 1688. He was succeeded at Hereford by his son, also Henry. Various canticle settings and five anthems were included by Tudway in his manuscript collection.

HENRY PURCELL, 1659 (London)–21st November, 1695 (London).
Chorister at the Chapel Royal under Cooke and later
Humfrey. Assistant to John Hingston, keeper of the King's
instruments (1673). Studied under Blow (1674) and became
organ tuner at Westminster Abbey. Composer in ordinary for
the violins (1677), organist of Westminster Abbey (1679), one
of the organists of the Chapel Royal (1682), organ maker and
keeper to the King in succession to John Hingston (1683),
member of the King's private music (1685). Died in London in
1695 and was buried in Westminster Abbey.

Purcell wrote a considerable amount of music for the stage,
many odes and welcome songs, vocal chamber music, instrumental pieces (including fantasias for viols and two sets of trio
sonatas for violins), seventy-one anthems (twenty-six with
strings), one complete service, one evening service (in G minor)
and one morning service with orchestral accompaniment.[23]

Although only a portion of Purcell's church music is at all
widely known, his whole output in this sphere is readily
accessible and has been duly assessed. The following chronological survey need only sketch in the outlines and encourage
the reader to make his own study of the music.

The most outstanding feature of Purcell's church music
(when it is realised that most of it was written within a single
decade) is not so much its quantity as its wide range in style and
form. It is understandable that the quality should be variable
when many anthems must have been written under pressure to
fulfil an immediate demand, but it is harder to see why the bulk
of his earlier anthems should often display a sureness of touch
which contrasts markedly with the emptiness of some of those
few composed in the last years of his life when he was writing
his finest music in other fields. The early anthems may not all
be of an equal standard, but the effort involved in forging a
distinctive style would seem to be as much to their benefit as a
too-ready facility in this style, once achieved, was to the detri-
ment of the later church music. The vocal pyrotechnics of the
later solo anthems, however effective originally, seem now very

conventional in comparison with the solo ensembles in the earlier verse anthems. The full, instrumental, and verse anthems composed in the last years of Charles II's reign possess a rugged individuality, after which the rough edges become worn away in a smoother, innocuous idiom.

Purcell, being educated in the Chapel Royal, could not have been better placed to assimilate the traditions of English cathedral music and to benefit from the experience gained by his seniors in adopting Italian and French influences. Naturally his indebtedness to their example is apparent in the earliest anthems, as is evident in the solo trios and the short final chorus of *Lord who can tell. I will love thee, O Lord* is in the form of the early Restoration anthem (a short chorus following the solos at the end of the first half, repeated at the conclusion of the whole work) and possesses close stylistic affinities with the music of other Restoration composers. The chorus is similar to many by Turner and Wise, and Blow could have been the model for a triple-time bass solo which begins with the following phrase, as could Humfrey for the recitative-like solo over a static bass which opens the second half.

Ex. 35
I will love thee, O Lord   Purcell

Locke's influence, too, is apparent in the vigorous opening tenor duet of *Let God arise*. *Out of the deep* begins to show Purcell finding his own independence. In the usual two halves, but the relation between the verses and choruses, and the individuality of each part, show it to be developing beyond Humfrey's example. A noticeable difference is the bass solo at the beginning of the second half which, instead of a recitative, is here an arioso on a two-bar ground bass.*

It has been conjectured that this anthem was composed in the year 1680. The large number of anthems that appeared in the years immediately following contain Purcell's greatest achievement in church music. Such a diversity as these represent can only be classified by whether or not they include parts for strings. The solo ensembles in verse anthems with organ such as *Let mine eyes run down*, or *Save me, O God* and *Hear me, O Lord, and that soon* are not far different from some chorus passages in the full anthems, and these in their turn generally included verses. The splendid eight-part *Blow up the trumpet in Sion*, although it has a sequence of three verses each followed by chorus sections, falls into neither of the accepted verse or full categories. In its more dissonant passages each vocal line

* A favourite device of Purcell's which, however, he only used in three other English anthems: *In thee, O Lord, do I put my trust; Awake, put on thy strength;* and *O sing unto the Lord.*

Ex. 36

Blow up the trumpet in Sion

Purcell

shows an obstinate disregard for its partners, creating sonorities
of a type that Purcell used to such effect in the great coronation
anthem *My heart is inditing*. The opening plain tonic–dominant
tuning up of Sion's trumpets soon moves into a minor key with
scope for such pungent harmony as in example 36.

The funeral anthem *Man that is born of a woman* follows the
same pattern, and though here Purcell wrote only in four parts
he creates in a masterly way an even more expressive
chromaticism. Yet the stature of this work must not overshadow such full anthems as *Lord, how long wilt thou be angry,
O Lord God of hosts, Remember not, Lord, our offences, Hear my
prayer, O Lord*, and *O God, thou hast cast us out*. All are different
in treatment and only the last is in the three-section form
(chorus–verse–chorus) that was adopted as standard in the
eighteenth century.

Such a consistently maintained level of interest as is revealed
in these full anthems is not always found in the instrumental
anthems that Purcell later wrote for Charles II's chapel. In a
few it is the quality of the string sections that redeems otherwise
rather ordinary material as, for instance, this lovely passage
from *I was glad*.

Ex. 37

I was glad   Purcell

Purcell recognised the formal cohesion that the strings could bring to these lengthy anthems. Occasionally he used them to accompany the voices, as in *Behold now, praise* and *In thee, O Lord, do I put my trust*; always the symphonies and ritornelli provide an essential part of the structure. Furthermore, in the last-named anthem, Purcell twice used a ground bass: for the opening symphony and for the final "hallelujah" section. An even closer link is achieved in *Awake, put on thy strength*, where the triple-time fugue of the opening symphony returns before the final "hallelujah" which in turn is constructed over the counter-subject of the fugue used as a ground bass. Typical examples of the string anthems are *The Lord is my light, Unto thee will I cry* and *It is a good thing to give thanks*. An opening symphony, generally a common-time section preceding a brisker triple-time movement, is followed by a series of verses (usually in three parts) and solos interlinked with further instrumental passages and concluded by a short chorus. The chorus is rarely used more extensively than this, *I will give thanks unto thee, O Lord* being one of the exceptions. The musical idiom is less angular than in the anthems with organ already mentioned, though the string passages still display that richness of texture that is one of their features. This is not uniformly so: there is a wide range between the lack of ebullience in the string writing of the rather prosaic Christmas anthem *Behold, I bring you glad tidings* and the bolder expression of *Why do the heathen*.

Yet the mastery that Purcell gained in these anthems, combined with his already assured technique of vocal writing, found its finest expression in one grand-scale work, *My heart is inditing*, performed at the coronation of James II.

All the above anthems are scored for a four-part orchestra. A few were subsequently composed that were scored for three-part strings, presumably for the Princess Anne's chapel during James II's reign. The best of these is *I will give thanks unto the Lord. O Lord, grant the King a long life* is shorter than usual. *They that go down to the sea in ships* (for counter-tenor and bass solos) provided an effective display piece for Gostling, but *Praise the*

Lord, O my soul, O Lord my God, while comparable in scoring and purpose, by reason of its greater length and slender content, is much inferior. With one notable exception, the remaining anthems with four-part strings are entirely unremarkable and were written for particular occasions, all probably in the year 1688. *My song shall be alway* is a solo cantata specially composed for a celebrity singer; *Blessed are they that fear the Lord* for the queen's pregnancy. Equally devoid of musical interest is *Praise the Lord, O Jerusalem* which foreshadows the empty bombast that marred so many early eighteenth-century occasional pieces. Placed in a class apart by its ingenuity and mastery of idiom is *O sing unto the Lord*. In this the vocal and instrumental resources are integrated in a purposeful scheme, and the solo voices are not dissipated in meaningless display as is the case in solo anthems (with organ) written in the last years of Purcell's life (example 38).

Ex. 38

The way of God is an undefiled way   Purcell

A verse anthem with short ritornelli for two violins written in 1693, *O give thanks*, stands well above this level; but Purcell's finest achievement is represented in the anthem he composed for the funeral of Queen Mary in 1695, *Thou knowest, Lord, the secrets of our hearts*. Quite unlike any other occasional piece, this miniature gem is unique for its utter sincerity and supreme simplicity.

An orchestral Te Deum and Jubilate in D for the 1694 Festival of the Sons of Clergy at St. Paul's Cathedral became a popular item at subsequent festivals. For regular liturgical use Purcell set the evening canticles in G minor and, at some time before the year 1682, a complete series in B flat of all the canticles that would have then been sung in cathedrals. The B flat service is brilliantly successful in presenting music of character within a succinct framework.

The two early Latin motets require brief mention. *Beati omnes qui timent Dominum* is not as outstanding as *Jehova, quam multi sunt hostes* (nothing can equal the section in the latter beginning "Ego cubui") but it is well worth singing, especially for its final "Alleluia" on a ground bass.

In addition to the services and anthems for liturgical use, Purcell set a number of sacred texts for domestic music-making. The solo songs contain music of great beauty, and some of the three- and four-part pieces could usefully find a place in modern cathedral repertoires, requiring as they do not so much brilliant vocal technique as sensitive musicianship. The ensemble pieces are a vocal equivalent (in purpose and even in style) of the fantasias for viols. Resembling the writing in some of the early anthems, they frequently outshine them in their freshness of invention and harmonic richness, as can be seen by a comparison of the metrical-psalm setting of *O Lord our governor* with the anthem of the same title.

For all Purcell's famed ability for setting words to music there are a number of anthems where the approach to the text is mannered and even superficial. This criticism can not be applied to the sacred songs in which the declamation fits the words naturally, their import at the same time being pro-foundly matched by the harmonic idiom. In these Purcell is freed to use his own voice, at his pleasure, and is not burdened by public speaking or obliged to adapt his manner to suit the oratory of others.

JAMES HAWKINS, c. 1662–1729 (Ely).

Organist of Ely from 1682 until his death. Of importance, not so much for the considerable number of anthems and services he wrote for Ely, as for the works of other composers he transcribed and which are still in the library there.

DANIEL PURCELL, c. 1663 (London)–1717 (London).

The exact birth date of Henry Purcell's younger brother, Daniel, is still not known. It is unlikely to have been earlier than 1663, as he was one of the choristers of the Chapel Royal who attended the King at Windsor in 1678. There is a possibility* that the two composers were sons not of Thomas but of Henry Purcell who died in August, 1664, which would effectively prevent Daniel being born later than April, 1665. Daniel Purcell was organist of Magdalen College, Oxford, and received his salary in this capacity from 1689 to 1696, although he had already moved to London in May, 1695. There he became involved in writing music for various stage productions. He also wrote odes and a little instrumental music. He took a church organist's post again (at St. Andrew's, Holborn) for a few years before his death, and at some time he was also organist of St. Dunstan's-in-the-East.

As a composer of church music Daniel Purcell is known solely by his evening service in E minor which, luckily, Stainer transcribed from an autograph organ book that used to be at Magdalen College, Oxford. Such is the quality and charm of this service that it is a matter of some regret that the present provenance of this book is not known, and that not only the service but five anthems† that preceded it are no longer accessible.

A collection of fifteen "anthems", reputed to be in the composer's hand, are in the Bodleian Library.[24] These, however,

* See Franklin Zimmerman's *Henry Purcell: his Life and Times* (1967). In this book the author refers to Daniel Purcell, and explores the genealogical puzzles of the Purcells.

† *O praise God in his holiness, Hear my prayer, Bow thine ear, O give thanks, I will alway give thanks.*

were not for liturgical use, being composed by special request for (apparently) private performance, and they lack for the most part the restraint and disciplined expression of the E minor service. More in the nature of solo cantatas than anthems, they are all written for a single voice and continuo, and only four have a brief concluding four-part chorus.* The pattern of a succession of arioso and recitative-type movements follows a predictable course in all these anthems, but there are moments where a particularly expressive solo rises above the general level. The harmonic richness of such passages contrasts with the orderliness in the more vigorous movements (typical of later, eighteenth-century writing) and demonstrates Daniel Purcell's transitional position between the Restoration composers and those of the eighteenth century.

Although these fifteen anthems contain music that is of but ordinary interest, there are some sections which show Daniel Purcell's talent as being more than a pale shadow of his brother Henry's. For instance: the opening of *My God, my God, look upon me*, the concise and well-balanced phrases of the concluding section of *Lord, let me know mine end* (to the words "Hear my prayer, O Lord"), or the sensitive word-setting of the first movement of *Put me not to rebuke*. But it is *Bow down thine ear, O Lord* which best illustrates his originality, and also the importance of his music in the stylistic developments at the turn of the seventeenth century. This particular anthem is in three sections: the opening, as below, in common time, which is followed by a faster triple-time section; the G minor solo "Among the gods" (reproduced on plate 11) which is introduced by a short recitative; and another recitative, in C minor, leading into a final brisk triple-time solo in the major key, "I will thank thee", the music of which is taken up by a short concluding chorus.

* An example of this genre, comparable in both form and style, is Clarke's *Lord, how long*. Similar pieces by Weldon (*Divine Harmony*, 1716) were prefaced as being "very proper not only in private Devotion, but also for Choirs, where they may be Sung either by a Treble or Tenor".

Ex. 39

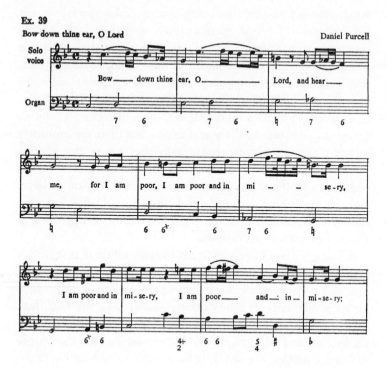

JOHN CHRISTOPHER PEPUSCH, 1667 (Berlin)–1752 (London).

When he was thirty Pepusch left the Prussian Court where he was employed, and after a period settled in London (*c.* 1700). Organist and composer at the future Duke of Chandos's chapel at Cannons (1712), for which he wrote some services and anthems. Following a period at Cannons he became much involved in various theatrical productions, including arranging and writing music for *The Beggar's Opera* (1728). But in 1737 he was appointed organist of the Charter House where he spent the rest of his life, continuing his teaching (Travers and Boyce were pupils of his), his theoretical work for which he was well known in his day, and his great interest in the Academy of Ancient Music.

JOHN GOLDING (Goldwin), *c.* 1667–7th November, 1719 (Windsor).

Chorister and pupil under Child. Lay-clerk at St. George's Chapel, Windsor (1689). Assisted Child in his declining years and succeeded him as organist (1697), being eventually appointed master of the choristers in 1703.[25]

Golding's anthems never achieved widespread use, but a complete service in F was included, deservedly, in Arnold's collection. This service, similar in type to Purcell's B flat setting, stands halfway between that and later more tedious eighteenth-century examples. With a judicious contrast of textures, between full and verse sections, chordal and imitative phrases, it maintains sufficient variety and achieves moments of more than ordinary interest.

JEREMIAH CLARKE, *c.* 1673–1st December, 1707 (London).

Possibly connected with a Windsor family, some of whom were lay-clerks at St. George's Chapel in the seventeenth and eighteenth centuries. Chorister at the Chapel Royal and a pupil of Blow. Sang treble at the 1685 coronation. Philip Hayes stated that he was organist of Winchester College (1692–1695). Organist of St. Paul's Cathedral (1699)* and almoner and master of the choristers (1703), gentleman-extraordinary of the Chapel Royal (1700) and joint organist there with Croft (1704).

Clarke wrote at least ten odes mainly for specific occasions such as the St. Cecilia's Day festival, commemoration of the death of Purcell, the Peace of Ryswick, and one for the "Gentlemen of the Island of Barbadoes" who had survived a hurricane there. He also composed songs and music for the theatre, harpsichord pieces, and at least twenty anthems and two services.

Of Clarke's two settings of the Te Deum and Jubilate, one, in G major, is exceedingly tame and perfunctory, but the other, in

---

* The date, 1699, of Clarke's appointment to St. Pauls Cathedral has been discovered by Watkins Shaw, correcting that (1695) given in previous biographies.

C minor, is more melodious. It is not only that Clarke is much more at home in the minor key, but that in the second setting he adopts a slightly more expansive lay-out, achieving interest with skilled use of tonality and a greater variety of rhythm. A Sanctus and Gloria in A minor is little more than a chant-like setting of the text which, apart from the final sentences, is set for three-part men's voices. Liturgical requirements, however, were much too restricting for Clarke's delicate talent, which found its happiest expression in music for solo voices. His ink is pale in comparison with that of Purcell's writing in this medium, yet his solos have a certain distinction in verse anthems such as *I will love thee, O Lord* and *How long wilt thou forget me?*, and more so in his sacred songs for domestic use. Playford included two in *Harmonia Sacra* from which examples 40 and 41 are taken.

Ex. 40

An Evening Hymn   Clarke

JOHN CHURCH, ?1675 (Windsor)–6th January, 1741 (London).
    Chorister at St. John's College, Oxford. Gentleman of the Chapel Royal (1697) and master of the choristers at Westminster Abbey (1704).

Ex. 41

Blest be those sweet regions   Clarke

There are various anthems and services in manuscript collections, and a service in F (full of finicky counterpoint) was printed by Ouseley in the nineteenth century.

JOHN WELDON, 19th January, 1676 (Chichester)–7th May, 1736 (London).

Educated at Eton College; later a pupil of Purcell. Organist of New College, Oxford (1694–1702). Gentleman of the Chapel Royal (1701), organist there (1708), and later granted a second composer's place for the Chapel Royal (1715). Was also organist of St. Bride's, Fleet Street, and (in 1726) of St. Martin-in-the-Fields.

Apart from the six solo anthems published in *Divine Harmony* [1716] there are many anthems by Weldon in manuscript.

Three books of songs were published and there are others in various collections.

Of the two anthems published by Boyce, *Hear my crying, O God* most deserves its modern reprint, though the counter-tenor and bass duet from *In thee, O Lord* makes this latter piece worthy of notice. Weldon's style belonging more to the eighteenth than to the seventeenth century, he was capable of a certain elegance of phrase—well oiled by sequences—and even some relatively bold harmony. A full anthem of his, *Who can tell how oft he offendeth*, ostensibly in seven parts, is an abysmal failure; but, encouraged perhaps by the celebrated singer Richard Elford for whom he compiled *Divine Harmony*, he was more successful in the verse anthem form. His writing for solo voices at times demands considerable vocal virtuosity, so it is not surprising that in the anthems the choruses are often outweighed. For instance, the five solo movements in *O God thou hast cast us out* take precedence over the three chorus sections, and important as the latter are structurally they cannot prevent this anthem from meandering tediously. The opening solo, however, is included here as a worthy example of Weldon's style.

Ex. 42

O God thou hast cast us out   Weldon

-- pleas'd, O__ turn thee, turn____ thee unto

us a-gain, thou hast al-so been displeased, hath al-so been displeased, O__

turn thee, O__ turn thee, O__ turn thee, O__ turn____

____ thee un-to__ us a - gain.

WILLIAM CROFT, 1678 (Nether Ettington, Warwickshire)–14th August, 1727 (Bath).

Chorister at the Chapel Royal under Blow. Organist of the new church of St. Anne's, Soho (1700–1712). Gentleman-extraordinary of the Chapel Royal (1700) and joint organist there with Clarke (1704), becoming the sole organist in 1707.

Master of the children and composer for the Chapel Royal, and organist of Westminster Abbey in succession to Blow. Doctor of music, Oxford (1713).

Croft wrote instrumental music for the theatre, chamber sonatas, harpsichord pieces, songs, and many anthems apart from the thirty he published in *Musica Sacra* in 1724.

The importance of *Musica Sacra* as being the first printed collection of church music in *score* is duly accepted, but the musical significance of these thirty anthems has been open to question. A long-lived personal reputation—"Dr. Croft was a grave and decent man"—became attached to his writing; both Croft and his church music were admired for respectability of manner.

> Doctor CROFT, who very successfully studied the Ancients, and his great Predecessor PURCELL, by happily uniting their various Excellencies, hath left behind him a noble Fund of Music, properly adapted to the most sublime Purposes of Devotion.[26]

Yet it was perhaps too great a dependence on the past that made it difficult for Croft to accept wholeheartedly the developments in musical styles that were taking place in his day. This may be the reason why the solos in his verse anthems often seem ill at ease, lacking, on the one hand, the vigour and expression of the late seventeenth-century composers and, on the other, the poise and fluency of later writers.

Croft appears less handicapped in setting the canticles which, by the nature of their function, demanded a conservative idiom and little vocal extravagance. The morning and communion service in A is the most traditional in idiom. The Te Deum and Jubilate has very little for verses, using the choir full, or else divided antiphonally, and there are the occasional touches that reveal seventeenth-century origins (example 43).

It is, however, only in the Creed that there is much evidence of real sympathy for the text. The change, for instance, from D major to D minor at the words "and was crucified" is both simple and imaginative. The Sanctus and Gloria of the B minor service are very ordinary, though the Te Deum and Jubilate in the same key achieves some variety in texture and a measure of contrapuntal interest. Yet even here the composer is straight-jacketed by the demands of brevity and only rarely allows a phrase to expand without the continued interruption of petty cadences.

Ex. 43

Te Deum and Jubilate in A   Croft

The E flat service (Te Deum, Jubilate, Cantate Domino, Deus misereatur) is more adventurous. Not only is there in this a wider variety of textures and scoring (antiphonal and full chorus, verses in various groupings) but there is also ample key contrast. The Te Deum never loses sight of the tonic, but there are frequent excursions into minor keys (B flat, C, G, F, E flat and A flat) as well as into A flat and B flat major. The majority of these modulations are structurally meaningful; and the work ends conclusively with a fugal section whose long-note theme gives it a sense of spaciousness. This short verse indicates how far, in this Te Deum, Croft had progressed from earlier models.

Ex. 44

Te Deum in E flat   Croft

The restrained expression and fitting homophonic idiom of
the Burial Service has ensured that this, alone of Croft's
liturgical compositions, has remained in continued use. That,

on the other hand, hardly any of his anthems are now sung seems an undeserved fate. Admittedly they are uneven in quality, but *Musica Sacra* is not solely a compendium of little more than historical interest.

The full anthems follow the accepted form of two choruses flanking a central verse section. Both *Hear my prayer, O Lord* and *O Lord grant the King a long life* develop much more interesting material than the still popular *God is gone up* (which Croft did not include in *Musica Sacra*), but it is the six-part *O Lord, rebuke me not* that is the finest example in this form. The verse

Ex. 45

O Lord God of my salvation   Croft

I

anthems do not always succeed in maintaining a consistent standard, though they often contain individual solos of some originality. The bass solos in *The heavens declare* or *O be joyful in God* have plenty of vitality. They are to some extent enhanced by the ostinato-type accompaniment, though elsewhere Croft uses this device to wearisome length. In a more restrained mood are the solos in *Out of the deep*, and *O Lord God of my salvation*. The ensemble passages can be equally effective such as the trio (example 45) from *O Lord God of my salvation* (in a style akin to passages in Humfrey's anthems).

Some of the most impressive anthems are those which are too ambitious in scope for performance in the present-day cathedral service. *This is the day which the Lord hath made* consists of eight main sections, is well-balanced in its disposition of solo and chorus passages and secures a fine sense of drama, though musically the most effective moment is a gentle solo for counter-tenor at the words "He maketh peace". More successful on every count is *O Lord, I will praise thee*. Able to stand comparison with Handel's English anthems, this increasingly generates excitement as it progresses from a graceful opening duet for treble and counter-tenor, through a bass solo, a vigorous movement for counter-tenor and bass, to a splendid solo quartet which develops chromatic phrases and rich suspensions in a masterly way (see below). This quartet has none of the tedium of some Croft movements where, having stated an idea, he simply repeats it and then, seemingly at a loss for what to do next, gybes off on a new tack. The final chorus is dramatic and spacious, ending with a fugue in which a strong touch is provided when the subject is stated three times in augmentation.

A number of anthems that Croft included in *Musica Sacra* were originally written to celebrate special events, ranging from a military victory to the Princess of Wales's first attendance at the Chapel Royal after giving birth to a son. Croft's setting for the latter occasion of Psalm 128, *Blessed are all they that fear the Lord*, is in its shape and some of its features related to the verse

Ex. 46

O Lord, I will praise thee

Croft

anthem of Charles II's time. But the handling of the material, especially in the solo movements, is typical of Croft's manner. Although these occasional anthems may have been first performed with orchestral accompaniment, Croft only published two in *Musica Sacra* with instrumental parts. *Rejoice in the Lord, O ye righteous* and *O give thanks unto the Lord* are extensive works and are both scored for chorus, solo voices, strings and oboes.

Croft also wrote an orchestral Te Deum and Jubilate in D for a thanksgiving ceremony, which was sung twice at the Chapel Royal before Queen Anne. A performing score of this work (some pages of which are in Croft's hand)[27] is of interest because it not only names the singers for certain solo passages, but also specifies that some of the trios be sung by "all voices", and that even a duet for tenor and counter-tenor be sung by two singers on each part.

A handful of other anthems that were not published in *Musica Sacra* appeared in print later in the eighteenth century. Such anthems as *Be merciful unto me* and *I will give thanks unto thee O Lord* deserve little attention. Of two that Boyce published, *Put me not to rebuke* is a creditable example of Croft's writing in the full anthem style, but it is the verse anthem *Give the king thy judgements* that is the more outstanding.

GEORGE FRIDERIC HANDEL, 23rd February, 1685 (Halle)–14th April, 1759 (London).

Organist of Halle Cathedral for one year (1702). At Hamburg in 1703, and a violinist in the opera there. Subsequently in Italy (1706–1710). Musical director at the Elector of Hanover's court (1710). In the same year he visited London for the first time. Leave of absence granted by the Elector of Hanover in 1712 for a second visit to England; while Handel was still there, the Elector acceded to the English throne as George I (1714). Handel then remained in England and, apart from various visits abroad to obtain opera singers, he settled there, becoming an English subject in 1726. Musical director for the future Duke of Chandos between 1717 and 1719, and for a brief period in 1720. Composer for the Chapel Royal (1726). Handel struggled for many years to establish Italian opera in London, but bitter rivalries and repeated failures brought about his bankruptcy and a breakdown in his health. He turned increasingly to writing and producing oratorios. His last oratorio was completed in 1751, the onset of blindness finally interrupting a life-time of composing in all spheres.[28]

Handel's church music is listed below. An aspect of his work that has often been neglected, it has neither gained a place in the English church music repertoire nor been considered more than a very insignificant part of Handel's vast total output. Admittedly his church music is puny in comparison with his operas or oratorios, and much of it is in any case reworked material with many cross references to his own and other people's writing. For instance, having just written a successful setting of the Jubilate for the Peace of Utrecht, Handel found it worth rescoring (with little other alteration) as an anthem for the Duke of Chandos. Also he would extract sections, or just basic ideas, from pieces that no longer served any further purpose and refurbish them for a new occasion. The anthems in their turn provided material for the later oratorios. Handel knew that a well-tried recipe stands repetition, and that there is no point in wasting good food.

But much of Handel's church music is nonetheless deserving of performance, especially the earlier, non-occasional pieces (e.g. the Chandos anthems and the B flat Te Deum). In any modern performance care should be taken to secure an appropriate vocal (as well as orchestral) scoring. The chorus plays as predominant a part in Handel's church music as in his oratorios, and Handel wrote for an all-male choir consisting of trebles, counter-tenors, tenors and basses. It is important also to capture the relative strengths of choir and orchestra. For his Chandos anthems (and his oratorios) Handel used a small number of performers, professional singers and instrumentalists. While for the occasional church pieces he used as large a number of both as possible. For instance, at the Coronation of George II in 1727 in Westminster Abbey there was a choir of forty-seven professional singers (twelve trebles, fourteen counter-tenors, seven tenors and fourteen basses), and the orchestra was reputed to have totalled 150 players. For Queen Caroline's funeral in 1737 there were eighty singers and a hundred instrumentalists. On the other hand, a performance of *Messiah* at the Foundling Hospital in 1758 was given by six soloists, a chorus of seventeen singers, twenty strings (6.6.3.3.2), four oboes, four bassoons, two horns, two trumpets, timpani and probably two continuo instruments. Handel went to some lengths to secure the best singers from collegiate and cathedral choirs, as for a performance (in 1744) of *Belshazzar* when he told Jennens that he had engaged "Mr. Gates with his Boyes and several of the best Chorus Singers of the Choirs" (of the Chapel Royal, St. Paul's Cathedral and Westminster Abbey). Cathedral singers were used in provincial oratorio performances, and one at Bristol procured them from as far afield as Worcester, and had two boys from the Chapel Royal.[29]

In the following survey Handel's church music is grouped into four categories and placed within them in approximately chronological order. The majority of these six Latin pieces he wrote before settling in England (the first psalm when he was still at Halle, the next three during his visit to Italy, the *Salve Regina* either in Italy or, soon after, in England, and the motet *Silete venti* probably during the years 1715-1720).

(A) LATIN CHURCH MUSIC

1 *Laudate pueri:* psalm for soprano, two violins and bass continuo.

2 *Laudate pueri:* second setting of this psalm for soprano ("concertato") solo, chorus (S.A.T.B.), two violins, two violas, two oboes and bass continuo.

3 *Dixit Dominus:* psalm for five-part solos and chorus (S.S.A.T.B.), two violins, two violas and bass continuo.

A magnificent, extended setting with brilliant (if difficult) writing for the chorus. It is hard to understand why a work, for instance, such as Bach's *Magnificat* receives frequent performances while *Dixit Dominus* remains for the most part on the shelf. The choir has a predominant role, and the chance to sing some of Handel's finest choruses.

The opening instrumental introduction has few surprises, but

with the entry of the chorus one feature after another is added
in succession, twice called to order (in a manner later used in the
Chandos anthems) by the introduction of a chorale-like
melody. Two arias for alto and soprano provide a moment of
relief before this dramatic entry of the chorus at the words
"Juravit Dominus".

Ex. 47
Dixit Dominus   Handel

The succeeding choral sections are diverse and imaginative,
combining skilful counterpoint and dramatic effect. The final
"Gloria Patri" starts innocently enough but, after the re-

introduction of the long note theme from the first chorus, it breaks into a complex fugal *allegro* ("Et in secula") with four distinctive phrases being combined and developed at length before the whole settles on a firm dominant pedal just before the final cadence.

4   *Nisi Dominus:* psalm for the same forces as *Dixit Dominus.* This opens with a fully scored chorus, and is then followed by four relatively insignificant and brief movements for the solo voices.

5   *Salve Regina:* a four-movement setting for soprano, two violins and bass continuo.

6   *Silete venti:* motet for soprano, two violins, violas, oboes, bassoons and bass continuo. The opening "symphonia" leads without a break into the soloist's first entry, which is followed by two extensive *Da Capo* arias and a particularly jubilant 12/8 final "alleluja". Richly orchestrated, and both effective and rewarding for the singer.

(B)   CHANDOS ANTHEMS

Between about 1717 and 1720 Handel wrote eleven anthems for performance at the future Duke of Chandos's private establishment at Cannons. These take a central place in Handel's church music. With origins in both the English instrumental anthem and Italian sacred pieces, in their turn they provided one of the bases for Handel's more formidable oratorios. They all open with an instrumental sonata, which is followed by a succession of choruses and solo movements with instrumental obbligati. They are scored for two violins and 'cello, oboes (occasionally doubling on flutes), bassoons and bass continuo (both organ and harpsichord). The first six anthems are for three-part chorus, the remaining five (written after the choir at Cannons had been enlarged) for four-part chorus.

1   *O be joyful in the Lord:* The Jubilate written to mark the Peace of Utrecht in 1713 here reproduced with little change except being re-scored for the smaller Cannons establishment and with the addition of an instrumental prelude.

2 *In the Lord put I my trust.*

3 *Have mercy upon me.*

4 *O sing unto the Lord a new song:* An adaptation of an anthem of the same title written for the Chapel Royal.

5 *I will magnify thee.*

6 *As pants the hart* (in E minor): The first of four versions of this anthem.

7 *My song shall be alway:* A summary of this particular Chandos anthem, although not necessarily the most outstanding, will indicate typical features. The opening movement is a brisk G major *allegro* (later used again in the concerto grosso, op. 3, no. 3) for three-part strings with an independent oboe part. The first sentence of the text is set for these instruments accompanying the trebles, with later a tutti unison entry for the rest of the choir developing into a four-part chorus. A recitative and vigorous aria for solo tenor follows, with obbligato parts for the oboe and violins. The text of the next two sections offers opportunities for word painting which Handel does not miss in a trio (for treble, tenor and bass) and a duet (for counter-tenor and bass) both with full instrumental accompaniment. A well-developed chorus contrasting homophonic and contrapuntal passages forms at this stage the real climax of the anthem, while the following *andante* for trebles (with delicate commentary from the oboe and violins) and the final, brief "alleluja" (tutti) bring the anthem to a satisfying conclusion.

8 *O come let us sing unto the Lord.*

9 *O praise the Lord with one consent.*

10 *The Lord is my light.*

11 *Let God arise* (in B flat): Some of the material of this version was later used in an anthem for the Chapel Royal. Possibly the best of the Chandos set. The most effective movement is the swinging 12/8 *allegro* chorus in D minor, "O sing unto God": an instrumental ritornello leads into a passage for counter-tenors and basses, the trebles and tenors enter later, and the whole proceeds with an inevitable momentum, and never a note wasted.[30]

I*

Handel's indebtedness to the English anthem is at its most apparent in these eleven. The opening phrase, for instance, of a bass solo in number 9, "That God is great", might well have been written by Purcell for Gostling. Even more typically Purcellian is a chorus passage from number 11, beginning with the words "Praised be the Lord". The setting of "the earth trembled and quak'd" in the tenth anthem has a parallel in Jeremiah Clarke's treatment of the same text in his anthem *I will love thee, O Lord*.

Te Deum (in B flat): The most likely home for this *Te Deum* would have been Cannons, as is indicated by its scoring for a three-part string orchestra and the usual woodwind (with the addition of a trumpet in one movement). It is an extended setting with relatively few solo passages and fine, well-developed choruses.

(c) OCCASIONAL CHURCH MUSIC

In 1713 Handel wrote a Te Deum and Jubilate to celebrate the Peace of Utrecht (on the strength of this work and the Birthday-Ode for Queen Anne that had been performed earlier in the same year he was awarded a £200 annuity by the Queen). After being appointed composer for the Chapel Royal in 1726 Handel produced further large-scale works for official occasions that were performed by equally large-scale choirs and orchestras, the singers being drawn from the Chapel Royal, St. Paul's Cathedral and Westminster Abbey. Unfortunately, not all the music merits having survived the occasion for which it was written.

1713. *Utrecht Te Deum and Jubilate* (in D): Scored for two trumpets, oboes and bassoons, four-part strings, continuo and chorus of from four to eight parts. Performed at St. Paul's Cathedral in July, 1713, with the solos taken by Chapel Royal singers, this subsequently became a popular item in the Festivals for the Sons of Clergy at St. Paul's, and at the Three Choirs Festivals. Set predominantly for chorus with the solo voices used mostly in ensembles.

1727. *Coronation Anthems*:
(i) *The King shall rejoice,*
(ii) *Zadok the priest,*
(iii) *Let thy hand be strengthened,*
(iv) *My heart is inditing.*

This is the order in which they were originally sung at the coronation of George II in Westminster Abbey, 1727. They contain many exciting effects showing Handel's mastery in producing the desired pomp and circumstance noises when required. Three of the anthems are scored for three trumpets and timpani in addition to five-part strings, oboes and bassoons, and this restricts much of the music to the key of D. Too much jingoist D major can pall, and some choruses, however exciting, lack the intrinsic musical interest of earlier anthems with their more evenly spread mixture of melodic appeal, vigorous counterpoint, and dramatic effect. It is no accident that the more delicate (if in places, obscure) sentiments of the text in *My heart is inditing* should encourage Handel to wander away from the beaten track. This particular anthem stands apart from the rest of the set, not only for the relief it gives from D major and trumpets (used sparingly only at the beginning and end), but also for its succession of flowing *andante* movements, and its more subtle use of the available resources. This is the only one of the set that uses solo voices (in brief ensembles preceding choruses), the remaining three being entirely for choruses of up to seven parts—Handel was, after all, making good use of the opportunity of having the three best choirs in the kingdom to sing these pieces. The third anthem, *Let thy hand be strengthened,* dispenses with the trumpets and is of compact proportions, in three balanced sections with its outer movements full of the strength and cheerfulness of the first two anthems without their magniloquence.

Te Deum (in A): Composed for George I's return from Hanover,[31] similarities in the vocal scoring of this Te Deum with the 1727 coronation anthems give pretext for associating it with them. It contains references to the Utrecht Te Deum and, more obviously, to the B flat Chandos Te Deum, though this in A is a shorter version.

1734. *Wedding Anthem: This is the day which the Lord hath made.* An extensive cantata arranged from other works for the wedding of Princess Anne, and scored for unusually large forces: eight-part chorus, four soloists, strings, flutes, oboes and bassoons, trumpets and horns, timpani, and continuo instruments including harpsichord, organ and theorbo-lute. Despite the obsequious words Handel rises to the occasion with appropriately monumental choruses to begin and end the work, separated by four arias rich in ideas and varied in scoring (e.g. the bass solo "Blessed is the man" with 'cello obbligato and double-bass, harpsichord and theorbo-lute continuo). But, after a dutiful series of concluding "allelujas", Handel has the last word on the occasion with an extraordinary penultimate chord.

Ex. 48
This is the day which the Lord hath made   Handel

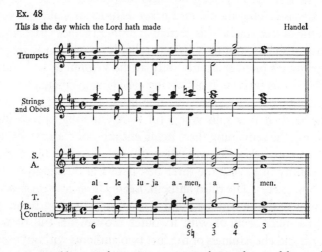

1736. *Wedding Anthem: Sing unto God.* For the wedding of the Prince of Wales. Although with not such ambitious orchestration as in the 1734 anthem, *Sing unto God* is an equally extensive work. The treble and bass soloists each have an aria to themselves, the counter-tenor and trumpet make a miniature double concerto of the opening chorus, while the tenor rivals this in a matching final chorus. The anthem is worth performing for this conclusion alone where the chorus with the strings and woodwind at first merely punctuate the virtuoso tenor solo part, but later, with the entry of the trumpets, gradually take precedence, all the forces combining in a splendid build-up to the final cadence.

1737. *Funeral Anthem: The ways of Sion*. Written for the funeral of Queen Caroline, and completed a week before the service took place in Westminster Abbey. This occasion obviously did not greatly inspire Handel, and the total effect is somewhat drawn-out. There are, however, some good moments such as the excellent penultimate movement (a solo quartet to the words "They shall receive a glorious kingdom") in which the treatment of the solo voices owes not a little to precedents in the late-seventeenth-century English anthem.

1743. *Dettingen Te Deum* (in D): Performed in the Chapel Royal to celebrate the victory of Dettingen, this Te Deum repeats *ad nauseam* the formula of earlier ceremonial pieces. A sort of interminable Hallelujah chorus for tutti choir and orchestra (with the usual trumpets), it is relieved only by two solo movements and some phrases for solo voices interlinked with the chorus.

1743. *Dettingen Anthem: The King shall rejoice*. Written for the same occasion as the above Te Deum, it is scored for the same forces and treads the same ground with scant easement from tutti jubilation.

1749. *Foundling Hospital Anthem: Blessed are they that consider the poor*. Produced not for a state occasion but for a concert at the Foundling Hospital. An effective concoction of new and old music (two of the four choruses are from the 1737 funeral anthem, and the final one is the Hallelujah chorus from *Messiah*). The anthem begins with a tenor solo and includes a movement for counter-tenor, both with obbligato string parts, and a particularly telling duet for trebles. The mixture could not fail to impress the patrons of the Foundling Hospital (Handel was subsequently made a governor, and devoted much of his time to this charity), and it remains sufficiently fresh to engage our interest today.

(D) CHAPEL ROYAL ANTHEMS

There remain seven anthems and a Te Deum which, it would appear, Handel adapted for use in the Chapel Royal (in some of them the soloists, all gentlemen of the Chapel Royal, are named in Handel's manuscripts).

O sing unto the Lord a new song: Written for the Chapel Royal (or at least the Chapel Royal singers) *c.* 1714, though perhaps never performed there. Parts of it were rescued and appeared shortly afterwards in the fourth Chandos anthem of the same title.

I will magnify thee: Only the beginning and end are borrowed from the fifth Chandos anthem of this title. The intervening movements appear in (or are taken from) other anthems.

As pants the hart (version ii): In D minor. Very freely adapted for the Chapel Royal choir (probably 1719-1720) from the sixth Chandos anthem, for larger forces (strings with violas and six-part chorus), with both new as well as reworked material.

As pants the hart (version iii): In D minor. A shortened version, excluding the orchestra, of the above anthem, but with a different ending.

As pants the hart (version iv): In D minor. The fourth version (*c.* 1720) of this anthem, and most closely related to the third. An adaptation on the lines of the English verse anthem for solo voices, chorus and organ continuo (possibly for repertoire use in the Chapel Royal when instruments were not used). The chorus sections are very similar to those in the third version, the main divergences being in the solo passages. The proportions of the verse and full sections are here better balanced, and the chorus have a slightly more significant role: five-part verse alternating with chorus, counter-tenor solo and chorus, bass recitative leading into four-part chorus, counter-tenor duet, four-part chorus. Handel named the soloists in his manuscript: Hughes,

Bell (counter-tenors), Wheely, Gates (basses). This anthem could well take a place in present-day cathedral services.

Let God arise (in A): A much altered and abbreviated version of the eleventh Chandos anthem for six-part chorus, four-part strings and woodwind. Two gentlemen of the Chapel Royal are named by Handel as soloists in the manuscript: Hughes and Wheely.

O praise the Lord, ye angels of his: This has been referred to as the twelfth Chandos anthem, but its more likely setting was the Chapel Royal. Scored for four-part strings, oboes, bassoons and trumpets, and containing more solo than chorus work, it is not the best of Handel's anthems.

Te Deum (in D): A relatively compact setting for five part chorus, four-part strings, flute and two trumpets, this Te Deum goes straight through the text with little repetition. The only extensive solo passages are for counter-tenor, which look as though they may have been written specifically for Elford. Probably composed *c.* 1714 soon after the Utrecht Te Deum (to which it contains a few references) and intended for use in the Chapel Royal. It shares features in the treatment of verse and full passages with the English anthem of the period, and (judging by the way the original manuscript has been well worn) may have gained a firm place in the repertoire.

WILLIAM HINE, *c.* 1687 (Brightwell, Oxfordshire)–28th August, 1730 (Gloucester).

Chorister at Magdalen College, Oxford. Studied under Clarke. Assistant organist to Stephen Jeffries at Gloucester Cathedral (1708) and his successor as organist (1714).

Hine's *Harmonia sacra Glocestriensis* was published posthumously by his widow, containing anthems, a morning service (the composition of which was shared with Henry Hall) and an organ voluntary.

Philip Hayes wrote of him: "an excellent organ player", but "being fix'd in a place, not very prone to encourage musical abilities found himself neglected; which made him the less solicitous about improving those talents that nature had given him, and thereby became a lost man to the musical world".[32] Hayes's impression is borne out by the music of "Hall and Hine in E flat", a setting of Te Deum and Jubilate by each composer respectively. Though Hine's share has some little character, both canticles wear the depressingly respectable mark of eighteenth-century anonymity.

CHARLES KING, 1687 (Bury St. Edmunds)–17th March, 1748 (London).

Chorister at St. Paul's Cathedral under Blow and Clarke. Married Clarke's sister, and succeeded him as master of the choristers at St. Paul's (1707). Organist of St. Benet Fink (1708).

King wrote several services and anthems. The fact that Arnold allots space for five complete services in his collection of cathedral music honours not so much King's quality as a composer, but rather reflects the decline of taste in the eighteenth century.

It was the stimulus of having to write services for daily consumption that were time-saving and, above all, easy to sing by choirs of uncertain ability that encouraged King and other minor eighteenth-century organist–composers to produce these vapid efforts. The pity is that many succeeding generations of choristers had to suffer their peculiar form of musical dysentery.

THOMAS KEMPTON, died 1762 (Ely).

Known only for his B flat service which for long remained in constant use. He was organist at Ely from 1729 until his death, and there are five services and three anthems by him in the Ely library.

THOMAS KELWAY, 1695 (Chichester)–21st May, 1744 (Chichester).

Chorister at Chichester Cathedral (1704). Admitted organist there "during good pleasure" (1720).

Kelway wrote three services (in B minor, A minor and G minor) which endured in cathedral lists for much longer than they deserved, and which can be said to have had nothing but a harmful influence, by their notoriety discrediting better and less frequently sung eighteenth-century church music. The monotonous feature of often-repeated cadences soon become as irksome as the inevitable clinch of hero and heroine in the worst sort of film.

MAURICE GREENE, 12th August, 1696 (London)–1st December, 1755 (London).

Said to have been a chorister at St. Paul's Cathedral under King and, in 1710, a pupil of Richard Brind. Organist of St. Dunstan's, Fleet Street (1714), and for two or three months of St. Andrew's, Holborn (1718). Organist of St. Paul's Cathedral (1718), and joint organist and composer for the Chapel Royal with Weldon (1727). Doctor of music, Cambridge (1730), where he also (in the same year) became professor of music. Master of the King's music (1735). He was buried at St. Olave's, Jewry, but in 1888 he was reinterred in St. Paul's Cathedral, next to Boyce.*

Greene wrote a considerable amount of choral music (sacred and secular), songs, and keyboard pieces. Apart from his *Forty Select Anthems* published in 1743, he wrote at least fifty-four anthems and one service in C. As master of the King's music he wrote many birthday odes and New Year odes. He set Pope's St. Cecilia's Day ode for Cambridge (1730) and an orchestral Te Deum in D for the Thanksgiving celebrations of 1745. Other choral works include two oratorios—*Jephtha* (1737) and *The Force of Truth* (1744), three dramatic pastorals, and the *Song of Deborah and Barak* (1732).

Greene was recognised by Samuel Wesley as "a composer of great Merit and Elegance", but his reputation foundered on the veiled criticism and innuendos of the historian Hawkins. The implication that Greene was less attractive in character than Boyce, and that his anthems lacked "that dignity and solemnity

* The correct dates of Greene's birth and of his appointment to St. Dunstan's, Fleet Street, have been discovered by H. Diack Johnstone.

which are essential in compositions for the church", has led to unwarranted neglect and misjudgement of his real achievements.[33]

Although Hawkins's views may subsequently have been widely adopted, at least his contemporaries appreciated Greene's music. The *Forty Select Anthems*, first published in 1743, were popular enough to receive more reprints during the eighteenth century than any other similar collection of church music, and a study of the contents show that this comparative popularity was not unjustified.

Few eighteenth-century church compositions, those by Croft and Boyce included, rival Greene's more inspired moments. A comparison of the two settings of *Like as the hart* by Boyce and Greene shows who possessed the more lively imagination. The latter's expressive range was much greater than that of Boyce. Similarly, Greene's pithy and original counterpoint was more masterly than Croft's, however sonorously effective that often is. Greene, like any of his contemporaries, could spin notes with a meaningless facility, and too large a portion of his music at one time can be indigestible. But though some of his anthems may seem to our ears unduly easy-going, excessively lengthy, even dull, a general level of interest is often maintained with rare consistency, and touches of brilliance are far from infrequent.

Greene's solos, after Boyce's, provide a breath of fresh air. Even an anthem of only average interest like *Acquaint thyself with God* is more inventive than many by Boyce. A natural vitality distinguishes the melodic writing where the phrases grow naturally, not in stilted chunks, developing logically rather than with aimless repetition, as in the second movement of the solo bass anthem *Hear, O Lord, and consider.* Much of the strength of Greene's melodies is due to a fluidity in the harmony which at its best assists a sense of progression and at least mollifies any incipient monotony. The idiom is illustrated in this excerpt from *O sing unto the Lord with thanksgiving.*

Ex. 49

O sing unto the Lord with thanksgiving   Greene

Vocal display for its own sake is rare. Exceptions (as in the bass solo anthems *My soul truly waiteth* and *The Lord, even the most mighty God*) only serve to highlight the sympathetic handling of the text in, for instance, the solos for tenor in *My God, my God*, or for counter-tenor in *Lord, how are they increased*. Although Greene composed effective ensembles for three or more singers, as in the trio quoted below (from *I will give thanks*), he seemed most at ease writing for a single voice or a duet for equal voices. Instances of treble duets are available in *Blessed are those that are undefiled* and the finer *Like as the hart*. There are good counter-tenor duets in *God is our hope and strength*, *The Lord is my shepherd*, and *O Lord I will praise thee*. *I will magnify thee O God* opens with an impressive duet for counter-tenor and bass. The same combination redeems an otherwise ingenuous piece, *O give thanks*, and the treble and tenor duet together with a succeeding treble aria places *O God of my righteousness* on a high plane.

Ex. 50

I will give thanks

Greene

The chorus in the verse anthems is usually more than an insignificant appendage. In one anthem, *O praise the Lord of heaven*, the chorus dominates the soloists, but more usually it adds supporting comment and develops phrases announced by the solo singers, as in *Arise, shine, O Sion*. In *Let God arise* the chorus succeeds in converting the opening trio from Boyce-like bravado to exciting drama at the words "Like as the smoke vanisheth".

In the full anthems the part-writing is taut and economical, and in the finest pieces Greene displays an original contrapuntal idiom. *Let my complaint, O sing unto the Lord a new song*, and *I will sing of thy power* are inferior to the justly famed *Lord, let me know mine end*, and the single-movement *O clap your hands*. But equally effective as these last two are *Lord, how long wilt thou be angry* (which combines homophonic phrases with pithy part-writing, using expressive harmony and dissonance) and *How long wilt thou forget me* (for double choir). In this the eight parts are not used all the time, but when they are there are no superfluous notes. The texture is dramatically varied. The momentum is gradually increased through each successive phrase of the opening section in A minor to the second half in A major and the brighter mood of the final phrases.

There are also six short full anthems, each in a different mode, that are curious exercises in an archaic language.[34] The same cannot be said of the C major service (Te Deum, Jubilate, Magnificat and Nunc dimittis) which although following honoured antecedents (the counterpoint has at times a seventeenth-century flavour) still finds space for uniquely eighteenth-century touches.

This service possesses unusual interest. Not excessive in length, it proceeds through the text with only a limited amount of repetition. Solo voices are scored in various combinations, placed between choruses generally in four parts, though increasing as occasion demands up to eight parts as in the Gloria of the Nunc dimittis. Strangely, this work never achieved popularity (one choirman pencilled in his copy at the end of the Te Deum the date 1842 and the comment "Never more I hope"!); but fortunately the evening canticles have now a scholarly, practical edition (O.U.P.).

Deserving revival along with the service in C are such anthems as the following: *Sing unto the Lord a new song* (good solo writing and an original "hallelujah" conclusion), *Let my complaint* (a fine counter-tenor verse anthem), *My God, my God* (for tenor solo with well integrated choruses), *Praise the Lord ye servants* (a notable opening treble duet), *Put me not to rebuke* (three solo voices in the first half lead naturally into the remainder where, over a running organ bass, the solo trio followed by the chorus gradually build up tension right to the final phrase), *O sing unto the Lord with thanksgiving* (tenor solo anthem), *God is our hope and strength* (effective solos for two counter-tenors and two basses with dramatic chorus writing), *The Lord is my shepherd* (counter-tenor duets and solos and a good final chorus).

Finally it is worth adding a comment on the importance of artistic realisations of the figured bass in Greene's anthems, especially as criticism of the anthems has been made on account of the apparent poverty of invention in the organ bass parts. In a few cases the composer himself sketched in the right-hand organ part, and as a guide to his intentions these four ritornello phrases from the third movement (a bass solo) of *O God, thou art my God* are extremely revealing. The opening organ introduction is given first (example 51, over).

Ex. 51

O God, thou art my God

Greene

(a)

(b)

JAMES KENT, 13th March, 1700 (Winchester)–6th May, 1776 (Winchester).

Chorister at Winchester Cathedral. Gentleman of the Chapel Royal under Croft. Through the influence of the sub-dean Dolben, became organist of Finedon, Northants (1717–1731), the seat of the Dolbens. Organist of Trinity College, Cambridge (1731–1737), and subsequently of Winchester Cathedral.

Late in his life Kent published twelve of his anthems. J. Corfe published, posthumously, a morning and evening service and eight anthems. It is hard to envisage now on what basis his music once enjoyed popularity. Certainly, the one anthem included by Arnold (*Hearken unto my voice*) has some effective moments, but the general level of his music can only serve to point, by way of contrast, the achievements of his close contemporaries, Greene and Boyce.

JOHN TRAVERS, *c.* 1703–1758 (London).

Chorister at St. George's Chapel, Windsor. A pupil of Greene and Pepusch. Organist of St. Paul's, Covent Garden (*c.* 1725), and subsequently of Fulham Church. He gave up the latter post when he became organist of the Chapel Royal in 1737.

Travers composed keyboard music, sacred and secular vocal music, including over twenty-five anthems and a service in F. Arnold included in his collection a Te Deum in D, a work laid out on a relatively ambitious scale (it may have been written for some special occasion). Here, although the muse runs fitfully, there are moments which could be made effective given a sympathetic performance. This unevenness is apparent in the familiar anthem *Ascribe unto the Lord* which for all its splendid solo passages finishes in a most facile manner, and in another verse anthem (for solo counter-tenor) *Ponder my words, O Lord,* though in this case it is the final chorus with its distinctive use of suspensions that is the best part.

WILLIAM HAYES, 1705 (Gloucester)–1777 (Oxford).

Chorister at Gloucester Cathedral under Hine. Organist of St. Mary's, Shrewsbury (1729). Organist of Worcester Cathedral (1731–1734), and subsequently organist and master of the choristers at Magdalen College, Oxford. Professor of music at Oxford (1741). He conducted some of the Three Choirs Festivals.

Hayes's published music is almost entirely vocal. His *Cathedral Music* did not appear until 1795, edited by his son, Philip. This contained a morning service in D, a communion and evening service in E flat designed as a continuation to Hall and Hine in the same key, twenty-one anthems, and an orchestral arrangement of the Old Hundreth psalm. His music is conservative in idiom, correct but uninspired, with scarcely more than a mechanical mastery of handling the voices in the full anthems (e.g. *Save Lord, and hear us*, and *Bow down thine ear*), and there is much tedium in the solo anthems. Emptiness of ideas is not compensated for by imaginative organ registration: *O God, thou art my God* calls for a diapason, a bassoon stop in conjunction with a counter-tenor, and a cornet stop. Appropriately, the solo "Thy wife shall be as the fruitful vine" is accompanied by a "Swelling Organ".

CHARLES STROUD, *c.* 1705 (London)–1726 (London).

Chorister at the Chapel Royal under Croft, but he died before he had time to make his mark except as the author of the anthem *Hear my prayer, O God*. The existence of this one anthem gave rise to exaggerated estimates of the composer's potential, curtailed by his early death. Not devoid of a rather mannered, polite form of expression, it nonetheless lacks contrapuntal development, and its anxiety not to cause offence (however much this may have been appreciated in the eighteenth century) renders it singularly characterless to modern ears.

THOMAS ARNE, 1710 (London)–5th March, 1778 (London).

He had little connection with church music, as his whole life was engaged in writing music for the theatre, mostly in London with two excursions to Dublin. But his success in this field draws attention to the existence of two motets, *O salutaris* (four-part chorus) and *Libera me* (five-part chorus and solo voices with organ). The latter work possesses an original charm, and is available in a modern edition.

WILLIAM BOYCE, (London) 1711–7th February, 1779 (London).

Chorister at St. Paul's Cathedral under King, and later a pupil of Greene. Organist of Oxford Chapel, Vere Street (1734). Composer for the Chapel Royal (1736). Organist of St. Michael's, Cornhill (1736–1768). Conducted the Three Choirs

Festival of Gloucester, Worcester and Hereford in 1737 and subsequent years. Organist of All Hallows' Great and Less, Thames Street (1749–1764). Succeeded Greene as conductor of the Annual Festival of the Sons of the Clergy (1735) and as master of the King's music (1755—though not sworn in to this office until 1757). One of the organists of the Chapel Royal (1758). By 1769 increasing deafness forced him to withdraw from active musical life and when he died at Kensington ten years later he was honourably buried in St. Paul's Cathedral.*

Boyce's compositions are many and cover a wide range. It is known that he wrote music for seventeen different stage productions, forty-three court odes and thirteen other such choral works, and various songs. He published twelve trio sonatas (c. 1745), eight symphonies (c. 1750–1760), twelve overtures (1770), and ten keyboard voluntaries (c. 1785). These brought him more fame in his lifetime than his church music, although he wrote a number of canticle settings and sixty-two anthems. Some of his own church music was published posthumously by his widow in two volumes (1780, 1790). In addition, Boyce completed the work begun by Alcock and Greene and (between 1760 and 1778) published a three-volume collection of *Cathedral Music* ranging from the Reformation to the early eighteenth century, which right to the end of the following century formed the basis of and, for better or worse, overwhelmingly influenced the repertoire of most cathedral choirs.[35]

Boyce's published settings of the morning canticles (in C, two in A, and a Te Deum in G) are workaday instances of service writing in the middle of the eighteenth century, competent but not thrilling. His anthems, however, have greater interest. Praise of these has been qualified, and even his best anthems have been wished, unreasonably, on to other writers. Boyce's

* See article by Donovan Dawe, "New Light on William Boyce", in the *Musical Times*, September, 1968, p.802. The writer deduces from the parish registers of St. James's, Garlickhythe, that Boyce was born at the beginning of September, 1711. He also relates some interesting information on the manner of Boyce's "resignations" from his two City organist posts.

active professional life must have left him only a limited amount of time for composing and it is not surprising that much of his music lacks ingenuity. He had a craftsmanlike ability to provide something suitable on demand for specific occasions, whether a royal birthday or a Chapel Royal service, but not always the inspiration to give such pieces substance.*

The omission of Boyce's own music in his collection of English cathedral music was made good by Philip Hayes, who edited two volumes after Boyce's death, and Vincent Novello, who supplemented these in the nineteenth century. But though the latter's collection may once have served a useful purpose, there is not much place for the greater part of their contents in the modern cathedral repertoire. *By the waters of Babylon* and *O where shall wisdom be found* are perhaps still generally sung; *The heavens declare* and *Turn thee unto me, O Lord* should also be in use. These last three anthems are, in their different ways, the most outstanding, but there are others that should not be entirely overlooked.

Boyce favoured verse anthems, and in some he does display original ideas which are at times convincingly developed; but his few full anthems deserve little consideration. *Turn thee unto me, O Lord* is the exception (immeasurably finer than the counter-tenor solo anthem setting of the same title). The subjective text provides a stimulus that is lacking in *O give thanks* (in B flat), where it is the central solo-quartet, and not the choruses, that is at all memorable. *Save me, O God*, consisting of a single movement for full choir, despite its expressive nature is better seen as an exercise in the style of similar choruses by Purcell than as a piece demanding performance in its own right.

The verse-anthem setting of *O give thanks* (in C) is both more convincing than the B flat version, and more typical of Boyce's

* For important events like the funeral of George II, and the wedding of George III, Boyce wrote *The souls of the righteous* and *The King shall rejoice* respectively. Instrumental anthems such as *Blessed is he that considereth* and *Lord, thou hast been our refuge* (an impressive piece) were written for the St. Paul's Festivals of the Sons of Clergy.

writing. The opening rumbustious trio is a little facile but not dull. A treble recitative introduces a charming arioso, and following this the treble solo gives the lead in a short chorus before another recitative and arioso (for bass), and a trio (A.T.B.). The trio and chorus alternate in a concluding cheerful "hallelujah". The anthem is compactly constructed and there is variety in key and mood throughout. Similar in approach is *Sing praises to the Lord*. The sequence of trio–solo–duet–solo–chorus is varied and well-proportioned. The music itself avoids exciting dissonance, allowing only some polite suspensions, but is tasteful and effective, as in comparable pieces like *O be joyful in God all ye lands* and *The Lord is King, be the people*. One of the most lively and rewarding verse anthems is *O sing unto the Lord a new song*. No singer could fail to enjoy a phrase like the following. Two of the three solo sections are a treble and bass duet, and these soloists take part in a spirited dialogue with the chorus in the final movement.

Ex. 52

O sing unto the Lord a new song   Boyce

Boyce appears happiest in anthems such as those demanding straightforward expression, and his occasional departures from an extrovert manner are rarely successful (*e.g. Hear my crying*). *Lord, who shall dwell in thy tabernacle* is somewhat unusual in its restraint and in its departure from the general verse-anthem pattern. The first section possesses a certain expressive quality, interspersing short phrases for solo voices with those for four-part ensemble, but the succeeding solo quartet (in the manner of a minuet) and the peremptory concluding chorus do not sustain the interest.

I have surely built thee an house is distinctive in that, apart from the trio at the beginning and the inevitable final triple-time "hallelujah", it is set in a mixture of recitative and arioso styles. For best effect this requires a performance that shows respect for its free character, and by subtly emphasising the underlying continuity unites the various sections.

A readily accessible and worthwhile example of the verse anthems is *The heavens declare*, which also displays in a bass aria Boyce's typically effective writing for a solo voice. Other anthems may be inferior to this yet still contain individual solos providing useful material for recitalists. There are good bass solos in *I have set God always before me, Give the King thy judgements, The Lord is my light,* and *The Lord is King, and hath put on.* There is an eloquent treble solo at the words "Lead me, Lord" in *Ponder my words,* the tenor discourses with a "bassoon stop" on the organ in *Sing unto the Lord,* and the counter-tenor has an equally impressive duet with the organ at the opening of *Teach me, O Lord.*

Ex. 53

Teach me, O Lord   Boyce

Teach me, O Lord, the way of thy sta-tutes
and I shall keep it un-to the end, and I shall
keep it un-to the end.

JAMES NARES, 19th April, 1715 (Stanwell)–1783 (London).

Chorister at the Chapel Royal, and educated under Gates, Croft and, later, Pepusch. Organist of York Minster (1735). Appointed one of the organists and composers for the Chapel Royal (1756) in succession to Greene, and in the following year master of the children. He held this last post until 1780.

He published various harpsichord pieces, six organ fugues,

treatises on singing, and a dramatic ode *The Royal Pastoral*, catches, and a set of *Twenty Anthems* (1778). After his death *A Morning and Evening Service and Six Anthems* were published (1788).

Nares's service in F, weak though it is, shows a little more imagination than some eighteenth-century settings, but it was through his anthems that he achieved popularity as a composer of church music. In a watered-down Handelian idiom, he repeated well-tried (and presumably successful) formulas, and in a succession of solo movements both gratified the singers and delighted the congregation. Understandably, as a renowned choir trainer, he set music for his boys which amply displayed their skill. Those anthems featuring treble solos (e.g. *The souls of the righteous, By the waters of Babylon, The Lord is righteous*—all for two trebles—and *God is our hope and strength* for three trebles) tend to possess more interest than those for men's voices, though even here there are some movements which could still sound effective given a stylish performance. *Behold, how good and joyful, Rejoice in the Lord, Unto thee, O God, The Lord is my strength* all contain some quite attractive solos and duets. After these lengthy displays the chorus do what is expected of them and neatly round off the anthem either in a semi-fugal style (*The souls of the righteous*) or in dialogue with a soloist (*O Lord my God, I will exalt thee*).

K

Appendix A

Royal Chapels

In the years immediately following the Restoration both the Queen Mother and the Queen had their separate royal chapels. That of the Queen Mother, Henrietta Maria, was at Somerset House. On her death in 1669 Charles II's Queen Catherine took possession, and she was in residence there from 1671. Matthew Locke was one of her organists. The Roman Catholic Queen continued the exercise of her own faith even during the reign of William and Mary. The chapel building at Somerset House survived until 1733 when, Hawkins tells us, "it was destroyed to make room for the Prince of Orange, when he came over to marry the Princess Anne".

At St. James's Palace, Inigo Jones had built a fine chapel *c.* 1623 (illustrated in *The Treasury of English Church Music*, volume 3) and it was again used by Charles II's Queen at the Restoration. Queen Catherine of Braganza brought to this Chapel her own Portuguese musicians who, apparently, failed at first to make much of an impression. Pepys went to the Queen's Chapel at St. James's on 21st September, 1662, "the first time it hath been ready for her", and was impressed with its furnishings. But, "I heard their musique too; which may be good, but it did not appear so to me, neither as to their manner of singing, nor was it good concord to my ears, whatever the matter was". Evelyn too had heard (on 9th June, 1662) "the Queen's Portugal music, consisting of pipes, harps, and very ill voices".

Nonetheless there was some improvement over the next few years with the introduction of Italian musicians, and with the placing of the establishment on a secure musical footing. An organ was installed and one Ferdinando was made master of the music over fourteen musicians and three choristers. When on Easter Day, 1666, Pepys "walked into the Park to the Queene's chappell, and there heard a good deal of their mass; and some of their musique", he could then say: "it is not so contemptible, I think, as our people would make it, it pleasing me very well; and, indeed, better than the anthem I heard afterwards at White Hall...".

Although the building still stands at St. James's Palace, the music at the Queen's Chapel ceased with her return to Portugal after the accession of William and Mary. The last relics of the Roman rites were disposed of, and in 1696 the organ in "the Chappell of St. James's, commonly call'd the Queen Dowager's Chappell" was given to the parish church of St. Anne's, Soho.

Another establishment served the Roman Catholic chapel of James II which was publicly opened in Whitehall on Christmas Day, 1686. On 29th December Evelyn "went to hear the music of the Italians in the new Chapel, now first opened publicly at Whitehall for the Popish service", and a month later he "heard the famous eunuch, Cifaccio, sing in the new Popish chapel . . .; it was indeed very rare. . . . much crowding—little devotion".

During this chapel's brief life of scarcely two years "Seignr. Fede" (as master) directed half a dozen soloists, ten "Gregorians", nine instrumentalists, a master and eight children. £200 was paid from the King's "secret services" account for their music for a quarter of a year, and "£100 for Mr. Brancourt [Prencourt], for the dyet of the boys, by advance". The same funds paid out the large sum of over £1,100 for a new organ by Harris. This was not completed until 1688, and could have been little used before being given away to St. James's, Piccadilly, in 1691:

> The Queene's Majesty hath been graciously pleased to give the great organ which is in the Great Chappell of Whitehall, which heretofore the Papist possessed, unto the parish of St. James.

The primary establishment, the King's Chapel Royal (known during the reign of James II as the "Princess's Chapel") accompanied the King wherever he resided. For the greater part of the year this was at the principal royal palace which, until William and Mary's reign, was at Whitehall. After the fire of 1698 which destroyed most of that palace, William III moved to St. James's, and that in the eighteenth century became the regular home of the Chapel Royal. Most fortunately, Inigo Jones's Banqueting Hall escaped destruction in the Whitehall fire, and this then came into use as a chapel, being opened on 9th December, 1698, with a specially composed anthem by Blow: *Lord, remember David and all his trouble.* In 1698 Bernard Smith was engaged to provide an organ there, "in the new Chappell at Whitehall". Smith had also built a new organ for the royal chapel at Hampton Court in 1690, and the palace here together with that at Windsor continued to be used by the royal family even after William III began to show a preference for Kensington Palace. In *The Old Cheque Book* there is (for 1720) a reference to his Majesty's Chapel Royal at St. James's and "the other Chapels Royal (viz): Hampton Court, Windsor, Kensington, etc. where his Majesty may reside any part of the year". Gradually, over the years, the Chapel Royal choir became less peripatetic, and the chapel in St. James's became not only its chief but also its sole home.[1]

Not mentioned in this summary because they had no distinct musical establishments are the Dutch Chapel, St. James's, founded by William III on his accession, and the German Lutheran Chapel, also at St. James's, founded by Queen Anne and her consort (Prince George of Denmark) at the beginning of the eighteenth century.

Appendix B

The music repertoire of
cathedral choirs

For some time after the appearance of printed collections of church music, each choir continued to rely on its own manuscript sets of part-books for the music in the daily services. When the provenance of these books is known they give some guide to the repertoire of any particular cathedral; but it is fortunate that a list of the music (although incomplete) sung at Durham Cathedral in June 1680 has survived, providing us with more precise information.[2]

Two key printed collections of services and anthems whose contents can be readily referred to cover the beginning and end of our period: 1641—Barnard's *The First Book of Selected Church Musick* (the contents were listed in editions of *Grove's Dictionary* previous to the current one); 1760 to 1778—Boyce's *Cathedral Music* (Grove's *Dictionary*, I 864-5). Of interest also are Clifford's book of anthem texts, *The Divine Services and Anthems*, 1663 and 1664 (the composers represented are listed in *Music and the Reformation in England* by Le Huray, page 367), and Tudway's six-volume collection of cathedral music in the British Museum (Harley MSS. 7337-42) transcribed as a historical rather than performing collection between 1715 and 1720 (contents listed in *Catalogue of Manuscript Music in the British Museum*, I, by Hughes-Hughes).

"A catalogue of severall Services and Anthems that have been transcribed into the books of his Majesty's Chapell Royall since anno 1670 to Midsummer, 1676" can be found in *The King's Musick* by Lafontaine (pages 305-7). A more comprehensive indication of the Chapel Royal's repertoire in the eighteenth century is provided by a set of six part-books in the music room of the British Museum (Royal Music 23, m. 1-6), which was compiled at the beginning of the century using pages dating back to 1677, and with subsequent additions. The contents of these books have not yet been noted, but

Watkins Shaw has discussed this important collection in *A Contemporary Source of English music of the Purcellian Period* (Acta Musicologica, XXXI, 38–44).

The repertoire of a provincial cathedral choir in 1767 is revealed in "A Catalogue of the Musick Books in the Choir of the Cathedral Church of Chichester October 3 1767", which has been printed by the Chichester City Council (*Chichester Papers*, no. 8). The majority of the music is of the eighteenth century, the only pre-Restoration composers represented being Gibbons (an evening service), Farrant (an evening service), Morley (a burial service), and Byrd (one anthem).

Durham Cathedral Service List, June 1680

Day	Morning	Evening
June 1 (Tuesday)	Short Service—*Allinson*	Evening Service—*Gibbons* O let me hear thy loving kindness
2	Short Service—	Short Service—*Bird* Almighty God ye fountain
3	——	Evening Service—*Farrant* O Lord thou hast searched
4	. . . mine enemies—	Setting in D sol re—*Child* Out of the deep—*Morley*
5	——	Evening Service—*Patterick* God standeth in the congregation
6 (Sunday)	——	Evening Service—*Bryne* Holy Lord God—*Batten*
7	. . . arise—*Tallis*	Setting in G sol re—*Farrant* Blessed by thy name O God
8	——	Evening Service—*Nichols* Let God arise (basses)—*Ward*
9	——	Second Service—*Foster* O how glorious art thou
10	. . . —*Child* O pray for the peace	Evening Service—*Child* If the Lord himself—*Smith*

Day	Morning	Evening
11	Second Service—*Foster*	Second Service—*Foster* O God the proud
12	Short Service—*Wilkinson* O Lord give	Short Service—*Read* When the Lord turned—*Foster*
13 (Sunday)	Short Service—*Tallis* I will magnify thee— *Hooper*	Evening Service—*Tallis* I will always give thanks— *King*
14	Short Service—*Shaw* O pray for the peace— *Child*	Evening Service—*Shaw* I call and cry
15	Short Service—*Hilton* Blessed be the Lord God— *Child*	Short Evening Service— *Hilton* I will give thanks—*Nichols*
16	Setting in ff fa ut—*Child*	Setting in ff fa ut—*Child* Save me O God
17	Setting in E sharp—*Child* O clap your hands—*Child*	Setting in E sharp—*Child* Behold how good—*Portman*
18	Short Service—*Loosemore*	Short Service—*Loosemore* I lift my heart to thee
19	Short Service—*Tomkins* Give laud unto thee	Short Service—*Tallis* Call to remembrance
20 (Sunday)	Short Service—*Gibbons* O give thanks—*Giles*	Short Service—*Batten* O praise the Lord—*Batten*
21	Short Service—*Strogers* O thou . . .—	Short Service—*Strogers* If the Lord himself—*Foster*
22	. . .—*Child*	I will magnify the Lord—*Pearson* O sing unto the Lord—*Hinde*
23	——	Short Service—*Farrant* Almighty God—*Gibbons*
24	—— . . . sing—*Child*	. . . *Pearson's* of Exeter Unto the Lord—*Wilkinson*
25	Setting in D sol re—*Child*	Setting in D sol re—*Child* O pray for the peace—*Nichols*

Day	Morning	Evening
26 (Sunday)	Short—*Bryne* Behold it is Christ	Short Service—*Bryne* O Lord I bow the knees
27	Short Service—*Tallis* Lift up your heads	Short Service—*Tallis* We praise thee O father
28	Short Service—*Wilks* O how glorious	Magnificat—*Nichols* Blow up the trumpet
29	Short Service—*Mundy* If the Lord himself	. . . —*Read* Lord God my heart prepared is
30	Short Service—*Hilton* . . . —*Nichols*	Short Service—*Hilton* O Lord let it be thy will

Appendix C

Psalm chants, 1661-1771

The following nine chants will serve to illustrate the development of the Anglican chant in the hundred years after the Restoration. Often set out as for the first verse of the Venite (this being the first psalm sung at Matins) the same chant would then serve all subsequent psalms, the reciting note (the first in each half) being adjusted to fit the varying number of syllables in each verse.

Ex. 54

1 One of Lowe's unison melodies for the Venite and the psalms for the day. (*A Short Direction for the Performance of Cathedral Service*, 1661.)

2 One of Clifford's thirteen unison melodies ("Common Tunes"). (*Divine Services and Anthems*, 1664.)

3 "Christ Church Tune" (Lowe).

4 "Imperial Tune" (Clifford).

5 Single chant by Blow.

6 Single chant by Wise. These two chants are the first and last of nine (the others being by William Turner, Edward and Henry Purcell, and Thomas Heywood) that appear at the end of an organ book in Wimborne Minster Library, bearing the date 1670, and containing twenty-one anthems, eighteen services, and organ music. Perhaps Wise introduced these chants to Salisbury (he became organist there in 1668) from the Chapel Royal, and the book eventually found its way to Wimborne.

7 Double chant from Boyce's *Cathedral Music* (Volume II, 1768).

8 Single chant by Alcock.

9 Double chant by Alcock. These last two are taken from ten single and two double chants, all with ample ornamentation, given at the end of Alcock's *6 and 20 Select Anthems* (1771).

British Museum Add. MS. 17784, a collection of seventeenth-century services and anthems (*c.* 1676), contains some interesting early chants. The service end of the book is preceded by two pages of twenty-one single chants: the "Imperial", "Canterbury", "Dr. Child's Windsor", nine by "Mr. Blow", six by "Mr. Turner", two by Thomas Purcell, and one by Humfrey (thus indicating a Chapel Royal provenance). The notation of these generally follows this pattern:

Appendix D

The working life of a cathedral organist

John Alcock (1715–1806) was organist of St. Andrew's, Plymouth (1737), St. Lawrence, Reading (1742), and Lichfield Cathedral (1750). He ceased to be organist at Lichfield, though retaining his lay-vicar's place there, and became organist at Sutton Coldfield (1761–1786), and Tamworth (1766–1790).

In 1771 Alcock published a volume of his own anthems (*6 and 20 Select Anthems*) and in his interesting Preface he reminisces on the days when he was a cathedral organist. Good old days in one respect, when there was never a service or an anthem that was not "worth hearing, even in Depth of Winter; and never less than a hundred Chants, in constant use". What he goes on to say, however, reveals a somewhat disgruntled nature, but it is given here verbatim as throwing light on the conditions in one cathedral organ loft.

> For I was forced to teach the Lads, *twice every Day, (in the School,* at *Nine o'Clock* in the Morning, and at *Three* in the Afternoon, and at *no other Place, or Hours*:) And also to attend the Church, as often, being not permitted to go out of Town, to my Scholars in the Country, more than two Days, in a Fortnight, or three weeks; (altho' I had only one Scholar in the Town, for the first seven Years:) Notwithstanding I had a large family to maintain; and my Son, who was sixteen Years of Age, and understood Music exceedingly well, (for he was chosen Organist, and Master of the Singing-Boys, at *Newark* upon *Trent*, entirely by Merit, when he was but seventeen;) always instructed them in my Absence, and yet, that was not, *at that Time*, thought sufficient, tho' some of the Vicars used to be absent from Church, for four, or five Months together, whilst others scarcely ever attended at all: As may be seen in the *Dedication* to my *Service*; when I can safely affirm, that in two and twenty Years, I have, but twice, (which was, when I went to *Oxford* to take my Degrees,) miss'd attending there, *so long as a Week*, except I was ill: *And am always in the Choir, before Prayers begin.*

Alcock may have suffered a persecution complex, but he felt he had much to complain of. One cathedral that would have been unlikely to buy his anthem collection prefaced with these words would have been Lichfield.

Tis incredible what a Number of base Artifices have been practiced by some People belonging to this Cathedral, in Order to prejudice me, in my Profession, and distress my Family, for no Cause whatever: Nay, even my Son, as soon as ever he began to play for me, was turned out from being a Chorister, tho' he had been in the Choir but *two Years,* and his Voice, (which was a very useful one,) not the least fallen; when many of the Lads, are continued in their Places, for *ten, twelve,* or *fourteen* Years, and *long after their Voices are broke:* Also, tho' he always officiated for me, yet I forfeited the same Money, when I went out of Town, as if the *Duty* had been totally neglected; Albeit the Salary *then* was *only* four Pounds *per Annum,* besides the Vicar's Place; and there was much more Duty when I was Organist, *than now,* being obliged always to play a Voluntary after Morning, and Evening Prayers, even in the severest cold Weather, when, every often, there was only one Vicar, who read the Service, and an Old Woman at Church, besides the Choristers; which not only brought, but fix'd the Rheumatism so strongly upon me, that I am seldom free from Pain, and sometimes confin'd to my Bed, for eight, or ten Days together, tho' I never had the least Complaint of that Kind, till then; and no Body can live more regular than I have always done, as every one of my Acquaintance, can testify; I likewise play'd the Organ all *Passion-Week,* (except Good-Friday), both which Customs, have ever since, *been discontinued.*

All the Time I was Organist, which was upwards of Ten Years, there was not a Book in the Organ-loft fit for use, but what I bought or wrote myself, (for which I never was paid one halfpenny,) and yet there have been as many Books purchased, within these few Years, as have cost, at least, Thirty Guineas.

References

The following list is intended to serve a dual purpose: to provide chapter and verse of matter in the text, and to be a guide to further reading—hence the editions named are those that are most easily referred to. To make for easier cross-reference, the second and subsequent entries for any one book give the chapter and number for the original reference (*e.g.* Chapter 1, Reference 5—Mace. *Musick's Monument*, etc. Chapter 4, Reference 17— Mace, *op. cit.* (1.5)). For the music discussed in Chapter 10, apart from the general guide to available editions in the first reference, no specific entries are given—sheet music has a habit of being in and out of print too quickly for references here to be of much use.

CHAPTER 1

1. L'ESTRANGE, NICHOLAS. *MS. Anecdotes* (British Museum, Harley MS. 6395, p. 493)
2. *Aubrey's Brief Lives*, ed. O. L. Dick (1962), p. 213
3. *The Life and Times of Anthony à Wood*, abridged from A. Clark's edition by L. Powys (1961), p. 163
4. WENDEBORN, F. A. *A View of England* (1791), II, p. 180
5. MACE, THOMAS. *Musick's Monument* (1676), p. 233 (facsimile reproduction—Paris, 1958)
6. *Roger North on Music*, ed. John Wilson (1959), pp. 249–250
7. ADDISON, JOSEPH. *The Spectator*, 21st March, 1711
8. AVISON, CHARLES. *An Essay on Musical Expression* (1752), pp. 2–4
9. HAWKINS, JOHN. *Memoirs of Dr. Boyce* (introduction to 2nd edition, 1788, of Boyce's *Cathedral Music*, I, p. xi)
10. North's views quoted in this and the nine preceding paragraphs are to be found in *Roger North on Music*, *op. cit.* (1.6) chapter 6.
11. AVISON, *op. cit.* (1.8) pp. 20–28
12. HAYES, WILLIAM. *Remarks on Mr. Avison's Essay on Musical Expression* (1753), p. 11
13. HAWKINS, JOHN. *A General History of the Science and Practice of Music* (1776), p. 919. This and subsequent entries refer to the Dover republication (1963) of Novello's 1853 edition.
14. *The Treasury of English Church Music*, III (Blandford Press, 1965), contains the anthems by Boyce and Travers (*Ascribe unto the Lord*)
15. HAWKINS, *op. cit.* (1.13) p. xxiii
16. HARRIS, JAMES. The second of *Three Treatises* (1744)

17. BROCKLESBY, RICHARD. *Reflections on Antient and Modern Musick, with the Application to the Cure of Diseases* (1749)
18. AUBREY, *op. cit.* (1.2), p. 235
19. NORTH, *op. cit.* (1.6), p. 124
20. WESLEY, SAMUEL. *Manuscript notes* (British Museum, Add. MS. 27593)
21. BYNG, JOHN. *The Torrington Diaries*, ed. C. B. Andrews (1934), p. 10
22. BURNEY, CHARLES. *A General History of Music (1776–89)*, from the Dedication written by Samuel Johnson. Subsequent entries refer to the Dover republication (1957) of the Mercer 1935 edition.
23. St. Mary's, Buriton, Hants.
24. *The Journey of Celia Fiennes*, ed. Morris (1949), p. 350
25. *The Diaries of Thomas Wilson*, ed. C. L. S. Linnell (1964), p. 39
26. EVELYN, JOHN. *Diary*, 2nd October, 1685, 10th November, 1661
27. GAUDEN, JOHN. *Considerations touching the Liturgy of the Church of England*
28. Hymns by Baxter and Addison respectively (*Hymns Ancient & Modern Revised*, numbers 371 and 170)
29. AUBREY, *op. cit.* (1.2) p. 351
30. BEST, WILLIAM. *An Essay upon the Service of the Church of England* (1746), p. 6
31. MACE, *op. cit.* (1.5), p. 272
32. DEAN, WINTON. *Handel's Dramatic Oratorios and Masques* (1959), p. 137
33. The ideas referred to in this and the preceding eight paragraphs are taken from the following:
    PLAYFORD, JOHN. *A Brief Introduction to the Skill of Musick*, preface to the 1672 edition
    GAUDEN, *op. cit.* (1.27), p. 35
    READING, JOHN. *A Sermon concerning Church-Musick* (1663)
    BRADY, NICHOLAS. *Church-Musick Vindicated* (1697)
    TATE, NAHUM. *An Essay for promoting Psalmody* (1710), p. 30 (quoting Collyer)
    ADDISON, JOSEPH. *The Spectator*, 14th June, 1712
    BISSE, THOMAS. *A Rationale on Cathedral Worship* (1720)
    BISSE, THOMAS. *Musick the Delight of the Sons of Men* (1726)
    ABBOT, HENRY. *The Use and Benefit of Church-Musick* (1724)
    SENHOUSE, PETER. *The right Use and Improvement of sensitive Pleasures* (1728)
    KEACH, BENJAMIN. *The Breach Repaired* (1691)
    MARLOW, ISAAC. *Truth Soberly Defended* (1692)

For easily readable summaries of the social background see the Batsford & Putnam English Life Series: *Life in Stuart England* (Maurice Ashley, 1964) and *Life in Georgian England* (E. N. Williams, 1962). For the religious background the most cogent approach is to be found in Norman Sykes's *The English Religious Tradition* (S.C.M. Press, 1961). See also the same author's *Church and State in England in the eighteenth century* (1934), and J. Wickham Legg's *English Church Life* (1914).

CHAPTER 2

1. FOSTER, MYLES. *Anthems and Anthem Composers* (1901), p. 60
2. PARRY, C. HUBERT. *The Music of the Seventeenth Century* (1902), p. 260
3. FULLER, THOMAS. *Thoughts and Contemplations*, ed. J. O. Wood (1964), p. 68
4. AUBREY, *op. cit.* (1.8), pp. 250, 24, 231
5. NORTH, *op. cit.* (1.6), p. 127
6. HAWKINS, *op. cit.* (1.13), p. 693
7. TUDWAY, THOMAS. *A Collection of the most celebrated Services and Anthems* (British Museum, Harley MSS. 7337–42), introduction to Volume II (1716)
8. AUBREY, *op. cit.* (1.8) p. 347
9. PEPYS, SAMUEL. *Diary*, 29th June, 1668; 15th September, 1667; 1st October, 1667; 12th August, 1660; 14th October, 1660; 22nd November, 1663
10. HEYLIN, PETER. *Ecclesia Restaurata* (1661), ed. J. C. Robertson (1849), II, p. 315
11. *The Old Cheque-Book of the Chapel Royal*, Da Capo Press reprint (1966) of Rimbault's 1872 edition, pp. 13–15
12. EVELYN. *Diary*, 8th July, 1660, 25th November, 1660
13. *The Old Cheque-Book*, *op. cit.* (2.11), pp. 81–84
14. ATKINS, IVOR. *The early occupants of the office of organist of Worcester* (1918), p. 48
15. *The Treasury of English Church Music* (Blandford Press, 1965), II
16. PEPYS. *Diary*, 21st August, 1667
17. PEPYS. *Diary*, 27th August and 4th September, 1664, 10th April, 1665
18. LAFONTAINE, HENRY CART DE. *The King's Musick* (1909)—a transcript of the Lord Chamberlain's records (1460–1700) relating to music— gives much of the information about the Chapel Royal Choir used in the last two sections of this chapter.
19. *The Old Cheque-Book*, *op. cit.* (2.11), pp. 28–29

CHAPTER 3

1. NORTH, *op. cit.* (1.6), p. 221
2. LAFONTAINE, *op. cit.* (2.18), pp. 133, 131
3. For this discussion of the number of string players involved in the Chapel Royal services see Lafontaine, *op. cit.* (2.18)
4. AVISON, *op. cit.* (1.8), p. 129
5. HAWKINS, *op. cit.* (1.13), p. 767
6. For this and the preceding three paragraphs see Lafontaine, *op. cit.* (2.18)
7. EVELYN, *Diary*, 21st December, 1662, 23rd April, 1661
   PEPYS, *Diary*, 27th February, 1668, 15th April, 1668
8. LAFONTAINE, *op. cit.* (2.18), pp. 128, 136, 147, 176, 253, 367
9. ASHMOLE, quoted in *The Old Cheque-Book*, *op. cit.* (2.11), p. 216
10. WOODFILL, WALTER. *Musicians in English Society* (1953), p. 149

11. Exeter Cathedral; *Chapter Acts* (MS. 3559, p. 492) for 27th August, 1664 (kindly supplied by Audrey Erskine)
12. *The Correspondence of John Cosin*, Surtees Society, LV, ed. G. Ornsby (1870)
13. NORTH, *op. cit.* (1.6), p. 40
14. Durham Cathedral Library; organ book B.1
15. LAFONTAINE, *op. cit.* (2.18), pp. 378, 245, 305, 422, 201, 212
16. LEWIS, JOHN. Introduction to *John Blow, Coronation Anthems* (*Musica Britannica*, VII)
    HUGHES, DOM ANSELM. "Music of the Coronation" (*Proceedings of the Royal Musical Association*, LXXIX)
17. LAFONTAINE, *op. cit.* (2.18), pp. 384–385
18. LAFONTAINE, *op. cit.* (2.18), pp. 373, 379
19. LAFONTAINE, *op. cit.* (2.18), p. 383
20. *The Old Cheque-Book, op. cit.* (2.11), p. 126
21. LAFONTAINE, *op. cit.* (2.18), p. 407
22. *The Old Cheque-Book, op. cit.* (2.11), pp. 129–130, 28
    HATTON, EDWARD. *A new view of London* (1708), p. 301
    HAWKINS, *op. cit.* (1.13), p. 740
    LAFONTAINE, *op. cit.* (2.18), p. 388
23. *The Old Cheque-Book, op. cit.* (2.11), pp. 86–87
24. SHEPPARD, E. *Memorials of St. James's Palace* (1894), pp. 215–216
25. HAWKINS, *op. cit.* (1.13), p. 740
26. TUDWAY, *op. cit.* (2.7)
27. BEDFORD, ARTHUR. *The Great Abuse of Musick* (1711), p. 179
28. CROFT, WILLIAM. *Musica Sacra* (1724)
29. HAWKINS, JOHN. *Memoirs of Dr. Boyce* (introduction to 2nd edition, 1788, of Boyce's *Cathedral Music*, I, pp. iv–v)
30. RILEY, WILLIAM. *Parochial Music Corrected* (1762), p. 14

CHAPTER 4

1. SCHOLES, PERCY. *The Puritans and Music* (1934)
2. BURNEY, *op. cit.* (1.22), II, pp. 307, 314
3. SCHOLES, *op. cit.* (4.1)—see chapter VI
4. See SCHOLES, *op. cit.*, quoting Prynne (pp. 217–218) and Earle (p. 226)
5. WOOD, ANTHONY. *Biographical notes on Musicians* (Oxford, Bodleian Library, MS. Wood D.19)
    Fasti Oxonienses, ed. P. Bliss (1815), II, p. 306
6. NORTH, *op. cit.* (1.6), p. 342
7. AUBREY, *op. cit.* (1.2), p. 243
    NEAL'S *History of the Puritans*, quoted in Scholes, *op. cit.* (4.1), p. 281
8. PINE, EDWARD. *The Westminster Abbey Singers* (1953), p. 116
9. AUBREY, *op. cit.* (1.2), pp. 348, 365.
10. LE HURAY, PETER. "Towards a Definitive Study of Pre-Restoration Anglican Service Music" (*Musica Disciplina*, XIV, 1960), pp. 183, 185

11. Norwich Cathedral Audit Books quoted by Noel Boston in *The Musical History of Norwich Cathedral* (1963), pp. 60–61
12. ATKINS, *op. cit.* (2.14), pp. 60–68
13. Exeter Cathedral; *Chapter Acts* (MS. 3562, pp. 405, 410)
14. WOOD, *op. cit.* (1.3), pp. 103–104
15. TUDWAY, *op. cit.* (2.7), II (1716)
16. HAYES, *op. cit.* (1.12), pp. 94–104
17. MACE, *op. cit.* (1.5), pp. 21–29
18. TUDWAY, *op. cit.* (2.7), VI (1720)
19. HAWKINS, *op. cit.* (1.13), p. 693
20. NORTH, *op. cit.* (1.6), pp. 268–271
21. BYNG, *op. cit.* (1.21), 25th August, 1782; 1st July, 1781; 8th July, 1781
22. HAWKINS, *op. cit.* (1.13), p. 796
23. FIENNES, *op. cit.* (1.24), pp. 226, 37, 136
24. WESLEY, *op. cit.* (1.20), f. 135
25. LYSONS, DANIEL. *Origins and Progress of the Meeting of the Three Choirs* (1895), p. 38
26. Salisbury Cathedral; *Act Book XX* (1696–1740). Entries for 8th February, 1711; 12th August, 1720; 7th October, 1747; 10th March, 1713; 23rd April, 1717; 22nd January, 1727; 24th July, 1752; 15th August, 1711; 8th October, 1745; 9th August, 1753; 5th September, 1755
27. HAWKINS, *op. cit.* (1.13), pp. 693, 859
28. NORTH, *op. cit.* (1.6), p. 41 (1742)
29. TUDWAY, *op. cit.* (2.7), VI (1720)

CHAPTER 5

1. ESTWICK, SAMPSON. *The usefulness of Church-Musick* (1696)—reprinted (1955) by Augustan Reprint Society (XLIX)
2. HAWKINS, *op. cit.* (1.13), p. 575
3. BEDFORD, *op. cit.* (3.27), pp. 180, 246, 221–226
4. CROFT, *op. cit.* (3.28)
5. TUDWAY, *op. cit.* (2.7), introductions to volumes I (1715), VI (1720), II (1716), IV (1717)
6. DINGLEY, W. *Cathedral Service Decent and Useful* (1713), p. 14
7. AVISON, *op. cit.* (1.8), pp. 93, 95–97, 101, 103
8. HAYES, *op. cit.* (1.12), pp. 45, 75, 92
9. HUGHES, WILLIAM. *Remarks upon Church Musick* (1763)
10. BROWN, JOHN. *A Dissertation on the Rise, Union, and Power of Poetry and Music* (1763), pp. 213–214, 231–232
11. MASON, WILLIAM. *A Copious Collection of Anthems* (1782); introductory "Essay on Cathedral Music"
12. AVISON, *op. cit.* (1.8), pp. 54–55
    HAYES, *op. cit.* (1.12), p. 56
13. ALCOCK, JOHN. *6 and 20 Select Anthems* (1771), preface

14. WESLEY, SAMUEL. *Lecture notes* (British Museum, Add. MSS. 35106, f. 60, 35105, f. 200)
15. BISSE, THOMAS. *A Rationale on Cathedral Worship* (1720), pp. 52–62
16. *The Spectator*, 8th December, 1714

CHAPTER 6

1. GAUDEN, *op. cit.* (1.27), p. 35
2. British Museum, Royal Music 23, m. 1–6
3. ALCOCK, *op. cit.* (5.13)
   NORTH, *op. cit.* (1.6), p. 40
4. Norwich Cathedral, *op. cit.* (4.11), p. 97
5. BRIDGES, ROBERT. *Collected Essays* (1935), XXII, p. 28
6. MILBOURNE, LUKE. *Psalmody Recommended* (1713), p. vii
7. HAWKINS, *op. cit.* (1.13), p. 539
8. PROCTER AND FRERE. *A New History of the Book of Common Prayer* (1901), pp. 172–173
9. NORTH, *op. cit.* (1.6), p. 269
10. BURNEY, *op. cit.* (1.22), II, p. 125
11. JEBB, JOHN. *The Choral Service* (1843), p. 305
12. BEDFORD, ARTHUR. *The Temple Musick* (1706), pp. 161–165
13. MASON, *op. cit.* (5.11), p. li
14. BUMPUS, JOHN. *The Organists and Composers of St. Paul's Cathedral* (1891), p. 85
15. ALCOCK, *op. cit.* (5.13)
16. Tenbury MSS. 797–803 and 1176–1182. Published (O.U.P.) in 1925, some have recently been reissued.
17. O.U.P.—C.M.S. Reprint 14
18. Blandford Press (1965)
19. Novello; O.U.P.
20. Blandford Press (1965)
21. Novello (1951)
22. Novello (1956)
23. Stainer & Bell (1953)
24. Birmingham, Barber Institute, MS. 5001, p. 185
25. Both anthems can be found in *The Treasury of English Church Music*, III (Blandford Press, 1965).
26. Novello; Stainer & Bell (1961)
27. Blandford Press (1965)

CHAPTER 7

1. FELLOWES, EDWARD. *Organists and Masters of the Choristers of St. George's Chapel* (1939), pp. 55–58
2. HAWKINS, *op. cit.* (1.13), p. 896
3. ALCOCK, *op. cit.* (5.13)
4. BURNEY, *op. cit.* (1.22), II, pp. 704–705

5. BISSE, THOMAS. *Musick the Delight of the Sons of Men* (1626)
6. HAWKINS, JOHN. *Memoirs of Dr. Boyce* (introduction to 2nd edition, 1788, of Boyce's *Cathedral Music*, I, p. xi)
7. WESLEY, *op. cit.* (1.20), f. 33
8. WESLEY, SAMUEL. *Lecture notes* (British Museum, Add. MS. 35105, f. 248)
9. ALCOCK, *op. cit.* (5.13)
10. Oxford Bodleian Library, MS. mus. sch. c. 44, f. 146
11. *Gentleman's Journal*, November 1692; but see an essay by Jeremy Noble in *Henry Purcell, Essays* (1959), pp. 60–61
12. NORTH, *op. cit.* (1.6), p. 238
13. FELLOWES, *op. cit.* (7.1), pp. 53–55
14. LONSDALE, ROGER. *Dr. Charles Burney* (1965), p. 4
15. GEE, HENRY. *Gloucester Cathedral, its Organs and Organists* (1921), pp. 19–20
16. Chester Cathedral; *Chapter Minutes* referring to Edmund White, 19th September, 1707; 14th May, 1708; 9th April, 1715
17. GEE, *op. cit.* (7.15)
    FELLOWES, *op. cit.* (7.1)
    Exeter Cathedral; *Chapter Acts* (MS. 3567, p. 362) for 8th December, 1744
    Note by Philip Hayes in British Museum Add. MS. 33235 (see also Hawkins's History, p. 784)
    WOOD, *op. cit.* (1.3), p. 347
18. Blow's complete organ works are published by Schott (1958), Purcell's by Novello (1957). Other modern editions of 17th- and 18th-century organ music are to be found in three series: *Tallis to Wesley* (Hinrichsen); *Early Organ Music* (Novello); *English Keyboard Music* (Stainer & Bell). O.U.P. have published a facsimile edition of Stanley's *Voluntaries*.
19. NORTH, *op. cit.* (1.6), p. 136
20. BEDFORD, *op. cit.* (3.27), p. 248
21. HAWKINS, JOHN. *Memoirs of Dr. Boyce* (introduction to 2nd edition, 1788, of Boyce's *Cathedral Music*, I, p. iii)
22. RILEY, WILLIAM. *Parochial Music Corrected* (1762), p. 18
23. *The Spectator*, Letter of 28th March, 1712
24. HAWKINS, *op. cit.* (1.13), p. 879
25. *Early Organ Music* (Novello, 1966), no. 24
26. HAWKINS, *op. cit.* (1.13), pp. xli, 826
27. HAWKINS, *op. cit.* (1.13), p. 911
28. BURNEY, *op. cit.* (1.22), II, p. 494, 1009
29. HAYES, *op. cit.* (1.12), pp. 81–82
30. e.g. *They that go down to the sea* (Purcell Society, XXXII; recorded on Argo RG.444)
31. King's College, Cambridge, Rowe Library MS. 262
32. Blandford Press (1965)
33. COLLES, H. C. *Essays and Lectures* (1945), p. 35
34. *The Old Cheque-Book, op. cit.* (2.11), pp. 14, 112

35. WILLIAMS, THOMAS (see Tudway, *op. cit.* (2.7), V)
36. Chichester Cathedral; *Chapter Records* for 2nd November, 1720 (see C. E. Welch, *Two Cathedral Organists*, Chichester City Council, 1957)

CHAPTER 8

1. WESLEY, SAMUEL. *Lecture notes* (British Museum, Add. MSS. 35106, f. 61, 35105, f. 202)
2. WESLEY, JOHN. Letter dated 20th September, 1757 (*Letters of John Wesley*, ed. Telford (1931), III, pp. 226–228)
3. MACE, *op. cit.* (1.5), chapters 1–10
4. BEDFORD, *op. cit.* (3.27), pp. 229–234
   MILBOURNE, *op. cit.* (6.6), p. 28
   BEDFORD, ARTHUR. *The Excellency of Divine Musick* (1733), pp. 28–30
5. Salisbury Diocesan Record Office; *The Dean's Miscellaneous Papers* for 1736 and 24th June, 1737
6. BROWN, *op. cit.* (5.10), pp. 214–215
7. BEDFORD, *op. cit.* (6.12), p. 226
   AVISON, *op. cit.* (1.8), pp. 89–90
   HAYES, *op. cit.* (1.12), pp. 77–78
   RILEY, *op. cit.* (7.22), pp. 15–18
8. GIBBON, EDMUND. *Directions* (1724), pp. 9–12
9. PORTEUS. *Works and Life of Secker* (1811), pp. 343–344
10. WICKHAM LEGG, J. *English Church Life* (1914), page 186 onwards
11. COX, J. C. *Notes on the Churches of Derbyshire* (1877), III, p. 338
12. NARES, JAMES. *Morning and Evening Service together with Six Anthems* (1788)
13. WENDEBORN, *op. cit.* (1.4), II, pp. 281–282
14. See for this and the following paragraphs:
    MACDERMOTT, K. H. *Sussex Church Music in the Past* (1922) and *The Old Church Gallery Minstrels* (1948)
    DITCHFIELD, P. H. *The Parish Clerk* (1907)
    RILEY, *op. cit.* (7.22)
15. Parish registers of Welford, Berks., quoted in Basil Clarke's *The Building of the Eighteenth-Century Church* (1964), pp. 31–32
16. ARNOLD, JOHN. *The Compleat Psalmodist* (1741), p. 16
17. WOODFORDE, JAMES. *Diary*, 9th and 26th February, 12th and 26th November, 17th and 24th December, 1769; 15th July, 1770; 16th April, 1775
18. LONSDALE, *op. cit.* (7.14), pp. 4–55
19. HAWKINS, *op. cit.* (1.13), p. 896
20. BOSTON AND LANGWILL. *Church and Chamber Barrel-Organs* (1967)

CHAPTER 9

1. PERKINS, JOCELYN. *Westminster Abbey: Its Worship and Ornaments* (1952), p. 111

2. SCHOLES, *op. cit.* (4.1), pp. 151, 144

3. WOOD, *op. cit.* (1.3), p. 313

4. HATTON, EDWARD. *A New View of London* (1708), p. 376

5. BURNEY, CHARLES. *The Present State of Music in France and Italy* (1771), p. 375

6. For discussion about the existence of pedals on English organs in the sixteenth and seventeenth centuries see B. J. MASLEN, "The earliest English organ pedals", in the *Musical Times*, September 1960, p. 578, and subsequent correspondence (November 1960, February 1961, April 1961)

7. BYNG. *Diaries, op. cit.* (1.21), 25th August, 1782
    EVELYN. *Diary*, 16th June, 1683

8. Salisbury Diocesan Record Office; *Faculty Petitions*, 8th October, 1723; 15th February, 1725; 11th September, 1726

9. James Hawkins's remark is quoted by A. W. WILSON in *Ely Cathedral. The Organ and Organists* (1908), p. 8. For a summary of the pitch problems (and essential references) see ROBERT DONINGTON'S *The Interpretation of Early Music* (1963), chapter 53.

10. PEPYS. *Diary*, 21st April, 1667

11. MACE, *op. cit.* (1.5), chapters 3–7, 10

12. TOWERSON, GABRIEL. *A Sermon concerning Vocal and Instrumental Musick in the Church* (1696)
    NEWTE, JOHN. *The Lawfulness and Use of Organs in the Christian Church* (1696)

13. DODWELL, HENRY. *A Treatise concerning the lawfulness of instrumental musick in Holy Offices* (1700)

14. BEDFORD, *op. cit.* (3.27), chapters 10–11

15. HAWKINS, *op. cit.* (1.13), p. 695

16. Salisbury Diocesan Record Office; *Faculty Petitions* for 1778

17. WENDEBORN, *op. cit.* (1.4), II, pp. 235, 285

18. Glasgow, Euing Library, R.d.62, f. 42

Much of the information used in this chapter can be found in CLUTTON AND NILAND, *The British Organ* (1693) and WILLIAM L. SUMNER, *The Organ* (1962). Both books are essential for further reading.

CHAPTER 10

1. e.g. *Grove's Dictionary of Music and Musicians*, ed. E. Blom (5th edition, 1954)—although only some of the articles from earlier editions have been revised. PULVER, JEFFREY. *A Biographical Dictionary of Old English Music* (1927)

Modern editions of the music are still relatively uncommon. Purcell's complete church music is in the Purcell Society Edition, volumes 13, 14, 17, 23, 28, 29, 30, 32, and a number of offprints are available (Novello). Watkins Shaw has edited some of Blow's church music (Schott, Stainer & Bell, O.U.P.). Handel's church music is in the German Handel Society complete edition (republished by the Gregg Press, 1965). Single pieces by various composers are published by Hinrichsen, Novello, Schott, Stainer & Bell, and O.U.P.. A representative anthology is *The Treasury of English Church Music*, III (Blandford Press, 1965). The most important eighteenth-century publications are Boyce's *Cathedral Music* (1760–1778) and Arnold's *Cathedral Music* (1790), Croft's *Musica Sacra* (1724), Greene's *Forty Select Anthems* (1743), and two volumes of Boyce's own anthems (1780 and 1790) later supplemented by Vincent Novello (1849). Some of the music of the earlier part of the period discussed in this chapter is to be found only in manuscript copies in various libraries, in particular those of the British Museum, the Fitzwilliam Museum, Cambridge, and St. Michael's College, Tenbury.

The music examples that are in the text are given in the briefest possible format, and the clefs used are those which present the illustrations in the clearest way to the reader. Original pitch and note values are used throughout. No attempt has been made to edit the examples by adding expression marks or by filling in the organ parts.

2. Fellowes, Edward. *Byrd* (1936), p. 85
3. e.g. Donington, Robert. *The Interpretation of Early Music* (1963)
4. Collier, Joel. *Musical Travels through England* (1774), p. 56
5. North, *op. cit.* (1.6), p. 40
   Avison, *op. cit.* (1.8), p. 118
6. North, *op. cit.* (1.6), p. 214
   Lampe, John. *The Art of Musick* (1740), p. 11
   Tans'ur, William. *A New Musical Grammar* (1746), p. 48
   Rameau, quoted in Donington, *op. cit.* (10.3), p. 453
   Burney, *op. cit.* (1.22), II, p. 9
7. Mace, *op. cit.* (1.5), p. 133
8. North, *op. cit.* (1.6), p. 218
9. Boyce, William. *Cathedral Music* (1760), I, footnote on p. xii
10. Cambridge, Fitzwilliam Museum, Griffin MS. 31. H
11. Avison, *op. cit.* (1.8), p. 137
    Alcock, *op. cit.* (5.13)
12. Burney, *op. cit.* (1.22) II, p. 488
13. Oxford, Bodleian Library, MS. mus.d.174
14. Bridge, J. C. "A great English choir-trainer" (*The Musical Antiquary*, II, p. 61)
15. MS. 5001. For a description of this important collection of composers' autographs see Watkins Shaw, "A Collection of Musical Manuscripts" (*The Library*, XIV, p. 126).
16. Lewis, Anthony. "Matthew Locke" (*Proceedings of the Royal Musical Association*, LXXIV, p. 57)
    Dr. Rosamond Harding has undertaken a thorough study of Locke's music, and I am grateful to her for letting me see her catalogue of Locke's church music.
17. Lafontaine, *op. cit.* (2.18), pp. 245, 244, 247
18. Pepys, *Diary*, 1st and 15th November, 1667
19. Hiscock, W. G. *Henry Aldrich* (1960)

20. LAFONTAINE, *op. cit.* (2.18), pp. 305-307
21. See article on Blow by Watkins Shaw in *Grove's Dictionary*, which includes a catalogue of the church music.
22. "John Blow as Theorist" (letter to the *Musical Times*, LXXVII, p. 835). See also: "Tradition and Convention in John Blow's Harmony" (*Music and Letters*, XXX, p. 136).
23. WESTRUP, J. A. *Purcell* (1965)
    ZIMMERMAN, F. B. *Henry Purcell, an analytical catalogue* (1963)
24. MS. mus.d.226.
25. FELLOWES, *op. cit.* (7.1), pp. 53-55
26. HAYES, *op. cit.* (1.12), p. 107
27. British Museum, Add. MS. 17845
28. DENT, EDWARD. *Handel* (1934)
    NEWMAN FLOWER's *George Frideric Handel* (1959) includes a full bibliography; see also DEAN, *op. cit.* (1.32).
29. DEAN, *op. cit.* (1.32), chapter 6
30 An Argo recording of Chandos anthems 9 and 11 demonstrates how they can and should sound (ZRG 5490)
31. See *A Catalogue of the Musick Books in the Choir of the Cathedral Church of Chichester, October 3, 1767* (The Chichester Papers, no. 8, 1957)
32. British Museum, Add. MS. 33235
33. Watkins Shaw has already expressed a due appreciation of Greene's church music (Church Music Society, Occasional Paper XXI). I am grateful to H. Diack Johnstone who has kindly given me the benefit of his thorough research which corrects our previous knowledge of Greene's life.
34. Oxford, Bodleian Library, MS. mus.d.48
35. Boyce's church music and the contents of his *Cathedral Music* are listed in *Grove's Dictionary*

APPENDIXES

1. LAFONTAINE, *op. cit.* (2.18), pp. 121, 144, 156, 167, 178, 400, 405, 431-433, 436
   The Old Cheque-Book, op. cit. (2.11), p. 88
   See North's account of Captain Prencourt, and the editor's footnotes in NORTH, *op. cit.* (1.6), pp. 51-54
2. Durham Cathedral Library, MS. C.17 (pasted on the inside front cover)

Index

Abbot, Henry 291
Abell, John 54
Abingdon 168
Addison, Joseph 290, 291
Alcock, John 121-2, 123, 272, 287,
 288-9, 294, 295, 296, 299
Aldrich, Henry 30fn, 69-71, 84, 90,
 101, 116, 120fn, 207, 209
Allinson, 282
Anne, Queen 23, 54-5, 58, 132fn, 214,
 222, 231, 248, 254, 256, 278, 280
Archer, Thomas 41fn
Arne, Thomas 152, 271
Arnold, John 297
Arnold, Samuel 108, 237, 260, 269,
 270, 299
 Service in A 109
Ashley, Maurice 291
Aston, Peter 191fn
Atkins, Ivor 292, 294
Attwood, Thomas 89
Aubrey, John 65fn, 290, 291, 292, 293
Avison, Charles 9, 90, 92fn, 182, 290,
 292, 294, 297, 299

Bach, J. S. 96, 156, 250
Bacon, Francis 108
Bancroft, Bishop 80
Banister, John 45
Banstead 12
Barnard, John 30, 66, 67, 93, 281
Batten, Adrian 19, 99fn, 104fn, 282,
 283
 Deliver us O Lord our God 109fn
 O praise the Lord all ye heathen 109fn
Baxter, Richard 291
Bedford, Arthur 85-6, 137-8, 143fn,
 173-4, 293, 295, 296, 297, 298
Bell, Thomas 259
Best, William 291

Bevin, Elway 99fn
Bisse, Thomas 291, 295, 296
Blagrave, Thomas 122fn, 200
Blow, John 14, 24, 25, 28fn, 29, 30fn,
 34-8 passim, 41fn, 42, 46, 47, 48,
 52, 54, 56, 57, 58, 83, 84, 86, 100,
 101, 108-12 passim, 116-17, 120fn,
 126, 127, 143fn, 165, 177, 185, 186,
 190, 200, 212-19, 220, 222, 226, 227,
 237, 241, 242, 260, 280, 287, 296,
 298, 300
 And I heard a great voice 217
 Awake, utter a song 181
 Blessed be the Lord my strength 181
 Blessed is the man that hath not walked
  217, 218
 Bow down thine ear 218
 Gloria Patri qui creavit nos 219
 God is our hope 215
 God spake sometime in visions 42,
  114fn, 217
 In the time of trouble 218
 I said in the cutting off of my days 217
 Let the righteous be glad 184
 Let thy hand be strengthened 215
 Lord, who shall dwell in thy tabernacle
  217
 My days are gone like a shadow 218
 My God, my God, look upon me 84,
  215
 O Lord God of my salvation 215
 O Lord I have sinned 215
 O sing unto the Lord a new song 114fn,
  216
 Paratum cor meus Deus 219
 Salvator mundi 219
 Save me O God 215
 Service in G major 107, 219
 Short services 219
 Venus and Adonis 213
Boston, Noel 294, 297

301

Boyce, William   5, 7fn, 11, 14, 41fn,
    85, 88, 93, 110, 117, 120–1, 126, 177,
    178, 180, 208, 221, 222, 236, 240,
    248, 261, 262, 266, 270, 271–6, 281,
    287, 290, 293, 296, 299, 300
  Blessed is he that considereth   91fn, 273fn
  By the waters of Babylon   273
  Give the King thy judgements   275
  Hear my crying   275
  If we believe that Jesus died   91fn, 120
  I have set God always before me   275
  I have surely built thee an house   275
  Like as the hart   262
  Lord, thou hast been our refuge   273fn
  Lord, who shall dwell in thy tabernacle
    275
  O be joyful in God all ye lands   274
  O give thanks (B flat)   273
  O give thanks (C)   273
  O sing unto the Lord a new song   274
  O where shall wisdom be found   273
  Ponder my words   275
  Save me, O God   273
  Services in A   272
  Service in C   109, 272
  Sing praises to the Lord   274
  Sing unto the Lord   275
  Teach me, O Lord   275, 276
  Te Deum in G   272
  The heavens declare   9, 273, 275
  The King shall rejoice   273fn
  The Lord is King, and hath put on   275
  The Lord is King, be the people   274
  The Lord is my light   275
  The souls of the righteous   273fn
  Turn thee unto me, O Lord   110, 273
Brady, Nicholas   135, 291
Bridge, J. C.   299
Bridge, Richard   163
Bridges, Robert   102, 295
Bristol   118, 166–7, 250
Brocklesby, Richard   291
Brown, John   294, 297
Browne, Thomas   15
Bryne, Albertus   190, 213, 282, 284
Bumpus, John   295
Buriton   291
Burlington, Lord   41fn
Burney, Charles   62–4,   123fn,   132,
    152–3, 165, 179, 183, 220, 291, 293,
    295, 296, 298, 299
Buxted   146
Byfield, John   163, 165–7
Byng, John   76, 291, 294, 298
Byrd, William   14, 40, 87, 88fn, 90, 96,
    99fn, 103, 107, 120 fn, 177, 282

Caddington   151

Caldara, Antonio   90
Calne   139
Cambert, Robert   48
Cambridge   29fn, 67, 75, 133, 159–61,
    221, 222, 261, 269, 296
Cannons   2, 236, 252, 254
Canterbury   29fn, 130–1, 159, 161, 168,
    213
Carissimi, Giacomo   90
Caroline, Queen   76, 115, 249, 257
Castle Cary   150–1
Catherine of Braganza   278, 279
Chandos, Duke of   2, 236, 248, 249, 252
Chapel Royal   18, 20–39 passim, 42–60
    passim, 67fn, 68fn, 75, 79, 81, 100–
    2, 113, 116, 123, 130–3, 143, 185,
    191, 199, 208, 212, 213, 220–2, 225–
    7, 230, 234, 237–42 passim, 248, 250,
    253–4, 257–61 passim, 269, 271–6
    passim, 278–80, 281, 287
Charles I   27, 62, 191
Charles II   13, 18, 20–7, 30fn, 33, 36,
    39, 42–9 passim, 52, 53, 54fn, 59, 68,
    102, 114, 130, 185, 186, 192, 227, 230,
    234, 247, 278
Chester   122, 123fn, 152, 296
Chichester   115,   133fn,   142fn,   260,
    282, 297, 300
Child, William   30fn, 34, 50fn, 80, 85,
    99fn, 101, 109, 120fn, 123, 143fn,
    201, 208, 237, 282, 283, 287
  O Lord grant the King a long life   109fn
  Praise the Lord O my soul   109fn
Church, John   238–9
Cifaccio   279
Clarke, Basil   297
Clarke, Jeremiah   58, 101, 117, 125fn,
    213, 237–9, 241, 259, 260
  An Evening Hymn   238
  Blest be those sweet regions   239
  How long wilt thou forget me   115, 238
  I will love thee, O Lord   238, 254
  Lord, how long   235 fn
  Te Deum and Jubilate in C minor   238
  Te Deum and Jubilate in G major   237
Clifford, James   98–9, 102, 104fn, 105,
    199, 213, 281, 287
Clutton, Cecil   298
Colles, H. C.   296
Collier, Joel   299
Cooke, Henry   23, 27–9, 33–9 passim,
    45fn, 47, 50, 53, 60, 122, 185–90,
    199, 200, 208, 212, 213, 225, 226
  Behold, O God, our defender   186
  Come let us pray, and God will hear   186
  We have sinned and committed iniquity
    188
  We will rejoice in thy salvation   186–7

Cooke, Robert: Service in G 109
Corelli, Arcangelo 89, 90
Corfe, Joseph 269
Cosin, John 51, 293
Coventry 156
Cox, J. C. 297
Creighton, Robert 101, *199*
 I will arise 109fn
 Lord thou art become gracious 109fn
Croft, William 5, 39, 58, 59, 86, 88,
  89, 92, 101, 110, 119, 120fn, 121,
  128fn, 131, 132fn, 180, 237, *241-8*,
  262, 269, 271, 276, 293, 294, 299
 Be merciful unto me 248
 Blessed are all they that fear the Lord 246
 Burial Service 110, 244
 Give the King thy judgements 248
 God is gone up 245
 Hear my prayer, O Lord 245
 I will give thanks unto thee O Lord 248
 Lord, thou hast searched me out 182
 O be joyful in God 246
 O give thanks unto the Lord 247
 O Lord God of my salvation 245, 246
 O Lord grant the King a long life 245
 O Lord, I will praise thee 246, 247
 O Lord, rebuke me not 110, 245
 Out of the deep 246
 O ye righteous 247
 Praise God in his sanctuary 132fn
 Put me not to rebuke 248
 Rejoice in the Lord 277
 Service in A 242-3
 Service in B minor 108, 242-3
 Service in E flat 243-4
 Te Deum and Jubilate in D 248
 The heavens declare 246
 This is the day which the Lord hath made
  246
Cromwell, Oliver 26fn, 61, 158, 159
Cuckfield 148

Dallam, George 68, 160
Dallam, Robert 159, 160, 166, 169
D'Avenant, Charles 185, 192
Daw, Donovan 272fn
Dean, Winton 291, 300
Dent, Edward 300
Dering, Richard 143fn, 197
Diack Johnstone, H. 261fn, 300
Dingley, W. 294
Ditchfield, P. H. 297
Dodwell, Henry 298
Dolben, John 267
Donington, Robert 298, 299
Dublin 184, 220, 271
Durham 51, 52, 102, 131, 159, 281,
  282-4, 293, 300

Edwards, Thomas 28fn, 38
Elford, Richard 131, 132fn, 240, 259
Elizabeth I 22, 27, 42, 156
Ely 159, 169, 234, 260
Erasmus 4
Estwick, Sampson 84-5, 294
Eton College 117, 184, 239
Evelyn, John 13fn, 29, 30, 40, 42-5
  passim, 49, 54fn, 278, 279, 291, 292,
  298
Exeter 28fn, 51, 68fn, 99fn, 168fn, 171,
  191, 225, 283, 293, 294, 296

Farrant, Richard 19, 282, 283
 Call to remembrance 109fn, 110
 Hide not thou thy face 109fn, 218
Fellowes, Edward 295, 296, 299, 300
Fiennes, Celia 291, 294
Finedon 132fn, 269
Flower, Newman 300
Foster, Myles 292
Foster 282, 283
Frere, W. H. 141fn, 295
Fuller, Thomas 21, 292

Galliard, John 118
Gasparini, Francesco 90
Gates, Bernard 39, 250, 259, 276
Gauden, John 291, 295
Gee, Henry 296
Geminiani, Francesco 90, 129fn
George I 59, 132fn, 183, 248, 255
George II 59, 249, 255, 273fn
George III 273fn
George, Prince of Denmark 280
Gibbon, Edmund 297
Gibbons, Christopher 99fn, *185*, 213
Gibbons, Edward 191
Gibbons, Orlando 40, 41, 85, 86fn,
  88fn, 90,99fn, 103, 107, 108, 120fn
  185, 282, 283
Gibbs, James 41fn
Giles, Nathaniel 99fn, 283
Glasgow 298
Gloucester 17, 123, 124fn, 134, 136fn,
  159, 175, 220, 259, 270, 272
Golding, John 101, 123, *237*
Gostling, John 24, 57fn, 59, 130, 231,
  254
Grabu, Louis 33, 199fn, 200
Green, Samuel 169fn
Greene, Maurice 5, 83, 89, 92, 93, 108,
  118, 127, 129fn, 177, *261-9*, 271,
  272, 276, 299, 300
 Acquaint thyself with God 262
 Arise, shine, O Sion 114, 266
 Blessed are those that are undefiled 264
 God is our hope and strength 264, 267

Greene (cont.)
  Hear, O Lord, and consider 262
  How long wilt thou forget me 266
  I will give thanks 264, 265
  I will magnify thee O God 264
  I will sing of thy power 266
  Jephtha 261
  Let God arise 266
  Let my complaint 266, 267
  Like as the hart 262, 264
  Lord, how are they increased 264
  Lord, how long wilt thou be angry 266
  Lord, let me know mine end 111, 266
  My God, my God 264, 267
  My soul truly waiteth 264
  O clap your hands 266
  O give thanks 265
  O God of my righteousness 265
  O God thou art my God 267–9
  O Lord give ear unto my prayer 91fn
  O Lord I will praise thee 264
  O praise the Lord of heaven 266
  O sing unto the Lord a new song 266
  O sing unto the Lord with thanksgiving
    262, 263–4, 267
  Praise the Lord ye servants 267
  Put me not to rebuke 267
  St. Cecilia's Day ode 261
  Service in C 108, 261, 266–7
  Sing unto the Lord a new song 267
  Song of Deborah and Barak 261
  Te Deum in D 261
  The Force of Truth 261
  The Lord, even the most mighty God 264
  The Lord is my shepherd 264, 267
Grove, George 281, 298, 300

Hackney 170
Hall, Henry 37fn, 225, 259, 260
  Service in E flat (with Hine) 259,
    260, 270
Hampton Court 48, 159, 169fn, 185,
    280
Hampton Town 213
Handel, G. F. 2, 6, 7, 16fn, 23, 39, 58,
    80, 88, 92, 113, 118, 126–31 passim,
    134, 166, 167, 176, 246, 248–59, 277,
    298
  As pants the hart (i) 253, 258
  As pants the hart (ii, iii, iv) 258
  Belshazzar 250
  Birthday Ode for Queen Anne 132fn,
    254
  Blessed are they that consider the poor
    257
  Chandos anthems 2, 249, 251, 252–4,
    258–9, 300

Dettingen Te Deum 257
Dixit Dominus 250–2
Have mercy upon me 253
In the Lord put I my trust 253
I will magnify thee (i) 253, 258
I will magnify thee (ii) 258
Jeptha 7
Laudate pueri 250
Let God arise (i) 253, 259
Let God arise (ii) 259
Let thy hand be strengthened 255
Messiah 16fn, 250, 257
My heart is inditing 255
My song shall be alway 253
Nisi Dominus 252
O be joyful in the Lord 252
O come let us sing unto the Lord 253
O praise the Lord with one consent 253
O praise the Lord, ye angels 259
O sing unto the Lord a new song (i) 253,
  258
O sing unto the Lord a new song (ii) 258
Salve Regina 250, 252
Silete venti 250, 252
Sing unto God 256–7
Te Deum in A 255–6
Te Deum in B flat 249, 254, 256
Te Deum in D 258, 259
The King shall rejoice (1727) 255
The King shall rejoice (1743) 257
The Lord is my light 253
The ways of Sion 115, 257
This is the day which the Lord hath made
  256
Utrecht Jubilate 58, 249, 252, 254
Utrecht Te Deum 58, 254, 255, 259
Zadok the Priest 91fn, 255
Hanslick, Eduard 110
Harblon, Lady Alice 142
Harding, Rosamond 299
Hardy, Thomas 149
Harley, Lord 221
Harris, James 10, 290
Harris, John 163
Harris, Renatus 121, 160–9 passim, 175,
  279
Harris, Thomas 159, 166
Hart, James 28fn, 47fn
Hartfield 154
Hatton, Edward 293, 298
Hatton, Lord 191
Hawkins, James 169, 234
Hawkins, John 9fn, 10, 45fn, 57fn,
  63, 64, 75fn, 80, 85, 124fn, 220, 261,
  262, 278, 290, 292, 293, 294, 295,
  296, 297, 298
Hayes, Philip 237, 259, 260, 270, 273,
  296

Hayes, William 9fn, 70–2, 90, 92fn, 133, 175, 270–1, 290, 294, 296, 297, 300
  Bow down thine ear 271
  O God thou art my God 271
  Save Lord, and hear us 271
  Service in D 270
  Service in E flat 270
Henman, Richard 68fn
Henrietta Maria (Queen Mother) 278
Herbert, George 77
Hereford 17, 136fn, 225, 272
Heylin, Peter 292
Heywood, Thomas 287
Hilton 283, 284
Hinde 283
Hine, William 259–60 (see also under Hall)
Hingston, John 52, 158, 213, 226
Hiscock, W. G. 299
Hobbes, Thomas 10
Holmes, Randle 50fn
Hooper 283
Hopkins, John 61, 104, 136
Howells, Herbert 109
Hughes, Dom Anselm 293
Hughes, Francis 132fn, 258, 259
Hughes, William 91fn, 294
Humfrey, Pelham 24–30 passim, 35, 38, 39, 42, 48, 52–4 passim, 60, 112, 176, 185, 195, 199–207, 212, 213, 217, 222, 226, 227, 228, 246, 287
  Almighty God, who madest thy blessed Son 205
  By the waters of Babylon 204–6
  Have mercy upon me, O God 202, 203
  Like as the hart 202
  O give thanks unto the Lord 205
  O Lord my God 112, 132, 202
  O praise the Lord 205
  Rejoice in the Lord, O ye righteous 202
  Service in E minor 107, 205–7
  Thou art my King, O God 202
Hunt, Thomas 94

James I 31, 32, 42, 62
James II 23, 44fn, 54, 55, 123, 217, 231, 279
James, John 153
Jebb, John 295
Jeffreys, George 191
Jeffries, Stephen 123–4, 259
Jennens, Charles 250
Johnson, Samuel 11, 108, 291
Jones, Inigo 41fn, 278, 279
Jordan, Abraham 163, 166

Keach, Benjamin 291

Kelway, Thomas 94, 109fn, 129, 133fn, 260–1
Kempton, Thomas 260
Kent, James 93, 269–70
  Hearken unto my voice 269
King, Charles 93, 94, 108–9, 260, 261, 271, 283
  Service in F 109
King's Lynn 152–3

Lafontaine, Henry Cart de 281, 292, 293, 299, 300
Lampe, John 299
Langwill, Lyndesay 297
Laud, Archbishop 27
Law, William 145fn
Lawes, Henry 64fn, 143fn, 185, 201
Lawes, William 34, 41fn, 143 fn, 201, 208
  Before the mountains 50
Le Huray, Peter 281, 293
L'Estrange, Nicholas 290
Lewis, Anthony 299
Lewis, John 293
Lichfield 29fn, 81, 118, 121, 123, 185, 288, 289
Lincoln 28, 29fn, 37fn, 131, 159, 222
Locke, John 1
Locke, Matthew 23, 30fn, 34, 41fn, 53, 122, 132, 185, 191–8, 201, 228, 278, 299
  Cantate Domino 197, 198
  I will hear what the Lord 194, 195
  Lord, let me know mine end 113, 192
  Not unto us, O Lord 194, 195
  O be joyful 195
  O Domine Jesu Christe 197
  Omnes Gentes 197, 198
  Sing unto the Lord, all ye saints 196, 197
  The Lord hear thee 197
  The King shall rejoice 42, 197
  Turn thy face from my sins 193
  When the Son of Man 193
Loggings, John 34, 38
Lonsdale, Roger 296, 297
Loosemore 283
Lotti, Antonio 90
Louis XIV 2, 43
Lowe, Edward 66, 67fn, 69, 97–8, 99, 102, 104fn, 105, 222, 287
Lowther Clarke, W. K. 141fn
Luton 151
Lysons, Daniel 294

MacDermott, K. H. 297
Mace, Thomas 73–5, 86, 133, 170, 290, 291, 294, 297, 298, 299
Marcello, Benedetto 90

Marlow, Isaac 291
Mary, Queen 23, 45fn, 53–7 passim, 88fn, 232, 278, 279
Maslen, B. J. 298
Mason, William 294, 295
Mendelssohn, Felix 89
Merbecke, John 103
Milbourne, Luke 295, 297
Milton, John 158
Morley, Thomas 90, 107, 157, 282
Mozart, W. A. 89
Mundy, William 99fn, 284

Nares, James 39, 143–4, 276, 277, 297
  Behold, how good and joyful 277
  By the waters of Babylon 277
  God is our hope and strength 277
  O Lord my God, I will exalt thee 277
  Rejoice in the Lord 277
  Service in F 108, 277
  The Lord is my strength 277
  The Lord is righteous 277
  The Royal Pastoral 277
  The souls of the righteous 114, 277
  Unto thee, O God 277
Neal, C. 293
Newark 28, 288
Newcastle 90, 139
Newte, John 171–2, 298
Newton, Isaac 1
Nichols 282, 283, 284
Niland, Austin 298
Noble, Jeremy 296
Norris, Charles 79
North, Francis 101fn
North, Roger 6–11, 24, 43, 50fn, 51, 75, 81, 164, 180, 290, 291, 292, 293, 294, 295, 296, 299, 300
Norwich 67fn, 102, 294, 295
Novello, Vincent 181, 273, 290, 299

Ouseley, F. A. G. 239
Oxford 64fn, 65fn, 66, 67fn, 69, 76, 77, 90, 116, 125 fn, 158–61 passim, 169, 184, 185, 191, 207, 220, 222, 234, 238, 239, 242, 259, 270, 288

Palestrina, G. P. 90, 96, 119
Parker, Archbishop 149fn
Parry, C. Hubert 292
Patrick, Nathaniel 94, 282
Peacham, Henry 5
Peak Forest 154
Pearson 283
Pease, Lancelot 159, 161, 168
Pepusch, J. C. 118, *236*, 269, 276
Pepys, Samuel 22, 26, 27, 29, 34, 38, 43fn, 45fn, 49, 52, 80, 122fn, 147, 158, 159, 170, 200, 278, 292, 298, 299
Perkins, Jocelyn 297
Peterborough 29fn
Pigott, John 117
Pine, Edward 293
Playford, Henry 143fn, 207, 238
Playford, John 143fn, 291
Plymouth 288
Pope, Alexander 15, 261
Porter, Walter 38, 65, 201
  Praise the Lord 34
Portman, Richard 99fn, 283
Potterne 168
Prelleu, Peter 118
Prencourt, Capt. 279, 300
Procter and Frere 295
Pulver, Jeffrey 298
Purcell, Daniel *234–6*
  Bow down thine ear, O Lord 235, 236
  Bow thine ear 234fn
  Hear my prayer 234fn
  I will always give thanks 234fn
  Lord, let me know mine end 235
  My God, my God, look upon me 235
  O give thanks 234fn
  O praise God in his holiness 234fn
  Put me not to rebuke 235
  Service in E minor 234, 235
Purcell, Edward 287
Purcell, Henry 4, 7fn, 14, 19, 24, 30fn, 34, 35, 41fn, 54, 57, 60, 76, 83, 88fn, 89, 93, 108, 111, 117, 120fn, 122, 125, 130–2, 143fn, 165, 176–80 passim, 183, 185, 193, 197, 200, 201, 205, 206, 213–15, 222, *226–33*, 234–9 passim, 242, 254, 273, 287, 296, 298
  Awake, put on thy strength 228fn, 231
  Beati omnes qui timent Dominum 233
  Behold, I bring you glad tidings 231
  Behold now, praise 231
  Blessed are they that fear the Lord 232
  Blow up the trumpet in Sion 228
  Hear me, O Lord, and that soon 228
  Hear my prayer, O Lord 230
  In thee, O Lord, do I put my trust 228fn, 231
  It is a good thing to give thanks 231
  I was glad 230
  I will give thanks unto thee, O Lord 231
  I will give thanks unto the Lord 231
  I will love thee, O Lord 227–8
  Jehova, quam multi sunt hostes 233
  Let God arise 228
  Let mine eyes run down 228
  Lord, how long wilt thou be angry 230
  Lord who can tell 227

Purcell (cont.)
  Man that is born of a woman 115, 230
  My beloved spake 113
  My heart is inditing 42, 230, 231
  My song shall be alway 232
  O give thanks 91fn, 232
  O God, thou cast us out 230
  O Lord God of hosts 230
  O Lord, grant the King a long life 231
  O Lord our governor 233
  O sing unto the Lord 113, 228fn, 232
  Out of the deep 228
  Praise the Lord, O Jerusalem 232
  Praise the Lord, O my soul, O Lord my
    God 232
  Remember not, Lord, our offences 110,
    230
  St. Cecilia Ode 122fn, 132fn
  Save me, O God 228
  Service in B flat 107, 219, 233, 237
  Services 226
  Te Deum and Jubilate in D 233
  The Lord is my light 231
  They that go down to the sea in ships
    231
  Thou knowest, Lord 88fn, 110, 232
  Unto thee will I cry 231
  Why do the heathen 231
Purcell, Thomas 199fn, 234, 287

Rameau, J. P. 299
Raphael 9
Read 283, 284
Reading 288
Reading, John 291
Rickmansworth 193
Riley, William 293, 296, 297
Rimbault, Edward 292
Robinson, John 128
Rochester 29fn, 159
Rogers, Benjamin 64fn, 85, 100, 101,
  184
Roseingrave, Daniel 220-1
Roseingrave, Ralph 220
Roseingrave, Thomas 118-19, 126, 220

St. Paul's Cathedral 34, 57fn, 75, 80,
  81, 98, 99, 117, 120, 131, 134, 136fn,
  159, 162, 167, 190, 208, 213, 222,
  233, 237, 250, 254, 260, 261, 271,
  272, 273fn
Salisbury 28fn, 29fn, 51, 67fn, 77-9,
  123, 133 fn, 139, 159, 162, 163, 168,
  174fn, 208, 220, 287, 294, 297, 298
Sandwich, Lord 34
Scarlatti, Domenico 119fn, 129fn
Schnitger, Arp 156
Scholes, Percy 293, 298

Schreider, Christopher 163, 165, 167
Schwarbrook, Thomas 163, 167
Selby Abbey 143
Senhouse, Peter 291
Shadwell, Thomas 192
Shaw 283
Shaw, H. Watkins 214, 215, 282, 299,
  300
Sheppard, E. 293
Shirley, James 185, 192
Shrewsbury 77, 152, 270
Shuttleworth, Obadiah 128
Silbermann, brothers 156
Smart, Peter 51
Smith, Bernard 121, 160-5, 167, 169fn,
  174, 280
Smith, Gerard 169, 171
Smith 282
Snetzler, John 163-5, 167, 169fn, 174
Spohr, Louis 89
Staggins, Nicholas 55
Stainer, John 234
Stanford, C. V. 109
Stanly, John 127, 128, 129, 296
Steele, Richard 80, 148fn
Sternhold, T. 61, 136, 140
Stevens, Denis 68fn, 119fn
Strogers, Nicholas 99fn, 283
Stroud, Charles 271
Sumner, William 298
Sutton Coldfield 118, 288
Swift, Jonathan 62
Sykes, Norman 291

Tallis, Thomas 30fn, 88fn, 90, 91, 98,
  99fn, 103, 120fn, 282, 283, 284
  O Lord, give thy holy spirit 110
Tamworth 118, 288
Tans'ur, William 299
Tate, Nahum 135, 291
Taylor, Silas 26
Temperley, Nicholas 143fn
Tenbury 295, 299
Thamar, Thomas 161, 168, 298
Three Choirs Festival 16, 17, 79, 91fn,
  254, 270, 271
Tillotson, Dr. 57fn
Tiverton 171-2
Tomkins, Giles 68
Tomkins, Thomas 19, 68fn, 99fn, 107,
  283
Towerson, Gabriel 171, 172
Travers, John 9, 51, 236, 270
  Ascribe unto the Lord 270, 290
  Ponder my words, O Lord 270
  Service in F 109fn, 269
  Te Deum in D 269
Trusley 143

Tucker, William 30fn, *191*
Tudway, Thomas 24–6, 30fn, 43, 45, 58, 67fn, 70fn, 75fn, 87–8, 132, *221–2*, 225, 281, 292, 293, 294, 297
Turner, William 28fn, 29, 30fn, 35, 37, 42, 47fn, 54, 132fn, 185, 189, *222–5*, 227, 287
  Behold now praise the Lord 224
  God sheweth me his goodness 224
  Hold not thy tongue, O God 222, 223
  Lord, thou hast been our refuge 222
  Lord, what is man 222
  O praise the Lord 224, 225
  The Queen shall rejoice 222
Tye, Christopher: *I will exalt thee* 85

Vanbrugh, John 41fn
Vicars, John 157

Walond, William 128
Ward, John 107, 282
Watts, Isaac 140
Weelkes, Thomas 41, 107
  Alleluia 110
  Gloria in excelsis Deo 110
Welch, C. E. 297
Weldon, John 101, 131, 183, 235fn, *238–41*, 261
  Hear my crying, O God 240
  In thee, O Lord 240
  O God thou hast cast us out 240–1
  Who can tell how oft he offendeth 240
Welford 142, 148, 297
Wells 168fn, 199
Wendeborn, F. A. 290, 297, 298
Wesley, Charles 140
Wesley, John 136, 297
Wesley, Samuel 89, 93, 120 fn, 261, 291, 294, 295, 296, 297
Westminster Abbey 34, 51, 65, 76, 79, 81, 115, 117, 128 fn, 131, 157–8, 185, 190, 191, 213, 222, 226, 238, 242, 249, 250, 254, 255, 257
Westrup, J. A. 176, 300
Wheely, Samuel 259
Wickham Legg, J. 291, 297
Wilkinson 283

Wilks 284
William III 23, 45fn, 53, 55, 56, 85, 278, 279, 280
Williams, E. N. 291
Williams, Peter 119 fn
Williams, Thomas 297
Wilson, A. W. 298
Wilson, John 191
Wilson, Thomas 291
Wimborne 287
Winchester 76, 168, 185, 220, 237, 267
Windsor 2, 28fn, 29fn, 33, 36, 46–50 passim, 54, 64fn, 80, 117, 118, 123, 124fn, 168, 184, 208, 234, 237, 269, 280
Wise, Michael 24, 28fn, 29, 35, 50fn, 78, 101, 123, 125, 185, 189, 206, *208–212*, 227, 287
  Awake; put on thy strength 211
  Blessed is he that considereth 208
  Blessed is the man that hath not walked 211, 212
  By the waters of Babylon 208
  How are the mighty fallen 209, 210
  I will arise 212
  Open me the gates of righteousness 210
  O praise God in his holiness 212
  Prepare ye the way of the Lord 212
  Service in E flat 107
  The Lord is my shepherd 208, 209
  The ways of Sion 183, 212
  Thy beauty O Isreal (see *How are the mighty fallen*)
  Thou, O God, art praised in Sion 208
Wood, Anthony 43, 158, 290, 293, 294, 296, 298
Woodfill, Walter 292
Worcester 17fn, 28fn, 29fn, 31, 51, 67–9, 76, 79, 91fn, 136fn, 160, 250, 270, 272
Wren, Christopher 41, 80
Wyrley Birch, Humphrey 76

York 28fn, 51, 91, 154, 159, 160, 170, 276

Zimmerman, Franklin 234fn, 300